D1318078

Great Bear Adventures
true tales from the wild

Introduction by Andy Russell

KEY PORTER·BOOKS

Copyright © 1987 by Key Porter Books Limited
ALL RIGHTS RESERVED

Canadian Cataloguing in Publication Data
Main entry under title:
Great bear adventures
ISBN 1-55013-014-5
1. Bears. I. Russell, Andy, 1915-
QL795.B4G73 1987   599.74'446   C86-095004-2

Key Porter Books Limited
70 The Esplanade
Toronto, Ontario
M5E 1R2

Designed by Marie Bartholomew
Printed and bound in Canada

87 88 89 90 5 4 3 2 1

Contents

THREE: CAPTIVE AND DOMESTICATED BEARS

FOUR: BEARS IN THE WILD

Introduction

ANDY RUSSELL

I had the good fortune to be born on the western edge of the prairies in southwestern Alberta, with the Rockies cleaving the sky two miles from our ranch house door. Mountain wilderness has been a major part of my life. In the sixty-odd years since I saw my first grizzly track with water welling up in it on the silty edge of a spring, I have lived in, and travelled through, bear country from Montana north to Alaska and the arctic coast and west to the rain forest regions of the Pacific rim. As a hunter I learned the virtue of observation, the quality of patience, the power of endurance and the difference between real fear and being just plain scared. Sometimes this was the dividing line between staying alive and being torn to shreds.

In the wilderness I learned the ways of nature and the joy of being a part of it, rather than a mere bystander. A subtle spiritual awareness grew inside me, too. I gradually understood that being there was one thing, but to crawl mentally inside an animal and to think like it was quite another.

There was a time when scientists, conducting tests in their laboratories, doubted that an animal could think. But they changed their minds when they ventured out to meet their subjects in their natural habitat. Here it was the scientists who found themselves being tested. And here the keen edge of bear intelligence was felt and finally appreciated. The scientists began to learn why primitive man revered these great animals, and why they elevated them to the status of powerful, sacred totems — strong medicine. From the very beginning, men have sat around their fires telling and retelling stories of adventures with bears.

ANDY RUSSELL

The great grizzly and his forbears have lived in North Africa, Europe, Asia and North America. The black bear along with its ancestral relatives has been even more widespread, but most numerous on this continent. Black bears are still to be found in substantial numbers from coast to coast, and from Mexico to the far reaches of the north. They have learned to make use of people in spite of quick changes to the environment. The grizzly is far more vulnerable due to its size, its fearsome reputation and its need for space.

What can be termed "grizzly country" is the wildest of the wild outdoors, limited as it is today by roads, industry, tourists and agriculture. It is where the sky and the earth meet: the snow-draped mountains reaching to the clouds, the mist dressing the mountain flanks in gentle grey undulations, the streams falling in white water cataracts that roar in exuberant play as they make the first long bounds on their journey to the sea. It is timberline country, where wind-bent trees and lichen-painted boulders are scattered in flower-spangled meadows green with alpine growth, and lovely blue lakes reflect the sky. In the valleys, the rivers flow through great groves of green timber. Silty flats are covered with horsetail, columbines, avens, grass and a host of other plants beneath forests of poplar, pine, spruce and fir.

On the steep slopes are the scars of old fires and avalanche tracks where the berries grow. Huckleberries, service berries, salmon berries, currants, raspberries, cranberries and sometimes gooseberries: all are sweet grist for the bear mill. Where Pacific salmon swim up the rivers in their phenomenal return, not only to the same river but the same riffle in which they were hatched, the grizzly comes to dine. In so doing he takes his part in the interlocking food chain significant to the region.

Grizzlies do not stay where food is not plentiful. They often leave their big, clawed paw marks on the slush, glacier ice and snowfields as they cross miles and miles of inhospitable terrain in search of new feeding grounds. Away in the far north, where the land slopes down to the coast of the arctic sea, some trail the caribou herds to their calving grounds. There, for three weeks or so, they feed on newborn calves between sessions of

2

grazing on the new spring vegetation. These are high-protein rations, but they are not available for long. When the calves learn to run with their mothers, the bears get sore feet trying to catch them. They soon give up and go looking for easier grazing and the new crop of berries. Then one sees them sharing the country with feeding caribou and moose and paying them no attention whatever, except to hijack wolf kills and sometimes getting into a ruckus as a result. Such encounters may leave the cubs with a lasting respect for wolves. Come fall when frost paints the leaves of the deciduous trees in brilliant colors the bears, having stuffed themselves for weeks on berries, are fat. They fill the remaining hollows by eating hibernating ground squirrels and marmots in the search for which they excavate great quantities of earth and rocks.

Over most of the mountain ranges grizzly and black bears share the spoils though they rarely mingle, for grizzlies are fond of black bear meat when they can catch it. The first winter snowstorms find them in their dens: the grizzlies in chambers dug into the ground somewhere up near timberline, where the snow drifts over them; the black bears lower down, wherever they can make a nest in a sheltered spot. This may be under an overhanging bank, a fallen log or sometimes in the hollow base of a big, standing dead tree. The bears in their dens snooze away the winter but they are by no means totally dormant. They are wakeful, semi-hibernators, unlike ground squirrels and marmots, which are totally comatose.

Bears have been around for a very long time. They came across the landbridge into North America from Asia during the ice ages. They shared trails with such exotic bygone beasts as hairy mammoths, woolly rhinocerii, Athabaskan bison, ground sloths and cave lions, to name a few. Among these was a mighty bear, six feet tall at the shoulder, rangy and very fast on its feet. Unlike its lesser cousins, it was a predator that fed on grass-eaters and about everything else it could catch. Even the great cave lion likely gave this bear the trail when they met. No doubt it also struck terror into the hearts of those tough and powerful men who regularly killed mammoths with their flint-topped spears. It is likely that they sat within the protection of their cooking fires at night telling stories of their encounters with the great bear, when their spears felt so puny and ineffectual. Thus, in the beginning, bears were given supernatural powers by men, for whom their very smell spelled a fast and bloody trip to the happy hunting grounds.

These were the ancestors of the tribes that populated North America. They survived many species, the giant bear included. But black bears and grizzlies also adapted to the changing times: the former populated most of the continent, while the latter lived in the ranges west of the Mississippi River and Lake Winnipeg.

Then the grizzly occupied the very peak of the life pyramid with man. Both of them ate many of the same things, though man's appetite probably ran more to meat. Both ate just about anything when really hungry. The bears did not eat men very often, for the two-legged one smelled very bad of tobacco and other unattractive things. Men did not tangle with grizzlies very often either, for even with an arrow or a lance through the heart, a grizzly could live long enough to destroy several hunters. A hunter with the bravery and the luck to win a fight with a grizzly instantly achieved great warrior status, and was on the way to becoming a medicine man. Not many men chose this way to fame.

Among the Old Crow Indians of the Yukon Territory, there were some among the hunters who were endowed with strong bear medicine. They were a special breed with powers passed on from father to son. These hunters killed the great bear by entering its den and stabbing it with a short-shafted spear. Even to this day Old Crow Indians claim that a bear will not fight in its den. They also say that some hunters have been known to fight a bear successfully in single-handed combat outside of the den. The man wrapped his left arm with a skin parka and gave it to the bear to chew while he pierced its throat with his spear.

The first recorded sighting of a grizzly by a white man in North America was made by a priest. He was the official recorder of a Spanish expedition which sailed into Monterey Bay in California in 1602. Father Antonio de la Ascencion described in his diary the grizzlies he saw feeding on a dead whale on the beach. A story teller of no little talent, he wrote that their tracks were a "good third of a yard long."

The first recorded instance of grizzly killed by a white man happened in Canada on August 19, 1692. Henry Kelsey, an employee of the Hudson's Bay Company, and his Indian guide, encountered two grizzlies on the edge of the prairie in what is now Manitoba. The Indian swiftly climbed a tree and Kelsey went up to the top of a clump of willows. He shot one bear dead with his musket. The other saw the puff of smoke and came looking for its source. Failing to locate it, the bear then went back to the tree which contained the Indian. Meanwhile, Kelsey reloaded his muzzle-loader and fired again, killing the second bear. A double on grizzlies with a 20-gauge smoothbore trade musket was an astounding feat but his diary is disappointingly brief and dry. To read it one would think he was shooting rabbits.

It was not until 1770 and again in 1772 that the Spanish came sailing back into Monterey Bay. They established two missions. Immediately, they suffered through a very severe drought which almost finished their colony. Had it not been for several mule loads of dried jerky made of grizzly meat, they would have had to eat their seeds and cattle. Killing grizzlies with lances while on horseback would have made an extraordinary story, but the record of it is scanty and modest.

The Spanish occupation spread and blossomed into the golden age of the Californios. The missions were farms using Indian slave labor to raise grain, vegetables and fruit. But the main industry was raising cattle for the tallow and hide trades. It was on the huge land grants owned by the dons, with their crews of bastard vaqueros, that the cowboy evolved. These vaqueros — all superb horsemen — developed the use of the rawhide reata to sheer art.

Their guns were crude and ineffective, and lances required getting too close to the grizzlies, so they roped the big animals from horseback. They caught them by the neck and feet and stretched them between their horses until the bears choked to death. A superlative roper, working alone, caught the bear by the neck, rode around a tree, then pulled the bear's head up against it. Leaving the horse to keep the rope tight, they went in on foot to kill it with a knife. One daring and reckless man, Don Jose Ramon Corrillo, fought bears with a sword inside a ring of mounted horsemen. He lived long enough to have his head blown off by an American desperado in a drunken brawl.

Following the Lewis and Clark expedition in 1805, when Lewis reported several adventures with grizzlies, the American fur trade was launched. The trade in Canada had been established for over a century, the Indians bringing their furs to strategically placed forts. The plains Indians were buffalo hunters and did not take beaver fast enough to meet the demand. So the skins were gathered in the American west by white trappers. These men were about as tough and daring as men can get. What with hostile Indians and lots of plains grizzlies, these trappers lived precariously: many of them went under. Each year the traders, trappers and Indians got together at a pre-arranged rendezvous to celebrate being alive, with whiskey and story-telling, fun and games with the girls, and contests of strength and skill with weapons. The stories were often unbelievable, rarely modest and generally hair-raising.

Perhaps one of the most unbelievable yet true stories told about man-bear conflict during this era was the remarkable adventure of Hugh Glass. He was out with a group of trappers exploring new beaver country, in the region of South Dakota, when he was attacked by a grizzly. He fought the bear, which finally left him and fell dead nearby. Some of his partners found Glass terribly torn, his scalp hanging over his eyes, his back chewed to naked bone and several ribs and a leg broken. Carrying him to camp they sewed his scalp back in place and tried to make him more comfortable. Not expecting him to live, they left him in the charge of two of his companions, young Jim Bridger and one Fitzgerald. Glass was so close to being dead that they dug his grave beside him, but he held on tenaciously, refusing to die. Surrounded by prowling, hostile Indians, whom they saw several times, the two finally gave up and left him.

Glass was periodically conscious, and when he realized that he had been deserted, he was so enraged that he swore to live, track down both deserters and kill them. He somehow splinted his broken leg, wrapped it with raw bear hide, then began to crawl. He stayed alive by eating insects, remnants of wolf kills and whatever else he could find, and drinking filthy slough water. He crawled on, suffering agonies for weeks, until he finally came to a river. Clinging to a dry cottonwood log, he floated downriver to a fort. He had come about 150 miles. When he had fully recovered, he proceeded to ride hundreds of miles to find Fitzgerald and Bridger. When he finally did catch up to them, Fitzgerald talked him out of shooting them.

When the beaver and the buffalo were about gone settlers poured into the west. By this time, a great many grizzlies had been wiped out by the hide hunters, and those that survived were mostly in the mountains. The last great California grizzly was killed near the turn of the century.

Hosea Sarber, the first salaried game warden in Alaska, had a great deal of experience with grizzlies. He said that most grizzlies will rarely bother a man unless wounded or encountered unexpectedly at close quarters. He reckoned that one in about every twenty-five might attack. Although the one exception is very dangerous, I can say that in two seasons, during 1962 and 1963, two of my sons and I made 204 close contacts without harm while filming and observing the big bears in their choicest ranges, here in British Columbia and in Alaska. We went completely unarmed except for our movie and still cameras for two reasons: first, the cameras were a heavy enough load to carry and, second, we felt that an unarmed man moves, thinks and generally gives off an aura less likely to get him into trouble. Movie camera lenses are more or less ineffective as interpretive instruments at long range, so most of our work was done within a hundred yards of the animals. Quite a bit of it was shot at fifty yards or less, and one memorable sequence, involving four bears, was filmed at a bit over fifty feet. We treated the bears honestly, never gum-booting around under cover, always approaching in the open where they could see us coming. Indeed, we religiously avoided heavy cover if possible to keep from surprising bruins snoozing in bed, which is an excellent way to get wiped out.

All bears are definite individuals, possessing unique characters. We dealt with them as such, getting to know which ones would tolerate us, and for how long. It took a lot of time and patience. By learning to move smoothly and respectfully, we collected thousands of feet of film, not only of grizzlies but other animals as well. To be sure, we sometimes made mistakes and were charged. Then we stood our ground or even moved a bit toward them before ordering them to back off, and we came through without a scratch. A charging grizzly upon finding himself faced by a man who doesn't run or show signs of panic is understandably surprised out of his socks. After all, just about everything runs from grizzlies. So every time we stood our ground, they veered away or stopped. It is not something that gets boring, nor is it conducive to low blood pressure. We were not afraid, but there were times when we were plenty scared, and we were always impressed. A charging grizzly is something to remember.

I definitely do not recommend that anyone else attempt to film bears in this way. It is necessary to have accumulated a great deal of experience of the animals in real wilderness country. It is not something one can learn by reading books, although the wild animal photographer interested in any species should have some considerable understanding of animal psychology, about which a lot has been written. Perhaps the most important thing is to learn to move like a wild animal moves — never in quick or jerky fashion, but always smoothly. This takes practice. It also takes patience and endless careful observation till one can crawl inside the fur-coated subject and think like it, and so anticipate where it will go and what it will do.

These stories reflect the experiences of people who have lived and learned in wild country, where they sometimes find themselves literally holding their lives in their hands. It is a sure way to learn that wilderness is a very necessary part of every one of us.

ONE

EARLY ENCOUNTERS

The White Bears

WILLIAM H. WRIGHT

Lewis and Clark, in their explorations of the American northwest, reported encounters with a number of grizzlies. They called them "white bears" to distinguish them from the black bears with which they were more familiar.

The history of the grizzly bear differs from that of all the other great beasts that have come into close contact with civilization. The story of the others begins with our beginnings. The lion and the tiger have been always with us. They helped to rock the cradle of the race, and lunched occasionally from its contents. When we were cave men, we barred them from the mouths of our caves, and drew pictures of them on the walls. Later, we charred the ends of sharpened sticks in our fires, and with these drove them into the jungle. We and they have grown up together.

But the first chapter of the history of the grizzly is the beginning of the story's end. When my grandfather was born, the grizzly had never been heard of. If my grandson ever sees one, it will likely be in the bear pit of a zoölogical garden.

The actual history of the grizzly bear begins on April 29, 1805, when, on the banks of the upper Missouri, at the mouth of the Yellowstone River, in what is now Montana, Captain Merriwether Lewis, of the Lewis and Clark Expedition, met one of these animals for the first time.

Before this, indeed, hints and rumours of a bear different from the Eastern variety had come back to civilization with returning traders and explorers. Edward Umfreville, writing in 1790 upon "The Present State of Hudson's Bay," had heard of them. In summing up the fauna of the North and West, he says: "Bears are of three kinds: the black, the red, and the grizzle bear." But he goes no further than to add, in regard to the two latter, that, "their nature is savage and ferocious, their power dangerous, and their haunts to be guarded against."

Sir Alexander Mackenzie, the explorer, during his second voyage, on May 13, 1795, mentions seeing bear tracks on the banks of the Peace River, some of which were nine inches wide. He says, "The Indians entertain great apprehension of this kind of bear, which is called the grisly bear, and they never venture to attack it except in a party of at least three or four." He never, however, seems to have seen one, nor does he describe it.

Lewis and Clark, on the other hand, not only entered in their journals full accounts of their various encounters with these animals, but made inquiries about them among the inhabitants of the regions where they were found, and took in them not only the interest of the fur trader and the hunter, but that of the naturalist. Moreover, for nearly fifty years these field notes of theirs were the chief, if not the only, source of information regarding these animals. Here and there, during that period, in the works of scientific writers upon natural history, an original observation, or an authenticated report of such observations, appears. But for the most part everything outside the categories of frank romance or alleged adventure that found its way into print, was an unblushing rehash or an unwarranted elaboration of their statements.

Their note of April 29, 1805, is as follows:

"Captain Lewis, who was on shore with one hunter, met, about eight o'clock, two white bears. Of the strength and ferocity of this animal the Indians had given us dreadful accounts. They never attack him but in parties of six or eight persons, and even then are often defeated with a loss of one or more of their party. Having no weapons but bows and arrows, and the bad guns with which the traders supply them, they are obliged to approach very near to the bear. As no wound, except through the head or heart, is mortal, they frequently fall a sacrifice if they miss their aim. He rather attacks than avoids a man, and such is the terror which he has inspired, that the Indians who go in quest of him paint themselves and perform all the superstitious rites customary when they make war on a neighboring nation.

"Hitherto, those bears we had seen did not appear desirous of encountering us; but although to a skilful rifleman the danger is very much diminished, yet the white bear is a terrible animal. On approaching these two, both Captain Lewis and the hunter fired and each wounded a bear. One of them made his escape. The other turned upon Captain Lewis and pursued him seventy or eighty yards, but being badly wounded the bear could not run so fast as to prevent him from reloading his piece, which he again aimed at him, and a third shot from the hunter brought him to the ground. He was a male, not quite full-grown, and weighed about three hundred pounds. The legs are somewhat longer than those of the black bear and the talons and tusks much longer. Its color is a yellowish brown; the eyes are small, black, and piercing; the front of the fore legs near the feet is usually black, and the fur is finer, thicker, and deeper than that of the black bear; add to which it is a more furious animal and very remarkable for the wounds which it will bear without dying."

Thus reads the first account of a meeting between a white man and a grizzly.

I quote at length from Lewis and Clark on this subject, not only because their notes are interesting, accurate, and instructive in themselves, but because, while they are scattered through the pages of a voluminous and unfamiliar report, a first-hand acquaintance with them is, in their field, the beginning of knowledge. On May 6, following, the record proceeds:

"Captain Clark and one of the hunters met this evening the largest brown bear we have seen. As they fired he did not attempt to attack, but fled with a most tremendous roar; and such was his extraordinary tenacity of life that, although five balls passed through his lungs, and he had five other wounds, he swam more than half [sic] across the river to a sand bar and survived twenty minutes. He weighed between five hundred and six hundred pounds at least, and measured at least eight feet seven and a half inches from the nose to the extremity of the hind feet, five feet ten and a half inches around the breast, three feet eleven inches around the neck, one foot eleven inches around the middle of the fore leg, and his talons, five on each foot, were four and three-eighth inches in length. This differs from the common black bear in having its talons longer and more blunt; its tail shorter; its hair of a reddish or bay brown, longer, finer, and more abundant; his liver, lungs, and heart much larger even in proportion to his size, the heart being equal to that of a large ox; his maw ten times larger. Besides fish and flesh he feeds on roots and every kind of wild fruit."

May 11, 1805. "About five in the afternoon one of our men (Bratton), who had been afflicted with boils and suffered to walk on shore, came running to the boats with loud cries and every symptom of terror and distress. For some time after we had taken him on board he was so much out of breath as to be unable to describe the cause of his anxiety; but he at length told us that about a mile and a half below he had shot a brown bear, which had immediately turned and was in close pursuit of him; but the bear, being badly wounded, could not overtake him. Captain Lewis, with seven men, immediately went in search of him; having found his track, followed him by the blood for a mile, found him concealed in some thick brushwood and shot him with two balls through the skull. Though somewhat smaller than that killed a few days ago, he was a monstrous animal and a most terrible enemy. Our man shot him through the centre of the lungs, yet he had pursued him furiously for half a mile, then returned more than twice that distance, and with his talons prepared himself a bed in the earth two feet deep and five feet long; he was perfectly alive when they found him, which was at least two hours after he had received the wound. The wonderful power of life which these animals possess renders them dreadful; their very track in the mud or sand, which we have sometimes found eleven inches long and seven and one-fourth inches wide, exclusive of the talons, is alarming; and we had rather encounter two Indians than meet a single brown bear. There is no chance of killing them by a single shot unless the ball goes through the brain, and this is very difficult on account of two large muscles which cover the side of the forehead and the sharp projection of the centre of the frontal bone, which is also thick."

May 14, 1805. "Toward evening the men in the hindmost canoes discovered a large brown bear lying in the open ground about three hundred paces from the river. Six of them, all good hunters, immediately went to attack him, and concealing themselves by a small eminence, came unperceived within forty paces of him. Four of the hunters now fired and each lodged a ball in his body, two of them directly through the lungs. The furious animal sprang up and ran open-mouthed upon them. As he came near, the two hunters who had reserved their fire gave him two wounds, one of which, breaking his shoulder, retarded his motion for a moment; but before they could reload he was so near that they were obliged to run to the river, and before they reached it he had almost overtaken them. Two jumped into the canoe, the other four separated, and concealing themselves in the willows, fired as fast as each could reload. They struck him several times, but instead of weakening the monster, each shot seemed only to direct him toward the hunter; till at last he pursued two of them so closely that they threw aside their guns and pouches and jumped down a perpendicular bank of twenty feet into the river. The bear sprang after them, and was within a few feet of the hindmost when one of the hunters on shore shot him in the head and finally killed him. They dragged him to the shore and found that eight balls had passed through him in different directions. The bear was old and the meat tough, so that they took the skin only."

May 22, 1805. "We have not seen in this quarter [since passing the Muscle Shell] the black bear common in the United States, and on the lower parts of the Missouri, nor have we discerned any of their tracks. They may easily be distinguished by the shortness of the talons from the brown, grizzly, or white bear, all of which seem to be of the same family, which assumes those colors at different seasons of the year."

June 12, 1805. On coming out to the Missouri River from an expedition inland, they this day saw two large brown bears and killed them both at the first fire — "a circumstance which has never before occurred since we have seen that animal."

June 14, 1805, at the Falls of the Missouri. "Captain Lewis met a herd of at least one thousand buffalo, and being desirous of providing for supper, shot one of them. The animal immediately began to bleed, and Captain Lewis, who had forgotten to reload his rifle, was intently watching to see him fall, when he beheld a large brown bear, which was stealing on him unperceived and was already within twenty steps. In the first moment of surprise he lifted his rifle, but remembering instantly that it was not charged and that he had no time to reload, he felt that there was no safety but in flight. It was in the open, level plain — not a bush or a tree within three hundred yards, the bank of the river sloping and not more than three feet high, so that there was no possible mode of concealment. Captain Lewis therefore thought of retreating in a quick walk, as far as the bear advanced, toward the nearest tree; but as soon as he turned, the bear ran open-mouthed and at full speed upon him. Captain Lewis ran about eighty yards, but finding that the animal gained on him fast, it flashed on his mind that, by getting into the water to such a depth that the bear would be obliged to attack him swimming, there was still some chance of his life; he therefore turned short, plunged into the river about waist deep, and facing about, presented the point of his espontoon. The bear arrived at the water's edge within twenty feet of him; but as soon as he put himself in this posture of defence, the bear seemed frightened, and wheeling about, retreated with as much precipitation as he had pursued. Very glad to be released from this danger, Captain Lewis returned to the shore, and observed him run with great speed, sometimes looking back as if he expected to be pursued, till he reached the woods. He could not conceive the cause of the sudden alarm of the bear, but congratulated himself on his escape when he saw his own track torn to pieces by the furious animal, and learned from the whole adventure never to suffer his rifle to be a moment unloaded."

June 20, 1805. "One of the men, who was sent a short distance from the camp to bring home some meat, was attacked by a white bear, closely pursued within forty paces of the camp, and narrowly escaped being caught. Captain Clark immediately went with three men in quest of the bear, which he was afraid might surprise another of the hunters who was out collecting the game. The bear was, however, too quick, for before Captain Clark could reach the man, the bear had attacked him and compelled him to take refuge in the water. He now ran off as they approached, and it being late, they deferred pursuing him till the next morning."

June 27, 1805. "As the men were hunting on the river, they saw a low ground covered with thick brushwood, where, from the tracks along shore, they thought a bear had probably taken refuge. They therefore landed without making a noise and climbed a tree about twenty feet above the ground. Having fixed themselves securely they raised a loud shout and a bear instantly rushed toward them. These animals never climb, and therefore, when he came to the tree and stopped to look at them, Drewyer shot him in the head. He proved to be the largest we had yet seen. His nose appeared to be like that of a common ox, his forefeet measured nine inches across, the hind feet were seven inches wide and eleven and three-quarters long, exclusive of the talons. One of these animals came within thirty yards of the camp last night and carried off some buffalo meat which we placed on a pole."

June 28, 1805. "The white bears have now become exceedingly troublesome, they constantly infest our camp during the night, and though they have not attacked us, as our dog, which patrols all night, gives us notice of their approach, yet we are obliged to sleep with our arms by our sides for fear of accident, and we cannot send one man alone to any distance, particularly if he has to pass through brushwood."

May 13, 1806, near the Kooskooskee River. "The hunters killed . . . a male and female bear, the first of which was large, fat, and of a bay color, the second, meagre, grizzly, and of smaller size. They were of the species common to the upper part of the Missouri and might well be termed the variegated bear, for they are found occasionally of a black, grizzly, brown, or red color. There is every reason to believe them to be of precisely the same species. Those of different colors are killed together, as in the case of these two, as we found a white and bay associated together on the Missouri; and some nearly white were seen in this neighborhood by the hunters. Indeed, it is not common to find any two bears of the same color, and if the difference in color were to constitute a distinction of species, the number would increase to almost twenty. Soon afterward the hunters killed a female bear with two cubs. The mother was black with considerable intermixture of white hairs and a white spot on the breast. One of the cubs was jet black and the other of a light reddish-brown or bay color. The poil of these variegated bears is much finer, longer, and more abundant than that of the common black bear, but the most striking differences between them are that the former are larger and have longer tusks, and longer as well as blunter talons, that they prey more on other animals, that they lie neither so long nor so closely in winter quarters, and that they never climb trees, however closely pressed by the hunters. These variegated bears, though specifically the same with those we met on the Missouri, are by no means so ferocious, probably because the scarcity of game and habit of living on roots may have weaned them from the practice of attacking and devouring animals. Still, however, they are not so passive as the common black bear, which is also to be found here, for they have already fought with our hunters, though with less fury than those on the other side of the mountain."

May 31, 1806. (On one of the upper branches of the Columbia River.) "Two men visited the Indian village, where they purchased a dressed bearskin, of a uniform pale reddish-brown color, which the Indians called *yackah,* in contradistinction to *hohhost,* or white bear. This remark induced us to inquire more particularly into their opinions as to the several species of bears; we therefore produced all the skins of that animal which we had killed at this place, and also one very nearly white which we had purchased. The natives immediately classed the white, the deep and the pale grizzly-red, the grizzly dark brown, in short, all those with the extremities of the hair of a white or frosty color, without regard to the color of the ground of the poil, under the name of *hohhost.* They assured us that they were all of the same species with the white bear; that they associated together, had longer nails than the others, and never climb trees. On the other hand, the black skins, those which were black with a number of entirely white hairs intermixed, or with a white breast, the uniform bay, the brown, and light reddish-brown, were ranged under the class *yackah,* and were said to resemble each other in being smaller, in having shorter nails than the white bears, in climbing trees, and being so little vicious that they could be pursued with safety. This distinction of the Indians seems to be well founded, and we are inclined to believe: First, that the white, grizzly, etc., bear of this neighborhood forms a distinct species, which, moreover, is the same with that of the same color on the upper part of the Missouri, where the other species is not found; second, that the black, reddish-brown, etc., is a second species, equally distinct from the white bear of this country and from the black bear of the Atlantic and Pacific Oceans, which two last seemed to form only one species. The common black bear is indeed unknown in this country, for the bear of which we are speaking, though in most respects similar, differs from it in having much finer, thicker, and longer hair, with a greater proportion of fur mixed with it, and also in having a variety of colors, while the common black bear has no intermixture or change of color, but is of a uniform black."

It may here be noted that scientific naturalists, in their latest classifications of bears, while upholding Lewis and Clark in their surmises regarding the grizzlies, overrule them in their assumption that the other "black, brown, etc., bear" of the Rocky Mountain regions form a different species from the common black bear.

July 15, 1806. At the Falls of the Missouri again. "At night McNeal, who had been sent in the morning to examine the cache at the lower end of the portage, returned, but had been prevented from reaching that place by a singular adventure. Just as he arrived near Willow Run, he approached a thicket of brush, in which was a white bear, which he did not discover till he was within ten feet of him. His horse started and wheeled suddenly round, throwing McNeal almost immediately under the bear, which started up instantly. Finding the bear raising himself on his hind feet to attack him, he struck him on the head with the butt end of his musket; the blow was so violent that it broke the breach of the musket and knocked the bear to the ground. Before he recovered McNeal, seeing a willow tree close by, sprang up and there remained, while the bear closely guarded the foot of the tree until late in the afternoon. He then went off; McNeal being released came down, and having found his horse, which had strayed off to the distance of two miles, returned to camp."

Bears in New Brunswick in the Olden Time

VENERABLE ARCHDEACON RAYMOND

These reminiscences were recorded in the papers of the New Brunswick Historical Society and published in 1928. They describe a period of Maritimes history which reaches far back into the nineteenth century.

In my young days stories about bears were often related by the old settlers. The farm of my grandfather in Lower St. Marys had as its lower line the boundary between the Counties of York and Sunbury . . . A road called the "County Line Road" here ran back at right angles to the River Saint John. The land that bordered this road was pasture and partly overgrown with bushes. Raspberries grew in abundance and cattle roamed at large. Bears were numerous along the County Line Road but were usually so well fed, owing to the abundance of berries, that they were little dreaded. One of my uncles, when quite a small boy, in going after the cows one evening was running heedlessly along the cow-path when he ran slap into a bear lying asleep in a hollow. He tumbled over him and rolled headlong. It was hard to tell which was the most frightened the boy or the bear. Each fled in a different direction.

The bears were, however, partial to sheep and very destructive to the farmer's flocks, and the government offered a considerable bounty in cash for the nose of every bear, young or old. This helped to stimulate a crusade and the life of bruin became very hazardous ere long. Bears were shot and caught in traps by the score.

On a Sunday afternoon, sixty-five years ago, one of my uncles and his young wife went for a walk out the County Line Road, having their baby with them in her small carriage. They encountered unexpectedly a she-bear and her two cubs. Not having his gun and the mother bear being rather cowardly, my uncle chased the cubs up a tree and ran home for his gun leaving his wife with her baby at the foot of the tree to keep the cubs there until he returned. The old bear growled threateningly, and prowled about in the underbrush. The cubs attempted to descend but the plucky young wife stoned them up the tree again and held her ground until the return of her husband with his gun. He shot the cubs and in due time received the bounty from the government, but could not manage to get a shot at the old bear, which kept out of reach of his musket. This plucky young woman was a girl born in our City of Saint John.

This story I had from my mother.

In Woodstock, N.B., the home of my childhood, our nearest neighbors were my father's uncles of the Beardsley family. Most of the men were tall powerful fellows (there were six brothers). Perhaps the most so of all was "Uncle Ralph," who was tall, well-proportioned, and weighed about 250 pounds. His strength was great, as the following story will show:

The brothers, John and Ralph, one day found the remains of a fine steer that had been killed and partly devoured by a bear. The creature they judged by his tracks to be a very large one. They decided to watch for the bear the next night, presuming that he would return to continue his banquet.

Armed with the old-fashioned flint-lock muskets, they lay in wait beside the remains of the steer. A thunder-storm came on and one of the brothers said, "the bear will come with the storm." This proved true. A flash of lightning revealed the bear beside the steer and taking aim as best they could in the uncertain light the brothers fired. The priming of Ralph's gun had been wet by the rain and the gun missed fire, but the ball from Uncle John's musket passed directly through the bear's head and he rolled on the ground. John ran forward eager to administer the *coup de grace* but tripped over a root and fell on his face, the bear rolling directly upon him.

Uncle Ralph seized his musket by the muzzle and swung the heavy brass-bound butt with all his strength upon the head of the bear. The butt was splintered by the mighty blow, but the bear was not rendered unconscious. Seizing the iron gun-barrel Ralph proceeded to pound the life out of the bear, and did not desist until he had smashed the barrel of the musket into three pieces. He said afterwards that blows on the creature's head seemed of no use, but that when he pounded him on the *nose* he soon got the better of him. To his great relief he succeeded in saving his brother uninjured. The bear was a very large one and Ralph Beardsley's feat was often spoken of in the neighbourhood in my young days.

Through the kindness of our corresponding member, Dr. W.F. Ganong, of Northampton, Mass., I have had the privilege of studying his photo-stat copy of P. Campbell's "Travels in the Interior parts of North America in 1791, 1792," printed in Edinburg in 1793. The photo-stat copy is from the volume in the library of Congress. The books are now very scarce and a copy was sold at auction some little time ago for $350.00.

I shall only venture to give some extracts relating to *Bears in New Brunswick:* These extracts I give *verbatim* without note or comment. He writes on September 2, 1791: "After we had passed Major Coffy's (Coffin's) beautiful seat, pleasantly situated on a point (Woodman's Point) on the west side of the river, we landed. Here I was informed that two men, in coming down the river, had attacked an old bear and two young ones, swimming across the river, which they killed. Another man, in his boat alone, met a bear swimming across, and struck him with his axe and wounded him; but by the force of the stroke the axe fell overboard. The wound exasperated the bear to such a degree that it was with the utmost difficulty the man could keep him from boarding him and in the struggle he bit one of his fingers; but at last he shoved off his boat and got quit of him.

"On an island, called Spoon Island, there were seven bears killed in one day. A gentleman and his son, near the house in which I then lodged, had been out working at the hay, having pitch-forks and rakes. Seeing a monstrous bear, quite close to the river, they pressed so hard upon him as to drive him into the water. They then thought they had him secure, as there was a boat near them, to which they immediately ran; and having pursued and come up with him, they struck and pelted him with the pitch-forks and shafts till they broke them to pieces. The exasperated monster now, as they had no weapon to annoy him, turned the chase on his adversaries; and fixing his forepaws upon the gunnel of the boat attempted to get in.

"They did all they could to keep him out, but their efforts were in vain — he got in. So that at last they had nothing else for it, but either to jump out into the water or stay in the boat and be torn to pieces. They chose the former and swam ashore. The bear, now master of the boat whence the enemy had battered him, was so severely galled with the strokes and wounds he had received that he made no attempt to follow, but continued in the boat, otherwise he might have soon overtaken them, and have had ample revenge as he could swim three times faster than they.

"They immediately ran to the house for guns, and when they came back saw him sitting in the boat, and dipping one of his paws now and then in the water, and washing his wounds; on which, levelling their pieces, they shot him dead.

"The landlord of the house I put up at, when this story was told, showed me one of the paws of this bear, which, on account of its great size, he kept as a show, and added that it was as big as a yearling calf. So that one may easily conceive the havoc and destruction committed in a country so much infested with such monstrous and ravenous animals, especially on sheep, the simplest and silliest of all creatures, which fall an easy prey to beasts of far less strength and size. Many of these harmless, yet useful animals were destroyed by bears in this very neighbourhood, where one man sustained the loss of thirty of his sheep within a short space; and even young cattle often were devoured, and carried off by them; yet they prefer swine, when they can get them, to any other meat.

"After satisfying myself with everything necessary for me to see in this part of the River Saint John, I left my coat in the boat, the day being warm and sultry, and proceeded in my waistcoat and trousers twelve miles on foot.

"I proceeded on the road, which had hitherto continued along the river side, but now struck off from it and led into a thick wood. No sooner had I entered this dreary wilderness than the many stories I had heard of the bears recurred to my mind, which made me so apprehensive as to be at a stand whether to return back or push forward. I chose the latter. My dog, who was along with me and to whom I trusted much in case of being attacked, kept ranging about for game and was but rarely in my sight; so that I had constantly to call on him to keep him in, lest a bear should spring out of the wood on me in his absence; for it being Sunday I had left my gun, along with my servant, in the boat, and I began to cut a stout stick with my pocket knife. While bent down at this work, such was my apprehension, that I kept constantly looking around me, lest a bear should seize me by the posteriors.

"After being fortified with this stick I proceeded on without any further concern. Had I been so well informed as I afterwards was, I would have been under no such apprehension, as it is very rare that a bear, no way molested by man, will attack him unless she happens to have young cubs. In that case it is dangerous to go near her den, but no bear would keep her young so near a place so much frequented by her mortal enemies, the human species, as that road was."

So much for bears in New Brunswick.

Bear Customs of the Cree

ALONSON SKINNER

The following excerpt, taken from the Ontario Historical Society Papers and Records of 1914, suggests both the status accorded to bears by North American Indians, and the fascination with which Indians were regarded by white intruders.

Among all the animals with which they are familiar, there is none more impressive to the minds of the Eastern Cree than the black bear. Its courage, sagacity, and above all, its habit of walking man-like, upon its hind legs, have convinced the Indians of its supernatural propensities.

The Eastern Cree are convinced that all living animals have souls or spirits whose good will must be secured or else they will prevent their species from being captured by the hunters. Because of this belief they take pains to return the bones of the beaver to running water, and prevent them from being devoured by dogs. The heads of ducks and geese, the teeth of the caribou and moose, the claws, chins, and skulls of bears, are carefully preserved as talismans and trophies, and mystical paintings are placed on the skins of fur-bearing animals to appease their manes. But the customs concerning the capture and treatment of the bear have become much more elaborated.

If a hunter, while in the forest, comes upon a bear and wishes to slay it, he first approaches and apologizes, explaining that nothing but lack of food drives him to kill it, and begging that the bear will not be offended at him, nor permit the spirits of other bears to be angry. On killing the bear, he cuts off the middle toe and claw of the right fore foot and returns with it to his camp. When he arrives he first smokes for some time, saying nothing of what he has done, but meanwhile mentally deciding whom he shall ask to take care of, bring in, and butcher the carcass. Usually, if he is a married man, the person chosen is the wife of the hunter. When the proper time, perhaps an hour, has elapsed, he gives the announcing claw to the person whom he has picked out, and states where the bear may be found. The recipient of the claw understands what is required, and, asking no further questions, takes a companion, goes out, and brings in the carcass. The announcing claw is wrapped in cloth, beaded, or painted, or both, and kept as a memento of the occasion.

In case two or more men kill a bear, it is laid out on its back in their canoe, and carefully covered. When the hunters approach their camp or post, the burden is seen from afar, and all the Indians crowd the river bank with cries of congratulation. When the canoe grates on the beach, it is at once surrounded by the small boys, who run down and draw back the blanket or covering enough to expose the bear's head, or at least, its teeth. It is then carried up and laid out, like a man, in front of its slayer's wigwam. After the bear had been laid out, and tobacco placed in its mouth, the hunter and the chief men present smoke over it.

Nowadays, when the bear is brought in, it is laid out upon a new blanket purchased from the Hudson's Bay Company for the occasion. While the ceremony is going on, the bear must be called Kawipätc mitcem (black food). Pointing with the finger at the carcass during this ceremony is strictly tabooed.

After the hunter and the chief men have smoked, the bear is butchered, and the flesh distributed to all the camp. Certain parts of the bear's flesh are at once burnt ("given to its spirit to eat"), including a small piece of the heart. The rest of the heart is at once eaten by the slayer, in order that he may acquire the cunning and courage of his victim.

Women are not allowed to eat of the bear's head or paws, nor men of its rump. The bones are never given away, unless the bear's flesh is served as a feast in the lodge of the slayer. In any event, they are carefully cleansed, saved, and hung up, or placed on a scaffold where the dogs cannot reach them. If wild animals, other than dogs, reach and devour them, no harm is done. The skull of the bear is cleaned, and the brains removed. It is dried and painted with vermillion and is placed in a safe place and kept from three to six months, when it is secretly taken by its owner and hung up on a tree in the forest.

Formerly, the Cree of Moose Fort, instead of smoking over the carcass of a dead bear, like those of the Eastmain, went through the following ceremony:

The head of the bear was first cut off and cooked, after which the men and boys of the camp sat down in a circle about it. A large stone pipe was laid beside the head and a plug of tobacco placed upon it. Then the man who had killed the bear arose from his place in the circle and filled the pipe with the tobacco, after which it was lighted and passed about the circle from left to right, the slayer smoking first. Each person had the alternative of smoking the pipe for several moments or merely taking a single puff before passing it on. After this the bear's head was passed about and everyone strove to bite out a piece of its flesh without touching it with his hands. The same ceremony was sometimes also gone through after the slaying of a caribou.

Another bear ceremony observed by the Moose Cree was as follows: The bear's intestines were removed, slightly cooked and smoked, after the passing of the head. They were then coiled up on a plate and passed about the circle by the slayer and offered to all the men present, each of whom bit off a piece. Women were allowed to be present at this part of the function but were not allowed to partake of the meat. This ceremony was quite recently observed.

The Cree of Rupert's House and Eastmain River Fort taboo pointing at a bear with the finger even if it is a live bear in the woods, for if this was done, the bear would turn and run away, even if he did not see the offender, for his medicine would warn him of the approach of danger. At the feast, after the slaying of the bear, a certain amount of food is always set before each guest, who is obliged to finish it at one sitting. If, however, he cannot eat it all at once, he is privileged to leave it at the house of the giver of the feast until the next night, when he must finish it. The Moose and Albany Crees do not now observe the majority of the bear customs, nor have they for many years. Those at Albany have forgotten their significance.

It is permissible to speak of a bear as **Muskwá** (the "angry one" or "wrangler") in his absence only, unless one wishes to anger it, or as an expression of reproof. It must never be used before his carcass. If a hunter comes upon a bear in the woods, and is obliged to speak of it, he may call it **Kawipätc mitcem** (black meat, or food) because this is the bear's proper name, and it will not be offended or frightened. This name may also be used before the dead body. Under the same circumstances as above, or when it is not desirable to let it know that it is being spoken of, it may be called **Tciceäk** ("old porcupine") because it will not know who is being talked about. When making fun of a bear, or joking about it, it may be called **Wakiuc** (crooked tail). This name must never be used before the carcass, but **Tukwaiâken** (short tail) may be used. **Pisesu** or **Pisistciu** ("resembling a cat," or lynx) is another term applied to the bear to avoid calling him by his real name. **Wakiu** may be another form of **Wakiuc,** and **Matsue** may be a variant of **Muskwá.**

TWO

THE WAR
BETWEEN
MAN AND BEAR

Black Bear in Chamba

SHIKARI

Throughout the nineteenth century, and in the early years of the twentieth, bears were hunted and killed in their thousands. It seemed then that the number of animals which nature had provided for the entertainment of sportsmen was inexhaustible. The following extracts from the diary of a British army officer who spent three months on a shooting expedition in Chamba State, in India, is typical.

Shortly after this I called at a house in the nullah to ask if bear had been seen, and the owner showed me his largest field of corn, which had been badly trampled. A she-bear and her cub had done the damage; they usually came at dusk, so I decided to stay till then. There was a big tree on the edge of the field, and I fixed on that as my observation-post. I had a clear view of the whole field from a safe position, because if a bear and cub be the quarry it is prudent, to say the least of it, to keep out of her way as much as possible. At dusk Gilja and I climbed the tree. We waited for a couple of hours, but nothing happened. It was a cloudy night which was most unfortunate, as it was nearly full moon. I was just preparing to descend when I heard a loud grunt below me. There was the outline of the bear and her cub only a few feet away—a situation I had not looked for but aiming as well as circumstances permitted, I fired. Both animals fled grunting and snorting, and I afterwards found that the bullet had passed through a branch of the tree and flattened itself on a stone almost on the spot where she had been standing! It was most disappointing, as quite evidently the branch had deflected the bullet. I felt no compunction in trying to bag the bear as the cub was quite old enough to look after itself, and between them they had spoiled half a field of corn. Anyhow they had got a good fright, and probably would not return again before the native had his crop gathered in.

Gilja attributed my bad luck with black bear to the fact that I had not made a sacrifice at the shrine on the hillside. We were walking one day when we came to a small pile of stones. I was just about to ask Gilja if it was a landmark, when I saw him get down on his knees and assume the attitude of prayer. I at once turned my back and walked slowly on. Presently he caught me up and suggested we should turn back, as it was getting late. On passing the mound again I noticed some red powder sprinkled on the stones, also some red cloth on the end of a wire, which I had not seen before, and I presumed Gilja had put them there. I did not ask him anything about it, but he volunteered the information that it was a wayside temple. He suggested it would be a good idea to bring with us next time we came a small goat as a sacrifice and urged that the goat would cost me only Rs.£2, and would bring luck. I said I would think about it, but I knew the goat would only remain at the shrine five minutes, after which it would certainly make a good meal for the *shikaris*. And that was exactly what did happen later, when I thought it was wise to humour them after ten very disappointing days. Three visits were paid to the nullah, and on each occasion we returned empty-handed. So a young goat was taken up, killed with great ceremony, and duly laid on the wayside temple. I strolled along the path in the evening, and noticed the goat had mysteriously disappeared. Between three of them it must have made quite a good meal. And so the Eastern changes little as the centuries pass for were not the sacrifices in the temple at Jerusalem the prelude to a hearty meal?

That afternoon I had an interesting time, for Muni Lal, a sheep-farmer from Dharmsala, and some other celebrities, forgathered in the courtyard and held a conference on things in general and life in particular. Their idea was that life would not be worth living if it were not for *pice* and women. The latter, one old greybeard asserted, caused him vast amusement, because he loved to see them fight with one another. Muni Lal said he never allowed his womenfolk to fight; if they started, he simply threatened to cut off their supply of *pice*, which immediately stopped trouble. I heard some of their remarks on British rule. Certain of these, while complimentary in a sense, did not show up the judgment of someone in authority in any very flattering light, and I gathered it was a Commissioner of some district. Gilja then broke in with a remark that rather tickled my fancy. 'Supposing,' he said, 'there were no British "Raj" here, my occupation would be gone, and you would get no backsheesh, so be content.' I think he summed it up rather neatly, and the others evidently agreed with him, as I heard murmurs of assent.

The next day I went up the nullah more determined than ever to bag that elusive black bear. Arriving at eleven o'clock, after the hottest climb we had experienced, a survey of the nullah through the glasses showed no sign of life. The heat was evidently too much for game of any description: they had all retired to their shelters. I followed their example, falling asleep and not waking till four in the afternoon. By that time the lower portions of the nullah were in shade, so, taking the Mannlicher and half a dozen rounds, I moved along the ridge towards some rocks, from which a good view was obtained. It was a glorious sight that met the eye. The nullah was roughly five miles long by two miles broad at the crests, narrowing down to about 400 yards at the bottom of the deep ravine. A swiftly flowing stream in the middle ran into the Ravi at one end, and had its source in two glaciers at the other. Above the glaciers was a range of mountains, whose highest peak was about 18,000 feet above sea-level. These snowclad peaks towering up against the blue sky, and, as one's glance fell lower, the white carpet dotted with rocks, and here and there a stunted fir tree, gradually mingled with grass and shrubs, till the snow limit was reached. Here the forest of fir trees and conifers of all descriptions gave a dark tone to the mountainside, and one could not imagine better shelter for wild animals than in its inmost recesses. A blue heat haze gave an impression of distance, although from where I was sitting it could hardly have been more than a mile and a half to the forest. There was not a breath of wind. A couple of big kites were sailing backwards and forwards overhead, seemingly taking no interest in mundane affairs, but in reality sweeping the ground beneath them with keen eyes for some tit-bit for their evening meal. Now and then one would make a dive for some unoffending bird, but it was rarely I saw a capture made. I crawled out of my hiding-place to get a better view of the immediate surroundings.

Gilja had told me a black bear had been seen, and as I was examining the plateau with my glasses I saw him grubbing among some rocks and bushes. Gilja, Kermitie and I lost no time, and immediately started off down the hillside with both the .450 and the Mannlicher. As the plateau was about three-quarters of the way up the nullah, and on the opposite side from the shelters, we had to go to the bridge, cross over, and climb up the other side. The ascent was very trying, and we sat down at the top and scanned the plateau. The bear was still where we last saw him, so Gilja and I moved on, leaving Kermitie to keep an eye on our prey. Silence was now imperative, but as I wore grass shoes, and Gilja padded behind me on bare feet, we did not make much noise. I reconnoitred, and could see Kermitie, but could not spot the bear, so I signalled to him asking for its position, and from his wild gesticulations it seemed it must be very near us.

I led the way to higher ground and, after going about fifty yards, climbed a rock and looked over the edge. The bear was now about twenty yards from me, standing on his hind legs and sniffing the air in a suspicious manner, with his back to me. Not wishing to make a bigger hole in him than necessary, I decided to use the Mannlicher. Gilja handed me the rifle cocked and with the safety catch forward. Pulling the latter back and taking aim, I squeezed the trigger. All that happened was a click, which, to my ears, sounded like a blow with a sledge-hammer. The rifle was not loaded! I peered quickly over the boulder, expecting to see the bear coming for us helter skelter. But no, there he was, still contentedly feeding. He must have been deaf. Taking a clip of cartridges from my pocket, I inserted them as quietly as possible and closed the bolt. Our friend was now strolling aimlessly to and fro straight in front. Now was my chance, and I took it. As soon as I fired he gave forth two panic-stricken howls and made off downhill. Gilja and I followed, and saw him crawling slowly down a snowy slope. I fired again, and this time he crumpled up and started rolling over the snow until stopped by a tree stump. Gilja and Kermitie both started running to where he lay, while I followed more leisurely. When I came on the scene they already had him stretched out and were waiting for my measuring tape. He was just over six feet, and in excellent coat. Skinning operations were soon in progress.

It was nearly eight o'clock when we reached camp, but Kermitie had hurried on in front and warned the bearer to have a hot bath ready, and into it I plunged immediately on arrival. When I had dressed again, a most delightful dinner awaited me. 'Kermitie informed me,' said my bearer, 'of Master's good luck and wonderful shooting, so something special had to be prepared for Master's meal.' At the risk of boring my readers, I give the menu, in order to show what a really good native cook can produce with only an hour's warning:

Tomato Soup
Curried Eggs and Rice
Roast Chikor
Walnut Sauce
Stewed Mulberries and Cream
Sardines on Toast

Each course had to be cooked separately on a small fire, and the bird was roasted in the mud oven. Be it confessed, the tomato soup was made from soup cubes, and the sardines and the cream, of course, were tinned, but the rest was entirely native produce.

Next morning, on examining the skull, I found that the front portion of the lower jaw had been completely shot away, probably some four or five years previously, as it was completely rounded off. He must have had great difficulty in feeding, and the front teeth of the top jaw can only have been used as a kind of scoop with which to assist the food on to his tongue. This malformation was annoying, but luckily the taxidermist to whom I sent the trophy was a very keen sportsman himself, and was able to supply the lower jaw of another bear which he had shot, but whose mask had not been mounted.

A few days later I was preparing to leave for the nullah again when Gilja introduced Mawr Singh, the headman of the village, whose crops had suffered badly from a black bear. Having given a deep salaam, he told his story in slow and distinct Hindustani:

'Last night, Master, the moon having risen over yonder hill, I was awakened from my couch by my wife, who, to my amazement and anger, was standing at the window and giving little cries of dismay. I chided her for having awakened her lord and master at such an unseemly hour, but she insisted I should come and look. I did, and behold one big bear in the middle of my field of peas! He was of enormous size and showed no fear, as was proved by the contempt in which he held the inhabitants. And then an inspiration came to me. Bears do not love water. So I caught up a "chatty," filled it with water, leant over the wall, and emptied it where I thought the bear was.'

'And do you think he will return?' I asked.

'Of a certainty, Master.'

'And when do you think he will return?'

'One cannot say, Master; it may be this evening or to-morrow evening, or a week hence, but most assuredly he will come back, for are not my peas more luscious than any other fruit which this accursed beast consumes? Yea, he will come back, but woe betide him if thou, Master, be present with thy guns with which to kill him.'

I felt at that point I should get up, bow, and make a speech, thanking him for his kind words and testimonial. I arranged to go over that night, and went at once to inspect the field of action. Having done so, I prepared the plan of campaign with Gilja and Kermitie, which was as follows. In case the moon, which was then full, should be clouded over at the critical moment, Gilja was to have a lantern placed on the wall, shielded by a black cloth. At a given signal, he would turn up the wick and pull off the cloth, so that I would have light to shoot by. I further arranged with Mawr Singh to have the peas in the field directly below us smeared with honey. I also had several trails of honey laid in the field, each starting at the edge and becoming stronger as they converged to the point to which I hoped to lure our black friend. After dinner I walked along to Mawr Singh's house and found the tiffin coolie already on guard. I made Gilja practise uncovering the lamp once more, and then lay down to sleep. I did not sleep long, and, getting bored doing nothing, I accompanied Kermitie on watch. I soon spotted a blacker shadow than the rest, which seemed to move. It was the bear! Kermitie took the Mannlicher, and Gilja meantime had the lamp properly covered up, and by a series of stealthy moves put it on top of the house wall. I stood leaning up against the wall, with the rifle resting on top of it, Gilja on my left, and Kermitie with the Mannlicher, also on the wall, on my right. The stage was now set. The shadow detached itself from the trees, and there once more was our old friend back to his favourite haunt, making a great feast of honey and peas. The fickle moon again failed us at the critical moment, and it was some minutes before I could pick up the black form again. He was following up the honey track, still some twenty yards off, and in the darkness it would be easy to make a mistake. I crouched down over my rifle, and Kermitie did the same . . . The signal given, the black cloth fell from the brilliantly lit lamp; then without a moment's warning the lamp toppled over the edge of the wall and fell, a flare of light and splintered glass, to the ground! Speech failed me, and when I awoke to the situation Kermitie was blazing away round after round in the darkness. I quietly told him it was useless, and bringing my rifle over the wall, I extracted the cartridges and put them in my pocket. I turned to Gilja, who was staring at me with a stupid grin on his face. 'Go away; go right away, and never let me see you again,'' I said; and telling Kermitie to follow me with the rifles, I trudged wearily back to camp. I may say that for some time I had been dissatisfied with Gilja, and had come to the conclusion that Kermitie was the better man. Next morning I woke at twelve o'clock and called my bearer. When he had made the bath ready he came round to the front of the tent and said that Gilja was now in the camp, and that he was sorry — very sorry. Gilja was sorry, was he? Really, that was very good of him. Only six more days' shooting, and a very fine bear missed owing to his carelessness. A most excellent joke! 'Tell him,' I said to the bearer, 'I much appreciate his kindness and sympathy, but if he is not out of the camp in two minutes he *will* be sorry.' I called Kermitie to the tent. 'Kermitie,' I said, 'I have dismissed Gilja, and you must carry on now as head *shikari*. What do you propose should be done?' He hummed and hawed, and I knew what was coming. 'Master, may not Gilja return as *chota shikari,* under me? He will be for ever Master's servant if he may; if he be dismissed, when he reaches Chamba Town he will be asked why he has come back alone, and his name will be taken off the list of *shikaris.*' There was a good deal more of the same description. After all, I thought, why not? So I called Gilja to the tent, and told him I had decided to keep him as *chota shikari,* on condition that he did absolutely as Kermitie told him. He was profuse in his thanks and salaams, and went back to the servants' quarters.

During the next few days we searched for that bear without success. At last I got desperate, and urged my *shikaris* to make another careful search to find his lair. Gilja, anxious to retrieve his reputation, worked like a Trojan, and was ultimately successful in finding the bear's cave, half a mile from Deole, and so we moved our camp.

While my servants were doing so, I attended the reception which followed the sixth wedding of my old friend, the egg-wallah, accompanied by Kermitie. On arriving at the house I was met by the old man himself, who salaamed most profusely, and vowed he was overcome by the honour I was doing him. He was dressed in his everyday garments, but festooned with strings of coloured tinsel till he looked like a Christmas tree. After watching the dancing for some time, I sent Kermitie back to my bearer for a couple of tins of sardines, which I presented to the bridegroom with my compliments. I had instructed Kermitie to tell the old man, as tactfully as he knew how, that I did not wish anything to eat, as I had only just finished a heavy lunch; for refusal to eat when anything is offered one on an occasion of that kind is considered a great insult. In reality my reason for not wishing to eat was that I had tried chupatties and other native delicacies, but my interior had always refused to compete with them. Kermitie's gentle hint took effect, but in a most unexpected way. The old fellow solemnly placed yards of tinsel and gaudy multi-coloured metal stars round my neck and hat. I left shortly afterwards, and on the way home I asked Kermitie what it was all about, and he told me that with the money obtained from my purchases of hens and eggs the marriage had been made possible then; otherwise, it could not have taken place for another three months.

I went to inspect the cave where the bear was thought to live, and which he seemed to leave nightly about six o'clock. It was formed by a collection of huge boulders on the hill-side, and just above the entrance was a projecting ledge of rock, which formed an excellent spot to watch the bear's exit. It had the disadvantage, however, that if he came out at a run, in a few seconds he would be out of sight among the tangled undergrowth of the wood directly facing the cave. I decided to watch the den on the two remaining evenings from six till eight o'clock.

The first evening we sat till seven o'clock, when grunts and growls were heard directly below us. This continued for some time, when suddenly the bear dashed out as if propelled from a catapult. Before I had time to get the rifle to my shoulder he was gone, and absolutely lost to sight in the wood. I did not lose hope, however, that the last evening would see him killed;

he would not catch me napping again, and I determined I would lie on the rock with the rifle to my shoulder all afternoon and evening rather than have a repetition of what had occurred.

Next morning, preparations were made for leaving the following day. The first day's march to Chanail would be an easy one of twelve miles, so an early start was not necessary. Towards evening I went along to the cave and settled down on the rock to watch. A strong wind was blowing up from the river; this was of great assistance, as the bear would not be likely to scent us. During the period of waiting I amused myself by practising aiming at imaginary objects. Opposite to me, about ten feet away and three feet from the ground, was a perfect miniature target — a white circular flower with a very dark centre. I aimed at this natural bull's-eye, and . . . hang it all, something is covering the target; what the . . . Oh! . . . I squeezed the trigger, but not at the flower. A penetrating howl rent the air, and the bear made off down the slope. His hind legs were useless now, but he managed in a most wonderful manner to drag himself a further 200 yards. In another couple of minutes it was all over. He was a magnificent specimen, not only on account of his size, but because the coat was in such perfect condition. The problem now was to get him to the camp, and eventually I had to send for a tent-pole. Tying his legs together, we slung the pole through them, and six natives from the crowd, which had by this time collected, carried him back in triumph, and all the servants, except my bearer, set to work at once skinning him. I had eaten nothing since mid-day, and was ravenously hungry. There was a fine dish of green peas served up, a gift from Mawr Singh, who had rushed out and picked them the moment he heard that the despoiler of his property was no more. After dinner, I stepped outside the tent to find him there waiting to congratulate me. What a charming old gentleman he was! When the crowd watching the skinning process became too large, with a few trenchant remarks from him they faded away. All the characters of Deole turned up 'to see the *balu* which had caused so much trouble even to a Sahib,' and of course the old egg-wallah was among them. It was midnight before the skinning was finished, the skin thoroughly impregnated with alum, and pegged out under a tarpaulin in case it should rain; it was essential that the skin should be quite dry by the morning and ready to pack up. After ten days' continuous hunting I had at last attained my desire; it was very pleasant. And so to bed.

We started off next day, and arrived safely at Chamba Town, where I bade good-bye to Kermitie and Gilja. Gilja had 'made good' after all, and received good backsheesh and an excellent *chit* (testimonial).

And now my three months' leave was almost over, and I had spent it in what is to my mind the ideal way. There are some who will spend their leave at Darjeeling in one continuous round of tennis tournaments and tea fights; there are others who will spend their leave in Central India with an elephant gun. To those who have never been in the hills, bent on sport pure and simple — it may be in Chamba, Kashmir, or elsewhere — I say, let them try it, and I am certain they will never regret the experiment.

Bear-Chasing in the Rocky Mountains

FREDERIC REMINGTON

This article, by the famous illustrator of western scenes, appeared in Harper's New Monthly Magazine in July 1895. It expresses very effectively the exhilaration of the chase — and a pang of regret after the kill.

Mr. Montague Stevens is an Englishman who for the most part attends to the rounding up of his cattle, which are scattered over the northwestern quarter of New Mexico; but he does not let that interfere with the time which all Englishmen set duly apart to be devoted to sport. His door-yard is some hundreds of miles of mountain wilderness and desolate mesa — a more gorgeous preserve than any king ever dreamed of possessing for his pleasure — with its plains dotted with antelope, and its mountains filled with cougar, deer, bear, and wild turkeys. The white race has given up the contest with nature in those parts, and it has reverted to the bear, the Navajo, and Mr. Stevens, land grants, corrals, cabins, brands, and all else.

General Miles was conducting a military observation of the country, which is bound to be the scene of any war which the Apaches or Navajos may make, and after a very long day's march, during which we had found but one water, and that was a pool of rain-water, stirred into mud and full of alkali, where we had to let our horses into the muddy stuff at the ends of our lariats, we had at last found a little rivulet and some green grass. The coffee-pot bubbled and the frying-pan hissed, while I smoked, and listened to a big escort-wagon-driver who was repairing his lash, and saying, softly, "Been drivin' a bloody lot of burros for thirty years, and don't know enough to keep a whip out of a wheel; guess I'll go to jack-punchin', 'nen I kin use a dry club."

Far down the valley a little cloud of dust gleamed up against the grey of the mountains, and presently the tireless stride of a pony shone darkly in its luminous midst. Nearer and nearer it grew — the flying tail, the regular beating of the hoofs, the swaying figure of the rider, and the left sleeve of the horseman's coat flapping purposelessly about. He crossed the brook with a splash, trotted, and, with a jerk, pulled up in our midst. Mr. Stevens is a tall, thin young man, very much bronzed, and with the set, serious face of an Englishman. He wore corduroy clothes, and let himself out of his saddle with one hand, which he also presented in greeting, the other having been sacrificed to his own shot-gun on some previous occasion. Mr. Stevens brought with him an enthusiasm for bear which speedily enveloped the senses of our party, and even crowded out from the mind of General Miles the nobler game which he had affected for thirty years.

The steady cultivation of one subject for some days is bound to develop a great deal of information, and it is with difficulty that I refrain from herein setting down facts which can doubtless be found in any good encyclopaedia or natural history; but the men in the mountains never depart from the consideration of that and one other subject, which is brands, and have reached some strange conclusions, the strangest being that the true Rocky Mountain grizzly is only seen once in a man's lifetime, and that the biggest one they ever heard of leaves his tracks in this district, and costs Mr. Stevens, roughly estimating, about $416 a year to support, since that about covers the cattle he kills.

At break of day the officers, cavalrymen, escort wagons, and pack-train toiled up the Cañon Largo to Mr. Stevens's camp, which was reached in good time, and consisted of a regular ranchman's grub-wagon, a great many more dogs of more varieties than I could possibly count, a big Texan, who was cook, and a professional bear-hunter by the name of Cooper, who had recently departed from his wonted game for a larger kind, with the result that after the final deal a companion had passed a .45 through Mr. Cooper's face and filled it with powder, and brought him nigh unto death, so that even now Mr. Cooper's head was swathed in bandages, and his mind piled with regrets that he had on at the time an overcoat, which prevented him from drawing his gun with his usual precision. Our introduction to the outfit was ushered in by a most magnificent free-for-all dog-fight; and when we had carefully torn the snarling, yelling, biting mass apart by the hind legs and staked them out to surrounding trees, we had time to watch Mr. Cooper draw diagrams of bear paws in the dust with a stick. These tracks he had just discovered up the Largo Cañon, and he averred that the bear was a grizzly, and weighed eighteen hundred pounds, and that he had been there two years, and that all the boys had hunted him, but that he was a sad old rascal.

After lunch we pulled on up the cañon and camped. The tents were pitched and the cooks busy, when I noticed three cowboys down the stream and across the cañon who were alternately leading their horses and stooping down in earnest consultation over some tracks on the ground. We walked over to them. There were Mr. Cooper, whose only visible eye rolled ominously, and Dan, the S.U. foreman, with another puncher.

"He's usin' here," said Cooper. "That's his track, and there's his work," pointing up the hill-side, where lay the dead body of a five-year-old cow. We drew near her, and there was the tale of a mighty struggle all written out more eloquently than pen can do. There were the deep furrows of the first grapple at the top; there was the broad trail down the steep hill for fifty yards, with the stones turned over and the dust marked with horn and hoof and claw; and there was the stump which had broken the roll down hill. The cow had her neck broken and turned under her body; her shoulder was torn from the body, her leg broken, and her side eaten into; and there were Bruin's big telltale footprints, rivalling in size a Gladstone bag, as he had made his way down to the stream to quench his thirst and continue up the cañon. The cow was yet warm — not two hours dead.

"We must pull out of here; he will come back to-night," said Cooper. And we all turned to with a will and struck the tents, while the cooks threw their tins, bags, and boxes into the wagons, whereat we moved off down wind for three miles, up a spur of the cañon, where we again camped. We stood around the fires and allowed Mr. Cooper to fill our minds with hope. "He'll shore come back; he's usin' here; an' cow outfits — why, he don't consider a cow outfit nothin'; he's been right on top of cow outfits since he's been in these parts, and thet two years gone now when he begun to work this yer range and do the work you see done yonder. In the mornin' we'll strike his trail, and if we can git to him you'll shore see a bar-fight."

We turned in, and during the night I was awakened twice, once by a most terrific baying of all the dogs, who would not be quieted, and later by a fine rain beating in my face. The night was dark, and we were very much afraid the rain would kill the scent. We were up long before daylight, and drank our coffee and ate our meat, and as soon as "we could see a dog a hundred yards," which is the bear-hunter's receipt, we moved off down the creek. We found that the cow had been turned over twice, but not eaten; evidently Bruin had his suspicions. The dogs cut his trail again and again. He had run within sight of our camp, had wandered across the valley hither and yon, but the faithful old hounds would not "go away." Dan sat on his pony and blew his old cow's horn, and yelled, "Hooick! hooick! get down on him, Rocks; hooick! hooick!" But Rocks could not get down on him, and then we knew that the rain had killed the scent. We circled a half-mile out, but the dogs were still; and then we followed up the Cañon Largo for miles, and into the big mountain, through juniper thickets and over malpais, up and down the most terrible places, for we knew that the bear's bed-ground is always up in the most rugged peaks, where the rim-rock overhangs in serried battlements, tier on tier. But no bear.

Rocks, the forward hound, grew weary of hunting for things which were not, and retired to the rear for consultation with his mates; and Dan had to rope him, and with some irritation started the pony, and Rocks kept the pace by dint of legging it, and by the help of a tow from nine hundred pounds of horseflesh. Poor Rocks! He understood his business, but in consequence of not being able to explain to the men what fools they were, he suffered.

The hot mid-day sun of New Mexico soon kills the scent, and we were forced to give over for the day. A cavalry sergeant shot three deer, but we, in our superior purpose, had learned to despise deer. Later than this I made a good two-hundred-yard centre on an antelope, and though I had not been fortunate enough in years to get an antelope, the whole sensation was flat in view of this new ambition.

On the following morning we went again to our dead cow, but nothing except the jackals had been at the bear's prey, for the wily old fellow had evidently scented our camp, and concluded that we were not a cow outfit, whereat he had discreetly "pulled his freight."

We sat on our horses in a circle and raised our voices. In consideration of the short time at our disposal, we concluded that we could be satisfied with taking eighteen hundred pounds of bear on the instalment plan. The first instalment was a very big piece of meat, but was, I am going to confess, presented to us in the nature of a gift; but the whole thing was so curious I will go into it.

We hunted for two days without success, unless I include deer and antelope; but during the time I saw two things which interested me. The first was a revelation of the perfect understanding which a mountain cow-pony has of the manner in which to negotiate the difficulties of the country which is his home.

Dan, the foreman, was the huntsman. He was a shrewd-eyed little square-built man, always very much preoccupied with the matter in hand. He wore a sombrero modelled into much character by weather and time, a corduroy coat, and those enormous New Mexican "chaps," and he sounded a cow-horn for his dogs, and alternately yelped in a most amusing way. So odd was this yelp that it caught the soldiers, and around their camp-fire at night you could hear the mimicking shouts of, "Oh Rocks! eh-h-h! hooick! get down on him, Rocks; tohoot! to-hoot!" We were sitting about on our horses in a little *sienneca,* while Dan was walking about, leading his pony and looking after his dogs.

When very near me he found it necessary to cross an *arroyo* which was about five feet deep and with perfectly perpendicular banks. Without hesitating, he jumped down into it, and, with a light bound, his pony followed. At the opposite side Dan put up his arms on the bank and clawed his way up, and still paying no attention to his pony, he continued on. Without faltering in the least, the little horse put his fore feet on the bank, clawed at the bank, once, twice, jumped, scratched, clawed, and, for all the world like a cat getting into the fork of a tree, he was on the bank and following Dan.

Later in the day, when going to our camp, we followed one of Dan's short-cuts through the mountains, and the cowboys on their mountain ponies rode over a place which made the breath come short to the officers and men behind. Not that they could not cross themselves, being on foot, but that the cavalry horses could they had their solemn doubts, and no one but an evil brute desires to lead a game animal where he may lose his life. Not being a geologist, I will have to say it was a blue clay in process of rock formation, and in wet times held a mountain torrent. The slope was quite seventy degrees. The approach was loose dirt and malpais, which ran off down the gulch in small avalanches under our feet. While crossing, the horses literally stood on their toes to claw out a footing. A slip would have sent them, belly up, down the toboggan slide, with a drop into an unknown depth at the end. I had often heard the cavalry axiom "that a horse can go anywhere a man can if the man will not use his hands," and a little recruit murmured it to reassure himself. I passed with the loss of a quarter of the skin on my left hand, and later asked a quaint old veteran of of four enlistments if he thought it was a bad place, and he said, "It's lizards, not harses, what ought te go thar."

Riding over the rough mountains all day sows poppy seeds in a man's head, and when the big medical officer opens your tent flaps in the morning, and fills the walls with his roars to "get up; it's four o'clock," it is with groans that you obey. You also forego washing, because you are nearly frozen stiff, and you go out and stand around the fire with your companions, who are all cheerfully miserable as they shiver and chaff each other. It seems we do not live this life on a cold calculating plane of existence, but on different lines, the variation of which is the chief delight of the discriminating, and I must record a distinct pleasure in elbowing fellows around a camp-fire when it is dark and cold and wet, and when you know that they are oftener in bed than out of it at such hours. You drink your quart of coffee, eat your slice of venison, and then regard your horse with some trepidation, since he is all of a tremble, has a hump on his back, and is evidently of a mind to "pitch."

The eastern sky grows pale, and the irrepressible Dan begins to "honk" on his horn, and the cavalcade moves off through the grease-wood, which sticks up thickly from the ground like millions of Omaha war-bonnets.

The advance consists of six or eight big bloodhounds, which range out in front, with Dan and Mr. Cooper to blow the horn, look out for "bear sign," and to swear gently but firmly when the younger dogs take recent deer trails under consideration. Three hundred yards behind come Scotch stag-hounds, a big yellow mastiff, fox-terriers, and one or two dogs which would not classify in a bench show, and over these Mr. Stevens holds a guiding hand, while in a disordered band come General Miles, his son, three army officers, myself, and seven orderlies of the Second Cavalry. All this made a picture, but, like all Western canvasses, too big for a frame. The sun broke in a golden flash over the hills, and streaked the plain with gold and gray-greens. The spirit of the thing is not hunting but the chase of the bear, taking one's mind back to the buffalo, or the nobles of the Middle Ages, who made their "image of war" with bigger game than red foxes.

Leaving the plain, we wound up a dry creek, and noted that the small oaks had been bitten and clawed down by bear to get at the acorns. The hounds gave tongue, but could not get away until we had come to a small glade in the forest, where they grew wildly excited. Mr. Cooper here showed us a very large bear track, and also a smaller one, with those of two cubs by its side. With a wild burst the dogs went away up a cañon, the blood went into our heads, and our heels into the horses, and a desperate scramble began. It is the sensation we have travelled so long to feel. Dan and Cooper sailed off through the brush and over the stones like two old crows, with their coat tails flapping like wings. We follow at a gallop in single file up the narrow dry watercourse. The creek ends, and we take to the steep hill-sides, while the loose stones rattle from under the flying hoofs. The rains have cut deep furrows on their way to the bed of the cañon, and your horse scratches and scrambles for a foothold. A low gnarled branch bangs you across the face; and then your breath fairly stops as you see a horse go into the air and disappear over a big log fallen down a hill of seventy degrees' slope. The "take off and landing" is yielding dust, but the blood in your head puts the spur in your horse, and over you go. If you miss, it is a two-hundred-foot roll, with a twelve-hundred-pound horse on top of you. But the pace soon tells, and you see nothing but good honest climbing ahead of you. The trail of the yelling dogs goes straight up, amid scraggly cedar and juniper, with loose malpais underfoot. We arrive at the top only to see Cooper and Dan disappear over a precipice after the dogs, but here we stop. Bears always seek the very highest peaks, and it is better to be there before them if possible. A grizzly can run down hill quicker than a horse, and all hunters try to get above them, since if they are big and fat they climb slowly; besides, the mountain-tops are more or less flat and devoid of underbrush, which makes good running for a horse. We scatter out along the cordon of the range. The bad going on the rimrock of the mountain-tops, where the bear tries to throw off the dogs, makes it quite impossible to follow them at speed, so that you must separate, and take your chances of heading the chase.

I selected Captain Mickler—the immaculate—the polo-player—the epitome of staff form—the trappiest trooper in the Dandy Fifth, and, together with two orderlies, we started. Mickler was mounted on a cow-pony which measured one chain three links from muzzle to coupling. Mickler had on English riding-togs—this is not saying that the pony could not run, or that Mickler was not humorous. But it was no new experience for him, this pulling a pony and coaxing him to attempt breakneck experiments, for he told me casually that he had led barefooted cavalrymen over these hills in pursuit of Apaches at a date in history when I was carefully conjugating Latin verbs.

We were making our way down a bad formation, when we heard the dogs, and presently three shots. A strayed cavalry orderly had, much to his disturbance of mind, beheld a big silver-tip bearing down on him, jaws skinned, ears back, and red-eyed, and he had promptly removed himself to a proper distance, where he dismounted. The bear and dogs were much exhausted, but the dogs swarmed around the bear, thus preventing a shot. But Bruin stopped at intervals to fight the dogs, and the soldier fired, but without effect. If men do not come up with the dogs in order to encourage them, many will draw off, since the work of chasing and fighting a bear without water for hours is very trying. The one now running was an enormous silver-tip, and could not "tree." The shots of the trooper diverted the bear, which now took off down a deep cañon next to the one we were in, and presently we heard him no more. After an hour's weary travelling down the winding way we came out on the plain, and found a small cow outfit belonging to Mr. Stevens, and under a tree lay our dead silver-tip, while a half-dozen punchers squatted about it. It appeared that three of them had been working up in the foot-hills, when they heard the dogs, and shortly discovered the bear. Having no guns, and being on fairly good ground, they coiled their *riatas* and prepared to do battle.

The silver-tip was badly blown, and the three dogs which had staid with him were so tired that they sat up at a respectful distance and panted and lolled. The first rope went over Bruin's head and one paw. There lies the danger. But instantly number two flew straight to the mark, and the ponies surged, while Bruin stretched out with a roar. A third rope got his other hind leg, and the puncher dismounted and tied it to a tree. The roaring, biting, clawing mass of hair was practically helpless, but to kill him was an undertaking.

"Why didn't you brand him and turn him loose?" I asked of the cowboy.

"Well," said the puncher, in his Texan drawl, "we could have branded him all right, but we might have needed some help in turning him loose."

They pelted him with malpais, and finally stuck a knife into a vital part, and then, loading him on a pony, they brought him in. It was a daring performance, but was regarded by the "punchers" as a great joke.

Mickler and I rode into camp, thinking on the savagery of man. One never heard of a bear which travelled all the way from New Mexico to Chicago to kill a man, and yet a man will go three thousand miles to kill a bear — not for love, or fear, or hate, or meat; for what, then? But Mickler and I had not killed a bear, so we were easy.

One by one the tired hunters and dogs straggled into camp, all disappointed, except the dogs, which could not tell us what had befallen them since morning. The day following the dogs started a big black bear, which made a good run up a bad place in the hills, but with the hunters scrambling after in full cry. The bear treed for the dogs, but on sighting the horsemen he threw himself backward from the trunk, and fell fifteen feet among the dogs, which latter piled into him *en masse,* the little fox-terriers being particularly aggressive. It was a tremendous shake-up of black hair and pups of all colors, but the pace was too fast for Bruin, and he sought a new tree. One little foxie had been rolled over, and had quite a job getting his bellows mended. This time the bear sat on a limb very high up, and General Miles put a .50-calibre ball through his brain, which brought him down with a tremendous thump, when the pups again flew into him, and "wooled him," as the cowboys put it, to their hearts' content.

While our bear-hunting is not the thing we are most proud of, yet the method is the most sportsmanlike, since nothing but the most desperate riding will bring one up with the bear in the awful country which they affect. The anticipation of having a big silver-tip assume the aggressive at any moment is inspiriting. When one thinks of the enormous strength of the "silver-tip," which can overpower the mightiest steer, and bend and break its neck or tear its shoulder from its body at a stroke, one is able to say, "Do not hunt a bear unless thy skin is not dear to thee." Then the dogs must be especially trained to run bear, since the country abounds in deer, and it is difficult to train dogs to ignore their sight and scent. The cowboys account for the number of the bear in their country from the fact that it is the old Apache and Navajo range, and the incoherent mind of the savage was impressed with the rugged mass of fur and the grinning jaws of the monster which crossed his path, and he was awed by the dangers of the encounter — arrow against claw. He came to respect the apparition, and he did not know that life is only sacred when in the image of the Creator. He did not discriminate as to the value of life, but, with his respect for death, there grew the speculation, which to him became a truth, that the fearsome beast was of the other world, and bore the lost souls of the tribe. He was a vampire; he was sacred. Oh Bear!

Polar Bear Shooting on the East Coast of Greenland

FRIDTJOF NANSEN

The writer was part of a seal-hunting expedition in the Arctic Ocean when, near the end of June 1883, their ship was ice-bound off Greenland. He and the captain took advantage of the opportunity to hunt bears, as these entries from his diary show.

The polar bear differs from its brown cousin not only in color, but in being the possessor of a more elongated body, higher hind quarters, and a longer neck. It considerably exceeds the former in size and strength, and by reason of its somewhat shorter ears and smaller eyes has a wilder expression. It is a majestic animal, moving in ordinary circumstances with the quietness and security of a despot conscious of his own invincible superiority; but though large and heavy it is remarkably agile, and can cover the most uneven ice with astonishing rapidity. The powerful fore-limbs are its usual weapon, and well it knows how to use them; a single blow is often enough to despatch a seal.

Its principal food consists of the flesh of seal and walrus, but it also condescends to the carcases of whales, the larger kinds of fish, and other aquatic animals, and even, for want of anything better, to marine vegetables. It wanders about continually in search of seal, generally against the wind, as it has a good nose. That it can smell the seal so far off must also be attributed to the pure air which uninterrupted sweeps the surface of the ice in these high latitudes. In catching its prey it often shows remarkable cunning. Although a good swimmer and diver, it cannot reach the seal in the water, but must take them on the ice. This is no easy task, for the seal is wary, hears and sees well, and always keeps close to the edge of the floe in order to be able to take to the water at the first approach of danger. The bear, however, knows well enough how to outwit it; it marks the seal at some distance, and then creeps forward under cover of projections and pieces of ice; to deaden the sound it twists its feet in such a way that the hairy side is underneath, and in this manner succeeds in coming noiselessly on its victim. If the ice be flat and offer no shelter, the bear dives under the floes and appears suddenly in the opening near which the seal is lying. Even when basking on a lonely floe in open water it is not safe, for the bear glides noiselessly down from the ice, swims out towards the floe with only its nose visible above the surface of the water, and, when at a suitable distance, dives completely under and comes up close to the seal. It has been observed how, like the Eskimo, the bear will lie for hours watching the seal-holes — holes which the seal keep open in the ice to enable them to get upon it — ready to strike with its paw the first which is incautious enough to stick its head up.

The smaller seal are an easy prey, while on the other hand the bladder-nose and walrus may cost it many a hard fight. I saw a place where a fight of this kind had taken place between a bladder-nose and a bear, and the marks in the snow showed them to have been two mighty warriors. The body of the bladder-nose was still lying there, part of the blubber had been eaten up, but the flesh lay untouched, and the marks and gashes proved that it had not given in without a struggle.

In the months of March and April the bear has happy days; it is then that the seal bring forth their young, which for the first three weeks cannot go into the water. In the breeding-places thousands upon thousands of them lie dotted about on the ice, and the bear can now revel in its favorite dainties of blood and blubber. It is said to often "play" with these poor innocents, much in the same way that a cat plays with a mouse — taking them in its mouth, tossing them into the air, rolling them like a ball across the ice, striking them so that they fall over — and then, perhaps after taking a bite, to leave the young seal half dead and begin its game afresh with a new one.

The polar bear is an intelligent and crafty animal, but it is cursed with an intense curiosity, which Arctic travellers have often discovered to their cost when they have left bags and such things behind them on the ice. The contents of these have often been thoroughly ransacked, everything eatable devoured, and what the bear has been unable to consume — such as tin boxes and articles of that kind — has been broken in pieces, while other things they have dragged with them a long distance.

Whether or not the polar bear hibernates during the winter has not yet been clearly established, but it seems probable that the female produces her young in a lair, as holes left by them have been found in the snow, while the males and barren females wander about the whole winter. The pairing season, too, has never been fully determined. Some think it occurs in August, while others, like Julius Payer, are of opinion that, unlike other animals, it is not confined to any particular time, as small cubs are to be met with all the year round. As a general rule, however, it probably pairs in the month of August, and in midwinter its two cubs are born, which follow the mother from one to two years. She shows the greatest tenderness for them, and never leaves them even in the utmost danger. Of this we find many examples. My own experience has been that she was most careful when she had small cubs, and often ran away with them. To make them keep up with her she uses many devices, sometimes running in front, at other times turning to hurry them along by pushing them in front of her with her paws, or by putting her head between their hind legs in order to throw them forward, and thus with another short run and a repetition of the former manoeuvres she manages to advance with astonishing speed. If one wounds one of the cubs, she does not leave it, but stands and defends it to the end. So long as they are young, too, the cubs do not readily leave the mother. I knew of an instance where the two small cubs, with signs of the greatest affection, followed the body of their mother, which had been shot, to the boat, jumped in after it, sat themselves down on it, and quietly let themselves be taken on board.

The polar bear is not a sociable animal, and the males and females do not go about in company; the two cubs generally keep together for some time after they have left the mother, and are also occasionally to be found near her after she has again had young ones; sometimes even all five are to be met with together, but as a rule it is a solitary animal. It is generally on the alert at night, but keeps quiet during the day.

On the subject of the polar bear's courage and ferocity there is great divergence of opinion; some maintain it is very dangerous, while others scorn it altogether. I think this difference of opinion is mainly attributable to the different circumstances in which it has been met. If it has plenty of food it cares little about human beings. Sometimes at the season for capturing the young seal it has come up, smelt at the skins, and quietly gone its way again without showing any signs of enmity. In Spitzbergen and South Greenland, where it is in the habit of meeting people and being pursued, it flees at the sight of them. But if met in a region where it seldom sees human beings, as, for instance, the east coast of Greenland, and with an empty stomach, one will soon find out that it is not to be trifled with. It happened several times during the German expedition to the east coast of Greenland in 1869–70, that the crew were attacked by bears, one of the members, Börgen by name, even being dragged a considerable distance. He had been out in the evening to read the thermometer, which was placed on land, and while on his way home to the vessel was suddenly attacked by a bear. Having no time to arm, he tried to frighten it with the bull's-eye lantern which he carried; but without taking the slightest notice of this, the bear threw him down, bit him in a couple of places in the head, and then dragged him some distance. His cries for help were heard on board, and his friends hastened to the spot. On hearing the shots which were fired with the intention of frightening it, the bear retired a few paces, but returned, and, seizing the man again dragged him with him at a gallop over the uneven ice. At last it ran away for good. Börgen was badly wounded, but recovered, and, thanks to the thick fur cap he wore, his head was saved from being crushed. But we have examples, too, of how easily the bear can be frightened at times.

One of Dr. Kane's followers who was awakened by the growling of a bear which had put its head in at the tent door, resorted to the expedient of thrusting a box of lighted sulphur matches under its nose, an insult which it magnanimously forbore to revenge and took itself off.

Polar bear shooting, with the present quick-loading guns, is not attended with any particular danger, though the animal is very tenacious of life. Even when shot through the heart it is able to go some distance before falling. A bullet through the brain or vertebrae of the neck is the most fatal, and it generally falls without moving a limb. Walrus-hunters, like the Eskimo, often use a harpoon; but this may have dangerous consequences, as it has powerful jaws and knows how to parry the strokes with the greatest adroitness. Scoresby tells us of a polar bear which bit an iron harpoon half an inch thick right across.

In hopes that it may be of interest, I propose to give a few extracts from my diary on polar bear shooting on the coast of Greenland.

After a sojourn of three and a half months in the Arctic Ocean, we were unfortunate enough at the end of June to get frozen in on the east coast at about 66° 50' N., where we continued to lie for a month. This was the more deplorable as it was just the best time for seal-catching; but one must submit to fate, and we consoled ourselves as well as we could by bear shooting. My diary, however, written on board the Viking, sealer, of Arendal, under the command of Captain Axel Krefting, shall tell the tale.

June 28. — As I lay peacefully this morning dreaming of bears which I never got hold of, I was awakened by a whisper in my ear, "You had better turn out, for we have got a bear right under the ship's side." Hardly had I heard the word "bear" before I sprang up, rubbed my eyes, gazed with astonishment at the second mate, who continued whispering as if the bear were outside the cabin door, "You must look sharp." And look sharp I did, for I was up and on deck in a moment with rifle and cartridges. Quite right—there was the bear within range, quietly and reflectively walking backwards and forwards, and stopping now and then to sniff the air and scrutinize the ship which was evidently a novelty. There is no hurry, I thought; I can very well wait and enjoy the sight of this splendid proud animal till the captain comes. But why does he not come? Yes, there he is at last, and I was just turning to speak to him when I heard a report; as if stung by a serpent I rushed up in order that I too might at least send a shot after the bear on his journey; but no, undisturbed by such trifles he still walked quietly about although the bullet had struck the snow close beside him. The shot was from one of the seal-shooters, who could no longer restrain himself. It was therefore best to make our way on to the ice without further delay; once down I crept along and was soon within range, but the bear had meanwhile caught sight of me, and had gone up on to a hummock or crag of ice to re-connoitre. It was a pretty sight. I aimed just behind the shoulder—one does not shoot in the head for fear of spoiling the skull and skin—pulled the trigger of my rifle, and—it missed fire. It was fatal, and to make everything complete the cartridge stuck fast, so that I nearly tore all my nails off in getting it out; at last, however, it slipped out, and I was ready to begin again. Luckily the bear, instead of running away as I had expected, approached, and showed me his broad breast. I aimed straight into the whirl of white fur, and this time there was a report. Bruin did not like his reception; he growled, bit the ground, fell over, but jumped up again directly, and started off. I put another cartridge into my rifle, and sent a bullet into his hind quarters, which were now the only visible part of him. A new growl, and a still more hasty retreat. I followed him from floe to floe, but at last they became too far apart for him to jump, and he had to take to the water. In this way I gained on him, and put a bullet between the shoulder-blades just as he was climbing up the other side of a large piece of ice. He was done for now, and fell back into the water, looking at me furiously out of his small, fiery black eyes, but could do no more. Another bullet, and his sufferings were at an end.

The fog meanwhile had become so thick that I could not see the vessel, but on board they had heard the shots, and concluded the bear had fallen a victim. Some of the men soon came up, and we dragged him on board. It was my first polar bear, and with no little pride did I receive the congratulations of the captain and the others. I was astonished that the first shot had not made short work of him; it proved, however, on closer examination, that the bullet (express bullet ·450) had hit him right enough, but had burst in the layer of fat, and only a portion of it had entered the breast. The same thing had happened with the other two; they had caused large external wounds, but had not penetrated far. I thought next time I went bear shooting I would take good care to use something stronger.

June 30. — It is 10 P.M. The captain and I have just finished our dinner — I may mention in passing that we are so far fashionable that we seldom dine before eight or ten, sometimes not till next day — when Hans, one of the shooters, comes in to say that there is a bear close by. We jump up, get our rifles, and start off, at our leisure be it said, for there is no hurry — the bear is engaged on the carcases of some seal, the remains of our last catch. We soon see and make towards him, but the ice is uneven, and we are obliged to take our time. At last we mount a high hummock, and the bear catches sight of us. We lie down, and without hesitating he comes straight in our direction with his slowly swaying gait; a well-grown fellow he is, and gets over the ground with speed although he seems to be taking it so quietly. He is already behind the hummock immediately in front of us, not fifteen yards away; there is his head visible over the edge, but we do not fire, as that is all we can see of him, and he does not run away. A fine head it is too, the forehead as broad as a barn door, not to exaggerate. He rolls it backwards and forwards for a little while, then disappears altogether. We hold our rifles ready, for it is impossible to know where he may show himself next. Yes, there is his whole body appearing on the side of the hummock, his breast towards us. Both our shots go off together, the bear growls, bites his breast, staggers back a couple of paces, and then falls. He soon draws his last breath.

He was a very large animal, seven feet seven and one-half inches long, and in such good condition that anybody who had not seen him would hardly believe that the layer of fat on his body was in some places three to four and one-half inches thick, and the intestines were surrounded and interwoven with fat. He gave altogether over thirty-eight gallons of oil. The bullets had hit him in the middle of the breast an inch from each other, and had penetrated the whole length of the body as far as the hind quarters.

July 3—In the evening, just as I am in the act of taking samples of deep-water, I am interrupted by the man in the crow's-next (a sharp lookout for bear is always kept) informing me that there is a bear to leeward of us. Everybody wakes up at once, the samples are incontinently left, and after having glanced in the before-mentioned direction and got a glimpse of him, I rush down to the captain and collect my things. This is soon done; the bear meanwhile has vanished behind a hummock, and after having taken our bearings for this we start off. The ice is less passable than usual, and we have to take many jumps and side routes. But there is no hurry, the most important thing just now being to keep well to windward, so that he may get our wind. Once he has scented us we may be sure he will not keep us long waiting.

At last there is only one jump more before we stand on the same floe as the bear. I jump, but alas! the crust of snow breaks beneath my feet, and I stand on my head, luckily to reach the edge of the opposite floe with my arms and part of my chest, so that I get off this time with the reminder and a pair of wet legs. The captain gets over, too, and we approach the hummock behind which it is to be hoped Bruin is still lying. Meanwhile everything is quiet, and we are almost beginning to be anxious when his head suddenly appears above the edge. Immediately we lie down flat on the ice. This we were in the habit of doing as much to arouse the bear's curiosity as to prevent him being too much impressed by our savage aspect and consequently taking himself off. He inspects us calmly with his usual annoying patience—it would be unjust to say he ever hurries himself—and then the head disappears every now and then behind the hummock just as slowly as it reappears. This promises to be a waiting game, and we have not selected the best of couches in the middle of a pool of water. At last he gets up and comes jogging along towards us, complacently sniffing the smell of warm meat; then he swings round, broadside on, and the moment has come. The captain fires first, then I; the bear plunges, then rears and falls growling backwards; a short death-rattle, and he is on his way to the happy hunting grounds.

The crew are on the spot immediately, for the whole incident has been watched with the greatest interest from mastheads and yards. The bear is hauled on board with the funeral procession due to him, and is soon skinned and portioned out, for young bear-hams are a commodity which with the bear-eating part of the crew (some of them retain their old prejudice and think bear's flesh is injurious) meets with an enthusiastic reception. The tongue and heart, especial delicacies, fall to the share of the hunters.

July 4. — We were not allowed to sleep long before a new bear was discovered in the distance, and we had to turn out. This time I again took my express rifle to make quite sure if solid bullets were really preferable to hollow ones, and Kristian, generally called the Balloon, a quick, plucky fellow, was allowed to come with us. The way to-day was rougher than usual, and it took us some time before we, at a distance of fifteen hundred feet, sighted the bear, who had already smelt us, for he rose up on his hind legs to get a better view, and then went up on to a high hummock of ice, where, seating himself on his haunches, he obviously began to lay his play of operations. We make use of the time meanwhile to get over some difficult places under cover and reach a high hummock which we thought would make a suitable waiting-place. As we draw near the edge we hold our rifles ready for any emergency. The last time we saw the bear he was advancing towards us at full speed, but when on the top we could not, to our astonishment, see him in any direction. We scanned the ice, but, although it was tolerably even, could see nothing. That the bear was in our immediate proximity we felt certain, but whereabouts was a riddle indeed. Meantime we lay down, with our rifles cocked, in order to be ready; he might be on us before we knew where we were. Then, at a distance of fifty yards or so, in the nearest open pool, we saw a faint ripple on the water, and a dark spot appeared in sight, which slowly made its way towards us. Spite of the unusual cunning with which this was done, we at once saw that this was the bear's nose, and were now witness of a sight which was much too interesting for us to wish to put an end to it before it was necessary. How long it lasted I cannot say, but, at any rate, over twenty minutes. The nose gradually worked its way towards us, until it was lost to sight under the edge of the floe lying nearest to us. A little while afterwards the forehead, as far as the eyes, came slowly and cautiously into sight over the edge as if to reconnoitre. Here he remained immovable for a good while, and I could plainly see how the small black eyes peered in all directions, and now and then sent a lightning glance at us.

The impression apparently was not a favorable one, for the forehead disappeared and the nose began to sail along the surface of the water again as quietly as before. Here he moved backwards and forwards for some time, while now and again the eyes appeared in sight. At last he vanished behind a hummock, and was away for some time. We began to look about, as he might have dived, when all at once the forehead and eyes became visible over the edge of the hummock, behind which he had disappeared. He must now have got up on the ice; after carefully considering us for a moment, he vanished again. This was repeated several times at long intervals; he had obviously plenty of time and meant to consider the matter well, but so had we, and found the situation far too amusing to wish to curtail it. We agreed to wait as long as possible, although the captain complained of the ice-compress round his stomach, and the Balloon, that he had no more tobacco from which to cut himself a consolatory quid.

At last the bear seemed to have come to a conclusion. He had been away longer than usual, but now came shuffling along as large as life. First he gave an appalling yawn, and in so doing swung his tongue nearly up to his eyes. "Oh, good-morning, good-morning!" exclaimed the Balloon, quite loud, and we could not help laughing, although we bade him hold his tongue. With his rolling gait, the bear now began tacking towards us, pretending the while to be unconscious of our existence. Every time he had to go about he gave another yawn and an amorous glance in our direction, but continued his journey from floe to floe, carefully trying the edges of the ice before trusting himself. In truth, he took matters with exasperating calmness. If a floe sank under him he stepped on to the next with perfect indifference and in the same lazy time as before. When tacking for the last time before reaching us, a piece of ice obstructed his path, so large that a man could hardly have turned it over, and there was plenty of room to go round, but the bear only gave it a casual slap with one of his fore paws and sent it splashing into the water. He did it with an air as haughty as an emperor's, and exhibited a strength that was almost uncanny. The Balloon exlaimed involuntarily, "Oh, the scoundrel!" Meanwhile the bear has headed straight for us, and is not more than ten paces away, so it is time to fire. It is my turn, and just as his hind legs are at an angle preparatory to a last spring up to us, I put a bullet right into the middle of his breast. He growls, bites, as usual, at the wound, reels over, but jumps up again, and begins to run away. The captain then sends a ball into his hind quarters to stop him a little. My cartridge stuck fast, and only after considerable trouble did I get it loose and another one in. We are both ready again, and the bear is now in the water. As he climbs up the next ridge his back comes conveniently into sight; we both fire simultaneously, and the bullets enter between the shoulder-blades. He falls back into the water, but manages to get on to the floe again, where he is stopped by a bullet from the captain. He falls back into the water, and, after a few gasps, everything is over.

He was an unusually large and fine bear. Although we were all three tolerably strong fellows, and the floe, which was not high, sloped down to the water's edge, we had our work cut out to get him up. We converted the Balloon's belt into a noose, which we put round his neck, but he showed remarkable ingenuity in slipping his collar; a couple of twists round his nose, however, soon put an end to this, and at length, after much vain exertion, we succeeded in hauling him up on the ice. It now proved that the first bullet had been well enough directed, but virtually had only caused an outward wound, and had torn the flesh and fat in all directions in a frightful manner, without penetrating any distance into the breast. The wound in the back from the express bullet was so large that I could put my hand in under the skin and move it about, while with a couple of fingers I could even feel the lungs; the most important wound was therefore an outward one, and consequently much less deadly than that caused by the solid bullet, which, though undoubtedly small, went right through. The captain affirmed all the time, and I think with reason, that in the hand of a good shot a solid bullet of somewhat soft lead would certainly be the best thing for this kind of sport.

July 6. — At our nine o'clock dinner the captain said he thought it was time for another bear. It was long since we had killed the last — two whole days. Shortly we heard a cry from the maintop: "Three bears to leeward!" All was life at once, ice and dietary afflictions were forgotten, and we were soon on the ice with our rifles. The Balloon was allowed to come too, and off we went in pursuit of the three, which were said to be a she-bear and two cubs. We soon caught sight of them, but so far off we could hardly distinguish them from the ice. Apparently their eyes were as good as ours, for they had already seen us; whether it was sight or scent—for the wind was good and bore right upon them—I do not know. They did not take long for consideration, however, but started off towards us as hard as they could come—the finest race imaginable. We also took up our usual position—all three in line, on our stomachs, at the top of a hummock—and watched with the greatest equanimity the race, of which we ourselves were the goal. Sometimes they divided, sometimes closed in again, according as the ice necessitated; first one led, then another; sometimes they were in the water when the lanes or pools were wider than they could jump, sometimes on the ice, but always in full career. Then one of the cubs began to get a decided lead, and was nearly within range, while the mother and the other youngster were three hundred yards behind. It got little thanks for its pains, however, for we were afraid of shooting it before the others were within gunshot. There was nothing to be done but to wait as long as possible and let matters take their chance. The care of the cub was entrusted to me, while the captain undertook to settle the mother. The cub was already on the floe in front of us, but it never slackened speed until at about a distance of fifteen yards; then it stopped, examined us carefully, gathered itself together, and came wriggling along like a cat about to spring. It was within fifteen paces—ten, eight; my rifle was at my shoulder and my finger on the trigger. I followed every movement, glancing now and then at the she-bear to see if she would not soon be within range. The cub has come right under the barrel of the captain's gun, and while he is wholly occupied with the mother it stops, its muscles contracted. There is no waiting any longer; there is a report. Two bullets enter its breast, and, mortally wounded, it rolls off the hummock. The mother, seeing her cub fall, presses still more wildly forward, but a bullet from the captain's sure hand makes her bite the dust, to use a figure of speech. The cub, having staggered on to its legs again, is made an end of by a bullet through its back and into the heart. Meanwhile the captain, with a long shot, has brought down the second cub, and the mother, having got up again, is met by a shot from each of us, and falls, never to rise again. But now the second youngster is on its legs and is beating a retreat; a bullet from me, however, brings it growling to the ground. It recovers itself and starts off anew, saluted by a couple of shots from me; but, unfortunately, it is out of range now, and I shoot wide. Still I soon catch it up, and in a pool give it its *coup de grâce.*

Then it was hauled over to its two comrades which lay side by side on the ice. In truth a handsome trio, and shot in a much shorter time than it takes to tell.

July 7. — We made a bonfire of the stale meats and kept it going for several days, feeding it meanwhile with blubber; this we did to entice the bear with the aroma of their favorite food, which if the wind be favorable they can smell many miles off. This proved successful, for during the following days no less than twenty bears were seen, though many were at a great distance. Whether they were twenty different ones it is difficult to say, and hardly probable, but at any rate it gives an idea of how numerous these animals are still in these parts.

July 8. — A bear was seen this morning, and we were called up in a hurry, but did not get him — our first failure. He was probably frightened by the noise of the scraping and cleaning in the rigging, forecastle, and funnel, which, now that the men had nothing better to do, had been taken in hand with an energy the noise of which baffles description.

But still it was interesting to see the mother's care for her young, her anxiety to make them keep up with her, and how she helped them from floe to floe, sometimes using love and sometimes severity to hasten them on.

On the same day, however, another bear was announced to leeward, the most favorable position. We started off again for the third time, I taking with me the express as an experiment. I had removed the copper tube from the bullet and inserted a solid iron plug in its place, which quite filled the hole.

The bear was so occupied in eating some seal's flesh that we came upon it unawares. When, however, it did see us, it did not hesitate long. We throw ourselves prone on the ice. He makes straight for us, till at about fifty yards' distance he stops, tricks us by jerking to one side behind a hummock, then reappears stealing along like a cat, and takes a sudden run preparatory to throwing himself upon us. It is the captain's turn, and he sends a shot into the bear which makes him fall together without moving. It was none too soon, for ten yards more and he would have been upon us. To our astonishment, however, he came to life again immediately, the bullets having only grazed the skull and hit the spine through the vertebrae of the neck; still, he could only use his fore limbs. I tried a couple of my bullets and sent them straight through the breast; they seemed to act well and not to burst too soon, but I think on the whole solid bullets are to be preferred. The bear meantime was more than usually tenacious of life and would not die, before I, for want of any better article of cutlery, made my way to his heart with a pocket-knife. On the way home we discussed as usual the advisability of waiting so long before firing. One's cartridge might miss fire and the — Yes, we all agreed that it was not to be commended, promised each other as usual that it should never happen again, and that we would be more careful for the future. Still, it is easier to promise than to perform; the next time we had a bear before us all our good intentions were forgotten. We both thought the sport far too exciting and interesting to be cut short too soon.

A little while after we had returned on board a bear was again sighted to windward, but a long way off; this was the seventh to-day. As the distance was too great we did not follow it, but, after having fed the bonfire, turned in to a well-earned repose.

July 9. — To-day, at morning watch, two bears were again seen to windward, but too far off to be of any use. Later, just as we were up, another was announced, and this time not so far off but that we could see it with the naked eye. We started in pursuit, but he was going hard against the wind, and, as the captain said, "That fellow sails within a point of the wind, and at a pinch will go to windward of that." At length, however, he made a halt at some seal's flesh and began a good meal, while we gained ground to windward and bore down on him. As I mentioned before, the ice was covered with this seal's flesh, which, after being skinned and the blubber removed, is left as food for sea-birds, etc. — a circumstance which was of great advantage to us, as the bear will generally stop to feed at it. Probably this was the reason why there were so many bears to be seen, as the smell of the flesh would be carried by the wind far over the ice. Our bear was deeply engaged, and we came tolerably near before he caught sight of us, though to shoot an enemy which had not seen us was more than we could bring ourselves to do. But now he lifts his head and comes rocking along. We throw ourselves down on the ice, and he, ambushed behind the hummock immediately in front of us, keeps out of sight for a while. It was now a question of having our eyes about us, for if he made his appearance at the top of the hummock he would very soon be on us. The tip of his nose soon became visible between two pieces of ice, then a bit of his chest. We both fired together, the captain aiming at the breast, I, for a change, at the head, and my bullet entered the mouth and came out at the nape of the neck. The bear reeled over, but game to the last, and, still carrying his head high, he turned towards us. Two more shots and he fell, and then another bullet from the captain put an end to his sufferings.

When we came on board a bear was seen about three miles off going against the wind. Some of the crew were allowed to go in pursuit, and, as was to be expected, returned without seeing anything at all. Scarcely had they got on board before a bear came strolling along from the very direction in which they had been. Of course they were well chaffed by the others, especially one of the shooters who came in last and was beginning to give himself airs. "You do just the opposite to the captain and Nansen; instead of going after bear, the bear go after you. Why didn't you shoot him, man?" To this there was little enough to be answered, and he restricted himself to scratching his head. Meanwhile we thanked him for decoying the bear, and started off in pursuit. A couple of the men were allowed to be of the party.

On the way I scrambled up on to a high hummock to survey the country, and discovered at a good distance the head of a bear just above a ridge of ice. It vanished from sight, and I concluded the animal must be lying there. After having taken our bearings for this we set off again and soon left the men behind us, as we preferred to be alone when we got to close quarters. The distance was diminishing, and just as we had come on to a large floe and were discussing behind which hummock it was I had last seen the bear, we discover the head not thirty paces away above the edge of an iceridge. As if swept over, we threw ourselves down, but he was as quick as we, and came growling towards us, showing his teeth like a tiger. There were not many seconds to spare, and as he made a little turn, we both fired simultaneously — the captain through the breast, I through the back of the head, just behind the ear.

Well, if he had faced us bravely and voraciously, he at any rate fell better than any bear I ever saw, for he expired without a movement, and was dead almost while he stood. This must be attributed to the shot through the back of the head, which, taken altogether, is the most deadly to all animals, and has the most instantaneous effect on the nervous system.

July 11. — The most beautiful weather this morning, with burning hot sunshine. Just as I was sunning myself on deck, in shirt-sleeves and slippers, and thinking of the summer at home in old Norway, I caught sight of a bear not far from us. I was down after the captain in a minute, and off we went. As we stood, the bear was absorbed in the contemplation of some seal's flesh, so that we could approach him comfortably over large, flat floes without his remarking us. We whistle, and at last he turns round broadside on. The captain's gun peals forth its sharp crack, but from mine is heard first the cap, then a whizz, and at last the shot. The cartridge, a wire one, had become wet, and the ball had, of course, gone in any direction but where I wanted it to. But the captain's bullet, which never used to fail, where was that? The bear turned and fronted us, then advanced forty paces or so and came to a standstill. I had just rammed in a new cartridge and now pulled the trigger. Again the cap is heard, again a whizz, and at last the shot; but all the same he dropped stone dead. It proved that the captain's bullet had gone straight through both lungs and the heart, and that it was the report of my rifle only which had killed the bear, for in spite of the most careful search over the whole body no trace of any bullets was to be found. It is a remarkable proof of the polar bear's tenacity of life that after a shot so deadly it was still able to go forty paces.

This bear was killed at midday — a rare occurrence.

July 12. — In the evening I went up into the crow's-nest to sketch the coast of Greenland. First I carefully scanned the ice with the telescope to make sure there were no bear about, and then began my drawing. The men had gone to rest and everything was still; only the step of the Balloon, whose watch it was, broke the silence. I was absorbed in my work, and had almost forgotten where I was, when the Balloon, who had come up on the forecastle, suddenly shouted out, "Why, look at the bear!" Like a flash of lightning I bounded up and looked over the side of the crow's-nest; a bear was standing under the very bows of the ship. Pencil and sketch-book were thrown aside, a descent by means of one of the backstays and rigging and on to the deck was the work of a moment, and so into the cabin after rifle and cartridges. In the doorway I met the captain, who had also heard the Balloon's voice. We seized our rifles and started off as hard as we could go. The bear, probably frightened by the shouts of the ingenuous Balloon, had fled. When we had gone a little way we made the discovery that there were two bears; the other had been close by, and both of them were now jogging out of sight. After pursuing them some distance the captain, who was heavily clad, gave up, but my own attire being of the lightest, a jersey and canvas shoes, I thought I would see a little more of the game, and off we went, first the bear, then I, over one great flat floe after another. But they began to get ahead of me horribly, and as repeated signals were being made from the ship for me to return, the chase had to be abandoned. Angry and crestfallen I turned my steps homeward, but promised myself that had I ever another chance of running a race with a bear I would not give in so easily.

July 14. — We had begun again to pine for bear, when in the afternoon, "a big one" was announced as being not far off. We went up to the crow's-nest to look at it, took our bearings, and started off. One of the sailors, Paul, came with us. We walked for a long time, but saw no bear, and this was the more mysterious as we thought we must long ago have arrived at the place where we had marked it from the ship. With the help of signals from the crow's-nest, we at length, however, caught sight of it. We learned afterwards that it had seen us for some while and had steadily retreated. According to our usual custom, we took up our position on the summit of a hummock, for the purpose of watching our quarry. We might very well have shot then, but thought, as the bear generally came nearer, there was no hurry. Meanwhile he strolled backwards and forwards, looking at us from different points of view. Then he disappeared behind a large hummock, and when we next saw Bruin he was out of range. It was now a question of speed, and he was going at a good pace. We ran after him, covering our pursuit as well as we could; but when one is in a hurry one is apt to forget to be careful, and thus I forgot the deceptive edges of the floes, hollowed out by the water with a thin, brittle crust, projecting over the surface of the pools, so that, seen from above, they seem perfectly safe and strong. We come to a broad lane of water, which, at a pinch, might be jumped and I pull myself together for the effort; but, as luck would have it, there is just such an edge here which breaks under me, and, instead of landing on the ice, I plunge head foremost into the water. It was rather cold, but the first thing to be thought of was my rifle. I try to throw it up on the other side, but the edge is high, it falls short of the top, and slides down again into the water; then I dive and succeed in finding it. Disgusted, I now fling it right up on the floe and swim round to a place where I can climb up and recover it. A hurried inspection of barrel and lock, and off again. The cartridges were not so important, as they were water-tight Remington ones. The captain, meanwhile, had got ahead of me; seeing me fall into the water and having ascertained that I was able to take care of myself, he jumped over at another place and went on. Happily I was also that day very lightly clad — a jersey, canvas shoes, and no coat — so that I had not much water to carry, and it ran off almost as quickly as it came on. I was not long in making up for lost time, and when I saw the bear vanish behind a hummock, I took a short cut towards it. Just as I had reached this and was poking my head over the ridge, I was confronted by the bear. I bring my rifle to my shoulder instantly, but Bruin is quicker than I, and throws himself off the floe and into the water; the bullet only hits him in the hind quarters as he disappears.

I scramble over the crest and down to the edge to shoot him in the water, but there is no bear to be seen. Where is he? I can distinguish something white deep down in the pool, and realize the situation. But the channel was broad, and it was necessary for me to reach the other side in order to receive him there. There were two small blocks of ice in the middle of the water; it was a long jump, but I was constrained to try it. I jump, and alight comfortably on one of them. It would only just bear me, and I stagger to regain my balance, when, like a flash of lightning, the bear thrusts his head up close by the bit of ice opposite and throws himself upon it, growling. He would have had me in a minute had I not luckily forestalled him by placing a bullet in his breast, blackening the fur with the smoke. He fell into the water and expired — I was going to say in my arms; such was not quite the case, however, as I was holding him by the ears. He showed signs of sinking, which was the more curious as at this time of the year the bear are generally fat and float easily. The others soon came up and helped me out of my embarrassing situation. We had nothing else to drag Bruin up with but my belt, which was little enough for the purpose.

However, we fastened it round his neck and "led" him away to a little creek in the floe. There was now no longer any danger of his sinking, and we could haul him up by degrees. He was an unusually fine fellow, one of the largest we shot, and his skin lies under my writing-table. I can truly say that I sit with my foot on the neck of my enemy.

The distance to the ship was long, and it was some time before any of the men came to help us, so meanwhile we set to work to "weigh him out." This, however, I was not allowed to assist in; the captain said I was wet and cold, and I must obey orders and return to the ship. Unreasonable as I thought this, I obeyed him, and started homewards. I had got into the habit of giving way to him, and had little reason to regret my obedience in this instance. As I neared the vessel I perceived three of the crew on the ice; two of them, as far as I could make out, were carrying rifles. I wondered where they could be going, and, upon my inquiry when I came on board, learned that they were gone after bear, but that there was no hope of my being in time, as they were already within range. Very well, I thought, I must be satisfied for to-day, and let them have the bear, but when I heard there were three of them it was too much for me. One they might have, but out of three surely I might expect one to fall to my share, and off I went as fast as my legs would carry me. I was wet before, and a little water more or less would not make much difference; besides, I need not now go round so often to avoid the pools. I soon caught the men up, and found them lying in wait for a bear which was coming towards them. I stopped at a little distance in order not to be in the way, but they, fearing I should steal a march on them, fired too soon, and only wounded the bear, which made off growling. Now it was clearly my turn. I sent him a shot in the breast which brought him down, but he got up again and fled; I gave chase, and, as he then turned and came towards me, put a bullet through his head which ended his life.

We had now to think about the next one. Signals were made from the ship, and we took the direction pointed out to us, and soon caught sight of the bear, which was standing eating some seal's flesh, so occupied with his meal that, unperceived, we were able to get within easy range. As I was not sure of the others, I thought it better to shoot from here, and whistled to make him look up; but no. Then I tried again with no better result, then a third time as loud as I could, and he lifts his head. I aimed behind the shoulder, and let blaze, and the other two fired simultaneously. The bear growled and reeled backwards into the water. I rushed to the edge, but, as I thought he had got enough, let him quietly swim over to the other side, intending when he had got up on the ice to give him his quietus, thus saving ourselves the trouble of hauling him up. But this time I reckoned without my host, for he took care to land under cover of a large hummock, climbed as lithe as a cat upon the ice, and away he went. I stood with a long face, and only achieved a useless bullet in the hind quarters; but then began a race which was ample compensation for all the disappointment suffered. Oluf, who had no rifle, and was only carrying an ice-axe and a rope, followed a little way, but came to a standstill at the first piece of water that was too broad to jump. I, who had no intention of going round, took to the water. I heard a guffaw behind me; it was Oluf, who had never seen anybody get over a pool in that way before, and, meaning to manage things better himself, he, with the ice-axe, guided a floe into the middle of the water, intending to jump on it, and from thence make a second spring to the other side. But now it was my turn to laugh. He managed to land on the edge in such a way that he fell into the water up to his middle, and of course his high seaboots filled immediately. Then followed such an emptying of boots as I, with my light canvas shoes, had no need of, and consequently no time for. The bear and I apparently were going to measure our speed alone, and both of us were resolved to do our utmost. He ran for life, I for honor. My bullet had undoubtedly hit him behind the shoulder, but by mistake I had got hold of a cartridge containing hollow bullets, which had only caused an outward wound, and did not seem to hinder him much. A good deal of blood was flowing from it, and the track was therefore easy to find. The bullets of the other men had not hit him. Meanwhile we tore over the ice as fast as our legs would carry us; sometimes I gained on the bear, sometimes he made head against me. Thus we continued from floe to floe; if the pools were too wide to jump, I swam them — there was no time to think of going round now. Mile after mile we went, and the bear showed no signs of giving in, but at last he began to make turns, and I took advantage of this to cut across, and thus gained on him considerably. I understood now that he was beginning to grow tired, and was taking it easier, until I saw him disappear behind a hummock. Covered by this I put on a spurt in hopes of getting a shot at him, but no, he saw through my device and renewed his exertions. He went a little further, and then slackened speed. I at last came within range, and sent a bullet through the breast; he made a couple of bounds in the air and fell. A shot behind the ear ended his career.

All very well, but here I was, alone with a dead bear! A rifle without cartridges and a penknife my only weapons! The captain had kept my large knife for the purpose of "weighing out" the bear. The first thing to be thought of, therefore, was to make signs to the ship, but nothing was to be seen of it except the masts. I mounted the highest hummock near at hand, and from thence waved my cap, disposed on the end of my gunbarrel. I then descended and set to work on the bear with my penknife with the intention of at least saving the skin. It was slow work, as the head and feet had to be cut through in order not to detach them from the skin, but with care and patience I was able to do it, and had nearly finished when I heard a voice in the distance. I went up on to a crag of ice to see, and it proved to be Oluf, who, after his transit over the floes, had at last caught me up. He was unfeignedly delighted to see me, for he had run all the way, with his heart in his mouth, for fear of — meeting the bear! His only means of defence were an axe and a packet of cartridges. We finished the skinning and then began our not very easy task of dragging it homewards, for, with its accompanying layer of fat, a skin like this may weigh as much as two hundred pounds.

Oluf and I, who thought we had done enough, then left them and went on. On the way home Oluf had a great deal to say about my method of crossing pools, which was quite new to him, and the scene when he was left behind with his boots seemed to have made an indelible impression on his memory. We had not gone far before we met an embassy from the captain bringing us beer and something to eat. I was quite touched at this kindness, and can safely say that both Oluf and I did ample justice to the fare. When I came on board I heard that the third bear had been close at hand, but had now moved off. We ought to have had that too, and so made up the score; as it was, we had to be satisfied with only nineteen.

That was our last hunt; a few days afterwards the ice gave, and we got out. The sealing season was now over, and we had nothing to do but to set our course homewards. Lightly the Viking sped over the waves, as fast as wind and steam could carry her, and great was the joy on board when the weather-beaten peaks of our dear old Norway appeared in sight rising from the sea.

Black Bear Honking in the Valley of Kashmir

J.C. GREW

The hunt was the mother of invention. The writer of this piece made use of the manpower that was available to flush out the bear as if it were a grouse.

One crisp and cloudless August morning in 1903 I stood at the summit of the Tragbal Pass in Baltistan, looking down for the first time in several months on the great valley of Kashmir, spread like a map in the morning haze far below. Behind towered the vast ranges and snow-clad spurs of the Himalayas, culminating far in the distance in the peak of Nunga Parbat, which rose like a giant among its fellows, catching and reflecting the newly risen sun.

Kadera, my worthy shikari, stood near by, looking down intently at the scene below; he was not given to soliloquizing on the scenery and when he gazed in that meditative fashion, it was fairly certain that something important was on his mind. I asked him the cause.

"Atcha bhalu jagah, Sahib," he softly replied. I followed his gaze and saw a mass of dark green wooded foothills across the valley very far below. "Good bear country" — ah, that was tempting. I knew to what he referred. It was the height of the fruit season: the mulberries were lying thick and luscious just along those ridges and the wild apricots below were ripening to the heat of midsummer. The black bear would have left the heights and be passing the days in the clefts and nullahs of those wooded hills, coming out at night to feast on his favorite delicacies. I had heard much about the sport of beating or "honking" these nullahs in the foothills, sport rendered more exciting by the fact that unlike our American black bear, the Kashmir animal *(ursus torquatus)* is not a coward. Here was a chance for consolation, and although I was due shortly in Calcutta, the opportunity was too tempting to let slip by.

Kashmir was no longer the green and fertile valley I had left it. News had come to me while in Baltistan of a terrible flood which had completely inundated the country, wrecking homes, destroying farms, and resulting even in much loss of human life. Now below me extended a vast lake as far as one could see, with only an occasional tree or housetop to mark where cultivated farms and dwellings had formerly stood. At Bandipur on the edge of the flood we camped for the night, and here an event occurred which made me sanguine of success.

Kadera came into my tent towards sundown to inform me that two large black bears had recently been seen in the hills directly behind the village, and suggested that we go back a few miles on the chance of running across one. We accordingly set out with a "gam wallah" or local guide, who led us up into the hills and placed us at the foot of a long slope covered with low furze bush, where we crouched for a couple of hours. Toward dark my eye was caught by a large object moving across the open hilltop some three hundred yards from our position. Its apparently enormous size made me think at first that it must be a stray bullock and the fact that the shikaris, usually so quick to sight game, remained motionless almost kept me from calling attention to it. Yet bullocks are seldom black, and there was that about the gait of this animal which told me it was something quite different. I touched Kadera on the shoulder and pointed. The result was startling; Kadera dropped on his stomach as if shot, while the gam wallah did the same, causing me to realize that the fast-disappearing object above us was one of the largest black bears I probably should ever have to fortune to run across. As we were about to stalk, a peasant came toward us in hot haste from the opposite direction and explained in some excitement that a bullock had been killed within the hour, not far from where we were, and that a bear was still at the carcass. As it was now much too dark to stalk the other successfully, we quickly shed all unnecessary garments and prepared to follow our new guide through a terrible tangle of underbrush. We were on our hands and knees most of the way and as we came toward the spot indicated by the peasant, our efforts to move silently were trying in the extreme. By the time we reached it the moon was shining through the undergrowth, making every stump exhibit such remarkably bear-like characteristics that more than one of them was in imminent danger of being shot.

The bear, however, must have heard our approach, for he was not with the body of the bullock, nor did he venture back to reward our long night's silent vigil.

Unfortunately there were no nullahs about here small enough to beat, and since Kadera assured me that at the head of the valley we should find several bears for every one we gave up here, I agreed on the following morning to start along.

The country through which we passed on this ride showed Kashmir at her loveliest and best. One felt as if one were continuously crossing the well-kept grounds of a huge private estate and any moment would come on the towers and chimneys of some lordly mansion. There was no road: one passed over the greenest grass, smooth and fresh as any lawn, extending as far as one could see, except where groves of wide spreading chenar trees cast their shade like oaks on a country park. Roses, not our wild ones, but such roses as at home are brought to flower only under hothouse panes, and wild flowers of all colors and species, grew along our way and filled the air with fragrance. In the midst of such surroundings, to come suddenly upon the dirty little hovels of a native village, with the fresh lawn extending to its very door and the chenar trees growing around, seemed indeed incongruous.

The beaters arrived at camp the following morning. They began to come in twos and threes, then in fives and sixes, and finally in dozens, so that by the time breakfast was over, the entire male population of some three villages were grouped about my tent. With the help of the shikaris, fifty of these were selected and each given a slip of paper bearing my signature, for when they came for their wages at the end of the day, I did not wish the friends and relatives of the beaters as well as the beaters themselves turning up for payment.

The din these fifty souls succeed in making as they move in a long line up the base and two sides of a wooded nullah shrieking, howling, cat-calling, setting off fire crackers and beating tum-tums, is enough to drive any self-respecting bear out of his seven senses. An army of battle-shouting dervishes could hardly create a greater amount of uproar, nor is it at all surprising that the bear should find a pressing engagement elsewhere at the earliest possible moment after finding his nullah thus rudely invaded. If he turns down the nullah, he encounters the invading army; if he tries to escape by the sides, he is met and driven back by beaters already posted. Therefore he does the most natural thing in the world by fleeing up the center of the nullah, directly away from the oncoming din. At the top of the cleft stands the sportsman. The undergrowth probably prevents the sportsman's seeing the bear or the bear seeing him until they actually meet.

I regret to say, in spite of Kadera's assertion that bears would be so thick in this country as practically to necessitate our looking carefully where we walked lest we stumble over them, it was not until after we had unsuccessfully honked nine separate nullahs, and I was beginning to think bear beating a snare and a delusion, that our first sport came.

The bear appeared on the scene of action so suddenly as to completely take my breath away. The beaters had been moving listlessly up a cleft, thickly wooded both with trees and undergrowth; this was to be the last honk of the day and two days unsuccessful searching had so plainly reacted on the spirits of the men as to change the dervish battle-shout into the mournful muttering of an Arab funeral procession. The line of beaters had almost reached me, my shikari with a last disgusted look had turned to go, when, all at once, the beaters who had been posted on the side of the nullah above where I was standing, set up a tremendous shouting, "Bhalu, Sahib, bhalu hai!" — "Bear, Sahib, bear coming!"

Now it is one thing to have a bear driven up to you from below, with plenty of warning that he is coming and time to choose an advantageous spot from which to shoot. It is quite another to find suddenly that the bear has somehow got above you, is being driven directly down upon you with all the impetus a steep hillside gives, and with the undergrowth extending to your very feet. I had barely time to wheel around when the bear came down the hillside aimed directly at the little clearing in which I was standing. A moment's glimpse of his back in the jungle did not afford me time to shoot. He disappeared into the undergrowth, but was still coming toward me as I could tell by the short yelps of excitement which he uttered, like a frightened dog, as the beaters closed in. Immediately as he emerged from the bushes he was met by both barrels of my .450-cordite-powder express, which, aimed and fired so suddenly from my hip at close range of less than two yards, seems to have missed him altogether, though the report turned and sent him lumbering down on the beaters below.

As the natives closed in, the bear went frantically around in a circle trying to break through the line. I ran down to the foot of the hillside where an occasional view of his back in the underbrush showed me that he had not escaped, though I dared not fire lest I should hit a beater. The fifty coolies were yelling like so many demons, the shikaris were out of their heads with excitement, and the bear, who was doubtless the most excited of all, continued his circular course inside the line of beaters as regularly as a planet on its usual orb.

I was now afraid that unless I stopped him he might escape through the line, and working up a little nearer fired several shots as he appeared from time to time, each of which I afterward found took effect. The bear was now thoroughly maddened and suddenly changing his course, came lumbering down the nullah directly toward me. The shikaris shouted to look out while the beaters doubled their cries and added to the confusion and my fear of shooting wild, by following the animal down hill. The thick underbrush annoyed me greatly, for though I could catch an occasional glimpse of his back, it was almost impossible when I saw him to fire quickly enough, and I knew that in a moment he would be on me. He was within four yards when a final shot brought him rolling almost to my feet, quite dead.

My faith in the .450 express was distinctly diminished when eleven holes were found in his skin. He was shot through and through, five shots at least having passed completely through and out of his body. The last, which finished him, had struck the shoulder fair. A bear certainly is game.

We had a triumphal procession on the way back to camp: first the two tum-tums, banging away like a regimental drum corps; secondly the bear, slung on a pole supported on the backs of two coolies; thirdly the sportsman, trying modestly to suppress an irrepressible grin; fourthly the shikaris, and last, but by no means least, the fifty honkers, all discussing the event like so many crows. As we passed through the village of Kaipora, the women and children — we had exhausted the place of men — turned out *en masse* to see the bear, and the occasion was all that could be desired.

A Colorado Bear Hunt

THEODORE ROOSEVELT

For Theodore Roosevelt, the bear hunt was a manly occupation. It was an occasion for the camaraderie of the campground, when presidents mixed with guides on equal terms. This article was published in October 1905, near the end of his first term as President.

In mid-April, nineteen hundred and five, our party, consisting of Philip B. Stewart, of Colorado Springs, and Dr. Alexander Lambert, of New York, in addition to myself, left Newcastle, Col., for a bear hunt. As guides and hunters we had John Goff and Jake Borah, than whom there are no better men at their work of hunting bear in the mountains with hounds. Each brought his own dogs; all told, there were twenty-six hounds, and four half-blood terriers to help worry the bear when at bay. We travelled in comfort, with a big pack train, spare horses for each of us, and a cook, packers, and horse wranglers. I carried one of the new model Springfield military rifles, a 30-40, with a soft-nosed bullet — a very accurate and hard-hitting gun.

This first day we rode about twenty miles to where camp was pitched on the upper waters of East Divide Creek. It was a picturesque spot. At this altitude it was still late winter and the snow lay in drifts, even in the creek bottom, while the stream itself was not yet clear from ice. The tents were pitched in a grove of leafless aspens and great spruces, beside the rushing, ice-rimmed brook. The cook tent, with its stove, was an attractive place on the cool mornings and in stormy weather. Fry, the cook, a most competent man, had rigged up a table, and we had folding camp-chairs — luxuries utterly unknown to my former camping trips. Each day we breakfasted early and dined ten or twelve hours later, on returning from the day's hunt; and as we carried no lunch, the two meals were enjoyed with ravenous pleasure by the entire company. The horses were stout, tough, shaggy beasts, of wonderful staying power, and able to climb like cats. The country was very steep and rugged; the mountainsides were greasy and slippery from the melting snow, while the snow bucking through the deep drifts on their tops and on the north sides was exhausting. Only surefooted animals could avoid serious tumbles, and only animals of great endurance could have lasted through the work. Both Johnny Goff and his partner, Brick Wells, who often accompanied us on the hunts, were frequently mounted on animals of uncertain temper, with a tendency to buck on insufficient provocation; but they rode them with entire indifference up and down any incline. One of the riders, "Al," a very good tempered man, a tireless worker, had as one of his horses a queer, big-headed dun beast, with a black stripe down its back and traces of zebra-like bands on the backs of his front legs. He was an atavistic animal, looking much as the horses must have looked which an age or two ago lived in this very locality and were preyed on by sabre-toothed tigers, hyenadons, and other strange and terrible beasts of a long-vanished era. Lambert remarked to him: "Al, you ought to call that horse of yours 'Fossil'; he is a hundred thousand years old." To which Al, with immovable face, replied: "Gee! and that man sold him to me for a seven-year-old! I'll have the law on him!"

The hounds were most interesting, and showed all the variations of character and temper to be expected in such a pack; a pack in which performance counted for everything and pedigree for nothing. One of the best hounds was half fox terrier. Three of Johnny's had been with us four years before, when he and I hunted cougars together; these three being Jim, now an old dog, who dropped behind in a hard run, but still excellent on a cold trail; Tree'em, who, like Jim, had grown aged, but was very sure; and Bruno, who had become one of the best of all the pack on a hot trail, but who was apt to overrun it if it became at all difficult and cold. The biggest dog of the pack, a very powerful animal, was Badge, who was half foxhound and half what Johnny called Siberian bloodhound—I suppose a Great Dane or Ulm dog. His full brother Bill came next to him. There was a Rowdy in Jake's pack and another Rowdy in Johnny's, and each got badly hurt before the hunt was through. Jake's Rowdy, as soon as an animal was killed, became very cross and wished to attack any dog that came near. One of Jake's best hounds was old Bruise, a very sure, although not a particularly fast dog. All the members of the pack held the usual wild-beast attitude toward one another. They joined together for the chase and the fight, but once the quarry was killed, their relations among themselves became those of active hostility or selfish indifference. At feeding time each took whatever his strength permitted, and each paid abject deference to whichever animal was his known superior in prowess. Some of the younger dogs would now and then run deer or coyote. But the older dogs paid heed only to bear and bobcat; and the pack, as a body, discriminated sharply between the hounds they could trust and those which would go off on a wrong trail. The four terriers included a heavy, liver-colored half-breed bull-dog, a preposterous animal who looked as if his ancestry had included a toadfish. He was a terrible fighter, but his unvarying attitude toward mankind was one of effusive and rather foolish affection. In a fight he could whip any of the hounds save Badge, and he was far more willing than Badge to accept punishment. There was also a funny little black and tan, named Skip, a most friendly little fellow, especially fond of riding in front or behind the saddle of any one of us who would take him up, although perfectly able to travel forty miles a day on his own sturdy legs if he had to, and then to join in the worry of the quarry when once it had been shot. Porcupines abounded in the woods, and one or two of the terriers and half a dozen of the hounds positively refused to learn any wisdom, invariably attacking each porcupine they found; the result being that we had to spend many minutes in removing the quills from their mouths, eyes, etc. A white bull-terrier would come in from such a combat with his nose literally looking like a glorified pincushion, and many of the spines we had to take out with nippers. The terriers never ran with the hounds, but stayed behind with the horses until they heard the hounds barking "bayed" or "treed," when they forthwith tore toward them. Skip adopted me as his special master, rode with me whenever I would let him, and slept on the foot of my bed at night, growling defiance at anything that came near. I grew attached to the friendly, bright little fellow, and at the end of the hunt took him home with me as a playmate for the children.

It was a great, wild country. In the creek bottoms there were a good many ranches; but we only occasionally passed by these, on our way to our hunting grounds in the wilderness along the edge of the snow-line. The mountains crowded close together in chain, peak, and table-land; all the higher ones were wrapped in an unrent shroud of snow. We saw a good many deer, and fresh sign of elk, but no elk themselves, although we were informed that bands were to be found in the high spruce timber where the snows were so deep that it would have been impossible to go on horseback, while going on foot would have been inconceivably fatiguing. The country was open. The high peaks were bare of trees. Cottonwoods, and occasionally dwarfed birch or maple and willows, fringed the streams; aspens grew in groves higher up. There were piñons and cedars on the slopes of the foot-hills; spruce clustered here and there in the cooler ravines and valleys and high up the mountains. The dense oak brush and thick growing cedars were hard on our clothes, and sometimes on our bodies.

Bear and cougars had once been very plentiful throughout this region, but during the last three or four years the cougars have greatly diminished in numbers throughout northern Colorado, and the bears have diminished also, although not to the same extent. The great grizzlies which were once fairly plentiful here are now very rare, as they are in most places in the United States. There remain plenty of the black and brown bears, which are simply individual color phases of the same species.

Bears are interesting creatures and their habits are always worth watching. When I used to hunt grizzlies my experience tended to make me lay special emphasis on their variation in temper. There are savage and cowardly bears, just as there are big and little ones; and sometimes these variations are very marked among bears of the same district, and at other times all the bears of one district will seem to have a common code of behavior which differs utterly from that of the bears of another district. Readers of Lewis and Clark do not need to be reminded of the great difference they found in ferocity between the bears of the upper Missouri and the bears of the Columbia River country; and those who have lived in the upper Missouri country nowadays know how widely the bears that still remain have altered in character from what they were as recently as the middle of the last century.

This variability has been shown in the bears which I have stumbled upon at close quarters. On but one occasion was I ever regularly charged by a grizzly. To this animal I had given a mortal wound, and without any effort at retaliation he bolted into a thicket of what, in my hurry, I thought was laurel (it being composed in reality I suppose of thick-growing berry bushes). On my following him and giving him a second wound, he charged very determinedly, taking two more bullets without flinching. I just escaped the charge by jumping to one side, and he died almost immediately after striking at me as he rushed by. This bear charged with his mouth open, but made very little noise after the growl or roar with which he greeted my second bullet. I mention the fact of his having kept his mouth open, because one or two of my friends who have been charged have informed me that in their cases they particularly noticed that the bear charged with his mouth shut. Perhaps the fact that my bear was shot through the lungs may account for the difference, or it may simply be another example of individual variation.

On another occasion, in a windfall, I got up within eight or ten feet of a grizzly, which simply bolted off, paying no heed to a hurried shot which I delivered as I poised unsteadily on the swaying top of an overthrown dead pine. On yet another occasion, when I roused a big bear from his sleep, he at the first moment seemed to pay little or no heed to me, and then turned toward me in a leisurely way, the only sign of hostility he betrayed being to ruffle up the hair on his shoulders and the back of his neck. I hit him square between the eyes, and he dropped like a pole-axed steer.

On another occasion I got up quite close to and mortally wounded a bear, which ran off without uttering a sound until it fell dead; but another of these grizzlies, which I shot from ambush, kept squalling and yelling every time I hit him, making a great rumpus. On one occasion one of my cow hands and myself were able to run down on foot a she grizzly bear and her cub, which had obtained a long start of us, simply because of the foolish conduct of the mother. The cub — or more properly the yearling, for it was a cub of the second year — ran on far ahead, and would have escaped if the old she had not continually stopped and sat up on her hind legs to look back at us. I think she did this partly from curiosity, but partly also from bad temper, for once or twice she grinned and roared at us. The upshot of it was that I got within range and put a bullet in the old she, who afterward charged my companion and was killed; and we also got the yearling.

One young grizzly which I killed many years ago dropped to the first bullet, which entered its stomach. It then let myself and my companion approach closely, looking up at us with alert curiosity, but making no effort to escape. It was really not crippled at all, but we thought from its actions that its back was broken, and my companion advanced to kill it with his pistol. The pistol, however, did not inflict a mortal wound, and the only effect was to make the young bear jump to its feet as if unhurt, and race off at full speed through the timber; for though not full grown it was beyond cubhood, being probably about eighteen months old. By desperate running I succeeded in getting another shot, and more by luck than by anything else knocked it over, this time permanently.

Black bear are not, under normal conditions, formidable brutes. If they do charge and get home they may maul a man severely, and there are a number of instances on record in which they have killed men. Ordinarily, however, a black bear will not charge home, though he may bluster a good deal. I once shot one very close up which made a most lamentable outcry, and seemed to lose its head, its efforts to escape resulting in its bouncing about among the trees with such heedless hurry that I was easily able to kill it. Another black bear, which I also shot at close quarters, came straight for my companions and myself, and almost ran over the white hunter who was with me. This bear made no sound whatever when I first hit it, and I do not think it was charging. I believe it was simply dazed, and by accident ran the wrong way, and so almost came into collision with us. However, when it found itself face to face with the white hunter, and only four or five feet away, it prepared for hostilities, and I think would have mauled him if I had not brained it with another bullet; for I was myself standing but six feet or so to one side of it. None of the bears shot on this Colorado trip made a sound when hit; they all died silently, like so many wolves.

Ordinarily, my experience has been that bears were not flurried when I suddenly came upon them. They impressed me as if they were always keeping in mind the place toward which they wished to retreat in the event of danger, and for this place, which was invariably a piece of rough ground or dense timber, they made off with all possible speed, not seeming to lose their heads.

Frequently I have been able to watch bears for some time while myself unobserved. With other game I have very often done this even when within close range, not wishing to kill creatures needlessly, or without a good object; but with bears, my experience has been that chances to secure them come so seldom as to make it very distinctly worth while improving any that do come, and I have not spent much time watching any bear unless he was in a place where I could not get at him, or else was so close at hand that I was not afraid of his getting away. On one occasion the bear was hard at work digging up squirrel or gopher *caches* on the side of a pine-clad hill; while at this work he looked rather like a big badger. On two other occasions the bear was fussing around a carcass preparatory to burying it. On these occasions I was very close, and it was extremely interesting to note the grotesque, half-human movements, and giant, awkward strength of the great beast. He would twist the carcass around with the utmost ease, sometimes taking it in his teeth and dragging it, at other times grasping it in his forepaws and half lifting, half shoving it. Once the bear lost his grip and rolled over during the course of some movement, and this made him angry, and he struck the carcass a savage whack, just as a pettish child will strike a table against which it has knocked itself. At another time I watched a black bear some distance off getting his breakfast under stumps and stones. He was very active, turning the stone or log over, and then thrusting his muzzle into the empty space to gobble up the small creatures below before they recovered from their surprise and the sudden inflow of light. From under one log he put a chipmunk, and danced hither and thither with even more agility than awkwardness, slapping at the chipmunk with his paw while it zigzagged about, until finally he scooped it into his mouth.

All this was in the old days when I was still-hunting, with only the rifle. This Colorado trip was the first on which I hunted bears with hounds. If we had run across a grizzly there would doubtless have been a chance to show some prowess, at least in the way of hard riding. But the black and brown bears cannot, save under exceptional circumstances, escape from such a pack as we had with us; and the real merit of the chase was confined to the hounds and to Jake and Johnny for their skill in handling them. Perhaps I should add the horses, for their extraordinary endurance and surefootedness. As for the rest of us, we needed to do little more than to sit ten or twelve hours in the saddle and occasionally lead the horses up or down the most precipitous and cliff-like of the mountain sides. But it was great fun, nevertheless, and usually a chase lasted long enough to be interesting.

The first day after reaching camp we rode for eleven hours over a very difficult country, but without getting above the snow-line. Finally the dogs got on the fresh trail of a bobcat, and away they went. A bobcat will often give a good run, much better on the average than a cougar; and this one puzzled the dogs not a little at first. It scrambled out of one deep valley, crossing and recrossing the rock ledges where its scent was hard to follow; then plunged into another valley. Meanwhile we had ridden up on the high mountain spur between the two valleys, and after scrambling and galloping to and fro as the cry veered from point to point when the dogs changed directions, we saw them cross into the second valley. Here again they took a good deal of time to puzzle out the trail, and became somewhat scattered. We had dismounted and were standing by the horses' heads, listening to the baying and trying to decide which way we should go, when Stewart suddenly pointed us out a bear. It was on the other side of the valley from us, and perhaps half a mile away, galloping downhill, with two of the hounds after it, and in the sunlight its fur looked glossy black. In a minute or two it passed out of sight in the thick-growing timber at the bottom of the valley; and as we afterward found, the two hounds, getting momentarily thrown out, and hearing the others still baying on the cat trail, joined the latter. Jake started off to go around the head of the valley, while the rest of us plunged down into it. We found from the track that the bear had gone up the valley, and Jake found where he had come out on the high divide, and then turned and retraced his steps. But the hounds were evidently all after the cat. There was nothing for us to do but follow them. Sometimes riding, sometimes leading the horses, we went up the steep hillside, and as soon as we reached the crest heard the hounds barking treed. Shorty and Skip, who always trotted after the horses while the hounds were in full cry on a trail, recognized the change of note immediately, and tore off in the direction of the bay, while we followed as best we could, hoping to get there in time for Stewart and Lambert to take photographs of the lynx in a tree. But we were too late. Both Shorty and Skip could climb trees, and although Skip was too light to tackle a bobcat by himself, Shorty, a heavy, formidable dog, of unflinching courage and great physical strength, was altogether too much for any bobcat. When we reached the place we found the bobcat in the top of a piñon, and Shorty steadily working his way up through the branches and very near the quarry. Evidently the bobcat felt that the situation needed the taking of desperate chances, and just before Shorty reached it out it jumped, Shorty yelling with excitement as he plunged down through the branches after it. But the cat did not jump far enough. One of the hounds seized it by the hind leg and in another second everything was over.

Shorty was always the first of the pack to attack dangerous game, and in attacking bear or cougar even Badge was much less reckless and more wary. In consequence, Shorty was seamed over with scars; most of them from bobcats, but one or two from cougars. He could speedily kill a bobcat single-handed; for these small lynxes are not really formidable fighters, although they will lacerate a dog quite severely. Shorty found a badger a much more difficult antagonist than a bobcat. A bobcat in a hole makes a hard fight, however. On this hunt we once got a bobcat under a big rock, and Jake's Rowdy in trying to reach it got so badly mauled that he had to join the invalid class for several days.

The bobcat we killed this first day was a male, weighing twenty-five pounds. It was too late to try after the bear, especially as we had only ten or a dozen dogs out, while the bear's tracks showed it to be a big one; and we rode back to camp.

Next morning we rode off early, taking with us all twenty-six hounds and the four terriers. We wished first to find whether the bear had gone out of the country in which we had seen him, and so rode up a valley and then scrambled laboriously up the mountain-side to the top of the snow-covered divide. Here the snow was three feet deep in places, and the horses plunged and floundered as we worked our way in single file through the drifts. But it had frozen hard the previous night, so that a bear could walk on the crust and leave very little sign. In consequence we came near passing over the place where the animal we were after had actually crossed out of the cañon-like ravine in which we had seen him and gone over the divide into another set of valleys. The trail was so faint that it puzzled us, as we could not be certain how fresh it was, and until this point could be cleared up we tried to keep the hounds from following it. Old Jim, however, slipped off to one side and speedily satisfied himself that the trail was fresh. Along it he went, giving tongue, and the other dogs were maddened by the sound, while Jim, under such circumstances, paid no heed whatever to any effort to make him come back. Accordingly, the other hounds were slipped after him, and down they ran into the valley, while we slid, floundered, and scrambled along the ridge crest parallel to them, until a couple of miles farther on we worked our way down to some great slopes covered with dwarf scrub-oak. At the edge of these slopes, where they fell off in abrupt descent to the stream at the bottom of the valley, we halted. Opposite us was a high and very rugged mountain side covered with a growth of piñon — never a very close-growing tree — its precipitous flanks broken by ledges and scored by gullies and ravines. It was hard to follow the scent across such a mountainside, and the dogs speedily became much scattered. We could hear them plainly, and now and then could see them, looking like ants as they ran up and down hill and along the ledges. Finally, we heard some of them barking bayed. The volume of sound increased steadily as the straggling dogs joined those which had first reached the hunted animal. At about this time to our astonishment, Badge, usually a staunch fighter, rejoined us, followed by one or two other hounds, who seemed to have had enough of the matter. Immediately afterward we saw the bear, half-way up the opposite mountain-side. The hounds were all around him, and occasionally bit at his hind quarters; but he had evidently no intention of climbing a tree. When we first saw him he was sitting up on a point of rock surrounded by the pack, his black fur showing to fine advantage. Then he moved off, threatening the dogs, and making what in Mississippi is called a walking bay. He was a sullen, powerful beast, and his leisurely gait showed how little he feared the pack, and how confident he was in his own burly strength. By this time the dogs had been after him for a couple of hours, and as there was no water on the mountain-side we feared they might be getting exhausted, and rode toward them as rapidly as we could. It was a hard climb up to where they were, and we had to lead the horses. Just as we came in sight of him, across a deep gully which ran down the sheer mountain-side, he broke bay and started off, threatening the foremost of the pack as they dared to approach him. They were all around him, and for a minute I could not fire; then as he passed under a piñon I got a clear view of his great round stern and pulled trigger. The bullet broke both his hips, and he rolled downhill the hounds yelling with excitement as they closed in on him. He could still play havoc with the pack, and there was need to kill him at once. I leaped and slid down my side of the gully as he rolled down his; at the bottom he stopped and raised himself on his fore quarters; and with another bullet I broke his back between the shoulders.

Immediately all the dogs began to worry the carcass, while their savage baying echoed so loudly in the narrow, steep gully that we could with difficulty hear one another speak. It was a wild scene to look upon, as we scrambled down to where the dead bear lay on his back between the rocks. He did not die wholly unavenged, for he had killed one of the terriers and six other dogs were more or less injured; the chase of the bear is grim work for the pack. Jim, usually a very wary fighter, had a couple of deep holes in his thigh; but the most mishandled of the wounded dogs was Shorty. With his usual dauntless courage he had gone straight at the bear's head. Being such a heavy, powerful animal, I think if he had been backed up he could have held the bear's head down, and prevented the beast from doing much injury. As it was, the bear bit through the side of Shorty's head, and bit him in the shoulder, and again in the hip, inflicting very bad wounds. Once the fight was over Shorty lay down on the hillside, unable to move. When we started home we put him beside a little brook, and left a piece of bear meat by him, as it was obvious we could not get him to camp that day. Next day one of the boys went back with a pack-horse to take him in; but half-way out met him struggling toward camp, and returned. Late in the afternoon Shorty turned up while we were at dinner, and staggered toward us, wagging his tail with enthusiastic delight at seeing his friends. We fed him until he could not hold another mouthful; then he curled up in a dry corner of the cook-tent and slept for forty-eight hours; and two or three days afterward was able once more to go hunting.

The bear was a big male, weighing three hundred and thirty pounds. On examination at close quarters, his fur, which was in fine condition, was not as black as it had seemed when seen afar off, the roots of the hairs being brown. There was nothing whatever in his stomach. Evidently he had not yet begun to eat, and had been but a short while out of his hole. Bear feed very little when they first come out of their dens, sometimes beginning on grass, sometimes on buds. Occasionally they will feed at carcasses and try to kill animals within a week or two after they have left winter quarters, but this is rare, and as a usual thing for the first few weeks after they have come out they feed much as a deer would. Although not hog fat, as would probably have been the case in the fall, this bear was in good condition. In the fall, however, he would doubtless have weighed over four hundred pounds. The three old females we got on this trip weighed one hundred and eighty, one hundred and seventy-five, and one hundred and thirty-five pounds apiece. The yearlings weighed from thirty-one to forty pounds. The only other black bears I ever weighed all belonged to the sub-species *Luteolus*, and were killed on the Little Sunflower River, in Mississippi, in the late fall of nineteen hundred and two. A big old male, in poor condition, weighed two hundred and eighty-five pounds, and two very fat females weighed two hundred and twenty and two hundred and thirty-five pounds respectively.

The next few days we spent in hunting perseveringly, but unsuccessfully. Each day we were from six to twelve hours in the saddle, climbing with weary toil up the mountains and slipping and scrambling down them. On the tops and on the north slopes there was much snow, so that we had to pick our trails carefully, and even thus the horses often floundered belly-deep as we worked along in single file; the men on the horses which were best at snow bucking took turns in breaking the trail. In the worst places we had to dismount and lead the horses, often over such bad ground that nothing less sure-footed than the tough mountain ponies could even have kept their legs. The weather was cold, with occasional sharp flurries of snow, and once a regular snow-storm. We found the tracks of one or two bears, but in each case several days old, and it was evident either that the bears had gone back to their dens, finding the season so late, or else that they were lying quiet in sheltered places, and travelling as little as possible. One day, after a long run of certainly five or six miles through very difficult country, the dogs treed a bobcat in a big cedar. It had run so far that it was badly out of breath. Stewart climbed the tree and took several photographs of it, pushing the camera up to within about four feet of where the cat sat. Lambert obtained photographs of both Stewart and the cat. Shorty was at this time still an invalid from his encounter with the bear, but Skip worked his way thirty feet up the tree in his effort to get at the bobcat. Lambert shot the latter with his revolver; the bobcat dying, stuck in the branches; and he then had to climb the tree to get both the bobcat and Skip, as the latter was at such a height that we thought he would hurt himself if he fell. Another bobcat when treed sealed his own fate by stepping on a dead branch and falling right into the jaws of the pack.

At this camp, as everywhere, the tiny four-striped chipmunks were plentiful and tame; they are cheerful, attractive little an-imals. We also saw white-footed mice and a big meadow mouse around camp; and we found a young brushy-tailed pack-rat. The snowshoe rabbits were still white on the mountains, but in the lower valleys they had changed to the summer pelage. On the mountains we occasionally saw woodchucks and rock squirrels of two kinds, a large and a small — *Spermophilus grammurus* and *armatus*. The noisy, cheerful pine squirrels were common where the woods were thick. There were eagles and ravens in the mountains, and once we saw sandhill cranes soaring far above the highest peaks. The long-crested jays came familiarly around camp, but on this occasion we only saw the whiskey-jacks, Clark's nutcrackers and magpies, while off in the mountains. Among the piñons, we several times came across straggling flocks of the queer piñon jays or blue crows, with their unmistakable calls and almost blackbird-like habits. There were hawks of several species, and blue grouse, while the smaller birds included flickers, robins, and the beautiful mountain bluebirds. Juncos and mountain chickadees were plentiful, and the ruby-crowned kinglets were singing with astonishing power for such tiny birds. We came on two nests of the red-tailed hawk; the birds were brooding, and seemed tame and unwary.

After a week of this we came to the conclusion that the snow was too deep and the weather too cold for us to expect to get any more bear in the immediate neighborhood, and accordingly shifted camp to where Clear Creek joins West Divide Creek.

The first day's hunt from the new camp was successful. We were absent about eleven hours and rode some forty miles. The day included four hours' steady snow bucking, for the bear, as soon as they got the chance, went through the thick timber where the snow lay deepest. Some two hours after leaving camp we found the old tracks of a she and a yearling, but it took us a much longer time before we finally struck the fresh trail made late the previous night or early in the morning. It was Jake who first found this fresh track, while Johnny with the pack was a couple of miles away, slowly but surely puzzling out the cold trail and keeping the dogs up to their work. As soon as Johnny came up we put all the hounds on the tracks, and away they went, through and over the snow, yelling their eager delight.

Meanwhile we had fixed our saddles and were ready for what lay ahead. It was wholly impossible to ride at the tail of the pack, but we did our best to keep within sound of the baying. Finally, after much hard work and much point riding through snow, slush, and deep mud, on the level, and along, up, and down sheer hillsides, we heard the dogs barking treed in the middle of a great grove of aspens high up the mountain-side. The snow was too deep for the horses, and leaving them, we trudged heavily up on foot. The yearling was in the top of a tall aspen. Lambert shot it with his rifle and we then put the dogs on the trail of the old she. Some of the young ones did not know what to make of this, evidently feeling that the tracks must be those of the bear that they had already killed; but the veterans were in full cry at once. We scrambled after them up the steep mountain, and then downward along ridges and spurs, getting all the clear ground we could. Finally we had to take to the snow, and floundered and slid through the drifts until we were in the valley. Most of the time the dogs were within hearing, giving tongue as they followed the trail. Finally a total change in the note showed that they were barking treed; and as rapidly as possible we made our way toward the sound. Again we found ourselves unable to bring the horses up to where the bear had treed, and scrambled thither on foot through the deep snow.

The bear was some thirty or forty feet up a tall spruce; it was a big she, with a glossy black-brown coat. I was afraid that at our approach she might come down; but she had been running hard for some four hours, had been pressed close, and evidently had not the slightest idea of putting herself of her own free will within the reach of the pack, which was now frantically baying at the foot of the tree. I shot her through the heart. As the bullet struck she climbed up through the branches with great agility for six or eight feet; then her muscles relaxed, and down she came with a thud, nearly burying herself in the snow. Little Skip was one of the first dogs to seize her as she came down; and in another moment he literally disappeared under the hounds as they piled on the bear. As soon as possible we got off the skin and pushed campward at a good gait, for we were a long way off. Just at nightfall we came out on a bluff from which we could overlook the rushing, swirling brown torrent, on the farther bank of which the tents were pitched.

The stomach of this bear contained nothing but buds. Like the other shes killed on this trip, she was accompanied by her yearling young, but had no newly born cub; sometimes bear breed only every other year, but I have found the mother accompanied not only by her cub but by her young of the year before. The yearling also had nothing but buds in its stomach. When his skin was taken off Stewart looked at it, shook his head, and turning to Lambert said solemnly: "Alex, that skin isn't big enough to use for anything but a doily." From that time until the end of the hunt the yearlings were only known as "doily bears."

Next morning we again went out, and this time for twelve hours steadily, in the saddle, and now and then on foot. Most of the time we were in snow, and it was extraordinary that the horses could get through it at all, especially in working up the steep mountain-sides. But until it got so deep that they actually floundered — that is, so long as they could get their legs down to the bottom — I found that they could travel much faster than I could. On this day some twenty good-natured, hard-riding young fellows from the ranches within a radius of a dozen miles had joined our party to "see the President kill a bear." They were a cheerful and eagerly friendly crowd, as hardy as so many young moose, and utterly fearless horsemen; one of them rode his wild, nervous horse bareback, because it had bucked so when he tried to put the saddle on it that morning that he feared he would get left behind, and so abandoned the saddle outright. Whenever they had a chance they all rode at headlong speed, paying no heed to the slope of the mountainside or the character of the ground. In the deep snow they did me a real service, for of course they had to ride their horses single file through the drifts, and by the time my turn came we had a good trail.

After a good deal of beating to and fro, we found where an old she-bear with two yearlings had crossed a hill during the night and put the hounds on their tracks. Johnny and Jake, with one or two of the cowboys, followed the hounds over the exceedingly difficult hillside where the trail led; or rather, they tried to follow them, for the hounds speedily got clear away, as there were many places where they could run on the crust of the snow, in which the horses wallowed almost helpless. The rest of us went down to the valley, where the snow was light and the going was easier. The bear had travelled hither and thither through the woods on the side-hill, and the dogs became scattered. Moreover, they jumped several deer, and four or five of the young dogs took after one of the latter. Finally, however, the rest of the pack put up the three bears. We had an interesting glimpse of the chase as the bears quartered up across an open spot of the hillside. The hounds were but a short distance behind them, strung out in a long string, the more powerful, those which could do best in the snow-bucking, taking the lead. We pushed up the mountain-side after them, horse after horse getting down in the snow, and speedily heard the redoubled clamor which told us that something had been treed. It was half an hour before we could make our way to the tree, a spruce in which the two yearlings had taken refuge, while around the bottom the entire pack was gathered, crazy with excitement. We could not take the yearlings alive, both because we lacked the means of carrying them, and because we were anxious to get after the old bear. We could not leave them where they were, because it would have been well-nigh impossible to get the dogs away, and because even if we had succeeded in getting them away, they would not have run any other trail as long as they knew the yearlings were in the tree. It was therefore out of the question to leave them unharmed, as we should have been glad to do, and Lambert killed them both with his revolver; the one that was first hit immediately biting its brother. The ranchmen took them home to eat.

The hounds were immediately put on the trail of the old one and disappeared over the snow. In a few minutes we followed. It was heavy work getting up the mountain-side through the drifts, but once on top we made our way down a nearly bare spur, and then turned to the right, scrambled a couple of miles along a slippery side-hill, and halted. Below us lay a great valley, on the farther side of which a spruce forest stretched up toward the treeless peaks. Snow covered even the bottom of the valley, and lay deep and solid in the spruce forest on the mountain-side. The hounds were in full cry, evidently on a hot trail, and we caught glimpses of them far on the opposite side of the valley, crossing little open glades in the spruce timber. If the crust was hard they scattered out. Where it was at all soft they ran in single file. We worked our way down toward them, and on reaching the bottom of the valley, went up it as fast as the snow would allow. Finally we heard the pack again barking treed and started toward them. They had treed the bear far up the mountain-side in the thick spruce timber, and a short experiment showed us that the horses could not possibly get through the snow. Accordingly, off we jumped and went toward the sound on foot, all the young ranchmen and cowboys rushing ahead, and thereby again making me an easy trail. On the way to the tree the rider of the bareback horse pounced on a snowshoe rabbit which was crouched under a bush and caught it with his hands. It was half an hour before we reached the tree, a big spruce, up which the bear had gone to a height of some forty feet. I broke her neck with a single bullet. She was smaller than the one I had shot the day before, but full grown. In her stomach, as in those of the two yearlings, there were buds of rosebushes and quaking aspens. One yearling had also swallowed a mouse. It was a long ride to camp, and darkness had fallen by the time we caught the gleam from the lighted tents, across the dark stream.

With neither of these last two bear had there been any call for prowess; my part was merely to kill the bear dead at the first shot, for the sake of the pack. But the days were very enjoyable, nevertheless. It was good fun to be twelve hours in the saddle in such wild and beautiful country, to look at and listen to the hounds as they worked, and finally to see the bear treed and looking down at the maddened pack baying beneath.

For the next two or three days I was kept in camp by a touch of Cuban fever. On one of these days Lambert enjoyed the longest hunt we had on the trip, after an old she-bear and three

yearlings. The yearlings treed one by one, each of course ne-
cessitating a stoppage, and it was seven in the evening before
the old bear at last went up a cottonwood and was shot; she
was only wounded, however, and in the fight she crippled
Johnny's Rowdy before she was killed. When the hunters reached
camp it was thirteen hours since they had left it. The old bear
was a very light brown; the first yearling was reddish brown,
the second light yellowish brown, the third dark black-brown,
though all were evidently of the same litter.

Following this came a spell of bad weather, snowstorm and
blizzard steadily succeeding one another. This lasted until my
holiday was over. Some days we had to stay in camp. On other
days we hunted; but there was three feet of new snow on the
summits and foot-hills, making it difficult to get about. We
saw no more bear, and indeed, no more bear-tracks that were
less than two or three weeks old.

We killed a couple of bobcats. The chase of one was marked
by several incidents. We had been riding through a blizzard on
the top of a plateau, and were glad to plunge down into a steep
sheer-sided valley. By the time we reached the bottom there
was a lull in the storm and we worked our way with considerable difficulty through the snow, down timber, and lava rock,
toward Divide Creek. After a while the valley widened a little,
spruce and aspens fringing the stream at the bottom while the
sides were bare. Here we struck a fresh bobcat trail leading off
up one of the mountain-sides. The hounds followed it nearly
to the top, then turned and came down again, worked through
the timber in the bottom, and struck out on the hillside opposite. Suddenly we saw the bobcat running ahead of them and
doubling and circling. A few minutes afterward the hounds
followed the trail to the creek bottom and then began to bark
treed. But on reaching the point we found there was no cat in
the tree, although the dogs seemed certain that there was; and
Johnny and Jake speedily had them again running on the trail.
After making its way for some distance through the bottom,
the cat had again taken to the side-hill, and the hounds went

after it hard. Again they went nearly to the top, again they streamed down to the bottom and crossed the creek. Soon afterward we saw the cat ahead of them. For the moment it threw them off the track by making a circle and galloping around close to the rearmost hounds. It then made for the creek bottom, where it climbed to the top of a tall aspen. The hounds soon picked up the trail again, and followed it full cry; but unfortunately just before they reached where it had treed they ran on to a porcupine. When we reached the foot of the aspen in the top of which the bobcat crouched, with most of the pack braying beneath, we found the porcupine dead and a half a dozen dogs with their muzzles and throats filled full of quills. Before doing anything with the cat it was necessary to take these quills out. One of the terriers, which always found porcupines an irresistible attraction, was a really extraordinary sight, so thickly were the quills studded over his face and chest. But a big hound was in even worse condition; the quills were stuck in abundance into his nose, lips, cheeks, and tongue, and in the roof of his mouth they were almost as thick as bristles in a brush. Only by use of pincers was it possible to rid these two dogs of the quills, and it was a long and bloody job. The others had suffered less.

The dogs seemed to have no sympathy with one another, and apparently all that the rest of the pack felt was that they were kept a long time waiting for the cat. They never stopped baying for a minute, and Shorty, as was his habit, deliberately bit great patches of bark from the aspens, to show his impatience; for the tree in which the cat stood was not one which he could climb. After attending to the porcupine dogs one of the men climbed the tree and with a stick pushed out the cat. It dropped down through the branches forty or fifty feet, but was so quick in starting and dodging that it actually rushed through the pack, crossed the stream, and, doubling and twisting, was off up the creek through the timber. It ran cunningly, and in a minute or two lay down under a bush and watched the hounds as they went by, overrunning its trail. Then it took off up the hillside; but the hounds speedily picked up its track, and running in single file, were almost on it. Then the cat turned down hill, but too late, for it was overtaken within fifty yards. This ended our hunting.

Hunting the Great Alaskan Bear

ANDREW J. STONE

Bears have been hunted for food, for sport, and finally in the name of science. The writer of this article led an expedition to Alaska in 1903, which was sponsored by the American Museum of Natural History, New York. He brought back a number of specimens, among them the largest bear then known to have been killed by man.

What percentage of people, even of those who feel an interest in wild animal life, really know that the largest flesh-eating animals in the world are found in America? People generally believe, and have believed for ages, that the African lion is the king of beasts. But he is not nearly as large or as powerful an animal as the large brown bear of Subarctic America. The bears are not as ferocious or combative as the lions, nor are they nearly as vicious as they are given credit for being; but the largest of them are much larger and more powerful than any of the lions. It is safe to say that the largest of the brown bears of the North would weigh three times as much as the largest specimen of lion, and is beyond all question greatly superior in strength.

Comparing these two powerful animals in action, if brought together in combat, the bear would at first appear very clumsy. It would not be capable of the quick rush or of the catlike spring of the lion. It would not attack, but would remain entirely on the defensive, meeting its adversary with blows of such rapidity and terrific force as at once to illustrate its superiority not only in strength, but in action. I do not believe that there is an animal in the world that can act more quickly or effectively or can aim its blows with greater certainty than the bear.

The large brown bears of the Alaska Peninsula, south of Behring Sea, are among the largest bears of the world, and it is evident that there is no part of the world outside of America in which such large flesh-eating animals are found. The bears are flesh-eaters, or carnivorous, yet there are none of them that depend upon flesh for food, and with most of them flesh comprises but a very small percentage of their food.

The large brown bears of the North and those of the Alaska Peninsula, to which I shall make special reference, usually travel to the sea when first leaving hibernation in the spring, and there they follow the beaches, picking up whatever food the generous waters may cast ashore and feeding upon the marsh grasses as they first begin to grow. As the snow begins to melt from the hillsides and the ground thaws, they travel to the hills in search of marmot and ground squirrels and mice, and will often dig to a depth of many feet in order to secure one of these small animals. At the same time they consume a great many roots and grasses. In July the salmon leave the sea and run up the small streams that come down from the mountains, and the bears wade into the streams and feast upon them to their hearts' content. In August, when the salmon begin to fail, the berries are ripening in the hills in great quantities and variety, and the bears live and fatten on these for the rest of the summer and fall, until it is time once more for them to hibernate or house for the winter. They are fond of the flesh of the caribou and moose and sheep, and more fond yet of the flesh of the mountain goat; but it is very rarely that they procure any of these animals, for they cannot overtake them in flight, nor can they very well creep on to such prey, for the reason of their own size and their inability to assume creeping positions; and beside, the other animals could almost always smell them before they approached dangerously near. Then, too, they are incapable of making any very quick rush upon such prey.

In the spring of 1903 a steamer landed myself and two assistants on Popoff Island, just south of the Alaska Peninsula where it stretches far to the west between the North Pacific and Behring Sea. The following day a little schooner in charge of two men, one a white man and the other a Russian Aleut, called for us and we crossed Unga Straits to the head of Portage Bay in the mainland of the peninsula.

We carried with us supplies for a six weeks' hunting trip, and the following morning the five of us set to work to carry them across the peninsula nine miles to the head of Herindeen Bay, on the coast of Behring Sea. We travelled a pass that cut through the mountain range of the peninsula in a most picturesque and beautiful country. Nowhere did our path rise to a height of more than five hundred feet above the sea, but at this time of year—the middle of May—the snow in most places was very deep and getting soft enough to let us through, making most difficult travel. Our heavy packs, added to our own weight, made our progress very difficult at times when we were breaking into the snow from one to two feet deep. But the days were long and the weather fairly good, and for each of the five days required to carry over our supplies we would make the round trip, carrying over our loads and walking back—a total travel of eighteen miles. This was strenuous enough for the beginning of the season's work, but no one complained and everything went smoothly.

The pleasure and excitement of the hunt awaited us. At the head of Herindeen Bay I secured an open boat and we loaded in our supplies and followed the coast of Behring Sea thirty-five or forty miles to a point on Muller Bay, where we pitched camp and decided to make our first hunt.

Moving our camp farther up the bay to new hunting grounds, an adult male bear, one of the largest ever taken, was secured on May 29th. This animal had just finished burying a full-grown caribou when killed, having first made a dinner from it.

Four more specimens were secured during the next few days, and on June 9th, while three of my party and myself were boating along the coast about nine miles from our camp, I sighted two large animals well up the mountain side. We rowed ashore and one of the men and myself commenced to climb the mountain.

Soon after we lost sight of the animals and did not see any more of them until we were very near them. The climb was a long one and in places very steep. There was nothing to be seen as I first peered over the rocks, and I was just lifting myself well above them, when my additional elevation extended my view. Glancing to the right I saw, not more than seventy-five yards distant, a huge brown creature lying in perfect composure against the face of a slide of decomposed rocks very nearly its own color. To every appearance the animal was asleep, and it seemed a pity to fire on it; but it was not a matter of sport, but a matter of securing exceedingly valuable specimens, and sentiment gave place to practical requirements. I drew back sufficient to get sight of the man behind me and waved him to keep quiet. Then drawing my rifle I fired at the animal's shoulder. All this time I had not caught sight of its mate, but at the report of my rifle, the huge beast I had fired on rose slowly to his feet and gave a deep groan. At the same instant its mate ran out from behind a ledge of rocks within fifty yards of me and I fired at it, breaking it down in the shoulders, and it went tumbling headlong down into a deep ravine. Turning to the first animal, I saw it slowly shambling forward into the same ravine. I fired two shots at it in quick succession and it plunged heavily forward and disappeared. I ran around the head of the ravine and down on the other side to a point of rocks from which I could look into the ravine and the country below, and I saw the second animal fired at, some distance below at the edge of some alders, trying to regain its feet, and I finished it with another shot. The first animal fired at lay lifeless at the bottom of the ravine, wedged in between a rift of ice and a wall of stone. They proved to be an adult male and female, and both of them very large.

A few days later, while hunting the country at the head of an arm of the same bay, I was sitting on the top of a high knoll overlooking a broad valley and the sides of the hills that fronted it.

I heard shots up the mountain side, evidently about a mile distant, that I knew were from some of my party. I fully expected that they had secured game, and I started to the foot of the hill, intending to follow along its base toward the vicinity where the shots were fired. When about half-way down the hill I had a splendid view of the mountain side and stopped to look it over with my glasses, hoping to locate the party. As my glasses came up over the country ahead of me, I saw a large bear at the foot of the mountain, about a half mile distant, running directly toward me.

There was a small water hole almost directly below me, and as I sat watching the animal every moment of its approach, I was deeply impressed by his magnificent size, his wonderful height, his stately bearing and his seeming great strength, as well as the magnificence and beauty of his light brown coat, that glistened in the sun like a moving mass of burnished gold. When he reached the side of the water hole he gave one great plunge and landed in the middle of it, evidently to cool his overheated body. He dipped himself several times with evident satisfaction, and as he was just taking one of his dips, I was foolish enough to fire at him, and I overshot him as he dropped beneath the surface. At the report of the rifle he sprang from the water with a terrific bound, and my second shot caught him fair as he started to run. He stumbled, but regained his balance, when my third shot very nearly brought him down; but he was fearfully excited and his blood was hot, which helped greatly to sustain him for a short period, and he continued his course through a small bunch of alders. As he appeared once more in the open on the other side of them, running diagonally from me, I fired again. His head dropped between his forelegs, and the momentum of his great body caused him to make a complete somersault, where he lay stretched full length on his back, perfectly dead, with all four feet in the air, never giving the slightest struggle. He proved a magnificent, large specimen, and one of the most beautiful animals I have ever seen.

The rest of my party came to me a little later, reporting having secured two animals. Before the night settled over the hills, all three animals were measured and skinned, and the skins and bones and skulls were carried to the beach, where we camped for the night, and the next morning we crossed the bay about ten miles back to our main camp with our beautiful and valuable trophies.

I now had ten perfect specimens of these very large bears and I decided to end the hunt, and on the morning of the 13th of June started on our return.

I have taken many bears of different species in many parts of the North, and I have made a very careful study of them; and I insist, contrary to popular sentiment, that bears are not ferocious animals. They are full of humor and have a great love of peace and a sincere regard for the superiority of man. They are very tractable and splendid reasoners, but when much excited, like most animals and people, sometimes display bad judgment.

A Bear Hunt in Montana

ARTHUR ALVORD STILES

The conflict between man and bear is unequal. The superiority of the hunter with a gun is beyond argument. But the mauling a maddened bear can inflict upon an unprepared man or woman is horrible to contemplate.

With the end of the hunting season in the Far West there comes to light a true and exciting bear story—one that well might have made the bravest hunter look to his safety, or even have thrilled the sportsman spirit of President Roosevelt himself.

The incident occurred last September in the forest of northwestern Montana. The party consisted of Dr. Charles B. Penrose, a well-known physician of Philadelphia, the victim of bruin's ferocious attack, and his two brothers, Spencer Penrose, of Colorado Springs, and Senator Bois Penrose, of Pennsylvania, now in Washington. The party had spent the early part of the season exploring a section of the Lewis and Clark Forest Reserve, where trails were to be found and where travel with the pack-horses was comparatively easy. Toward the end of the summer, however, Senator Penrose desired to see a part of the country hitherto unsurveyed and without trails or passways of any kind. It is a section of high and rugged mountain peaks, snowfields, and living glaciers, wholly uninhabited except by the wild animals, and wellnigh inaccessible save in the dead of winter, when some adventurous soul of doubtful judgment might make his way thither on snowshoes.

As it happened, a small party of topographical surveyors of the U.S. Geological Survey was then penetrating into this God-forsaken region, carrying with them their pack-train of mules, camp equipment, and map-making instruments. This was the first pack outfit of any kind to enter into the territory. Senator Penrose and his brothers joined the government party, and by them were conducted well up among the snow-capped peaks of the range.

Continued bad weather having stopped the work of the surveyors and made all mapping impossible, the writer who was chief of the government party, offered to take Senator Penrose out for a hunt. The Senator and his younger brother, however, were tired out with the long and difficult journey to the government camp, so Dr. Penrose, who had endured the hard climb better than his brothers, volunteered to accompany me to a distant glacier basin, where they expected to find big game. The saddle horses were left at the head of this basin, and, little knowing of the fate that awaited them, the two men separated.

I had just sighted a fine buck deer and was on the point of creeping away from it so that Dr. Penrose might come and kill it, when I heard three shots in rapid succession. I gave no special heed to the reports, which came from the other side of the ridge, and was about turning to shoot the deer myself, when I heard two more shots; a moment more and another report rang out. Immediately becoming alarmed, I ran back in the direction from whence the shots came. I suppose I reached the doctor in about five or ten minutes. As I came around a mass of broken boulders I saw Dr. Penrose wandering aimlessly around in the canyon bed. He had no gun. His hat was gone, his coat torn off, and his trousers rent. Blood poured from his head and neck, and he gripped his left arm in his crimson right hand. When I reached him he murmured piteously, "Water, water." I ran and brought water in my big sombrero from the other side of the rocks. He drank it like a thirsty horse, and I thought I saw part of it run out through a gash in his cheek. Then he said: "Stiles, I am all in; I have had a fight with a bear."

With signal cloth I hurriedly began to tie up the worst of his wounds, and as I did so the picture and the bleeding man told me the story. A few rods down the gulch lay a grizzly cub, so large as to appear full-grown, except to the careful observer. Near by was the huge carcass of a mother grizzly, and near her the doctor's Mauser rifle, cast aside and empty. All was plain now. In his excitement Dr. Penrose had not noted that the bear which his first three shots had so promptly slain was yet a young cub, whose grief-stricken and enraged mother might then be making her way from the rocks and brush to avenge the death of her offspring. Going down to examine his prize, he placed his rifle on a rock, fortunately not far away.

He was stooping over the dead cub when there came from behind him a rush and an awful cry. He turned and saw the mother bear coming upon him, then not sixty feet away. With almost superhuman presence of mind Dr. Penrose caught up his Mauser again and fired two shots into the enraged beast. Instantly he took from his pocket his last remaining cartridge, worked it into the rifle, and sent a third steel-jacketed bullet into the onrushing bear. Swift and sure as were the little bullets, the bear's fury was not checked in time. With one stroke of her paw she sent him into the gulch, eight feet below. She sprang down after him and caught him in her mouth and shook him as a cat might shake a mouse. She dropped him. Again she caught him up, his face between her glistening tusks. She tore his scalp; his eyes narrowly escaped. A tusk penetrated into his mouth from the side of his cheek; another tore open his throat. There were five gaping wounds in his chest. His thigh bore an awful, irregular tear, and the flesh hung in ragged pieces from the wound, half as wide as your hand. His left wrist was twisted and broken, and the bones stuck out through the quivering flesh. The bear tried once more to shake her half-dead victim, but she sickened with her own awful wounds, and staggering, fell dead at his feet.

The little Mauser bullets, fired a moment before, had finally had their deadly effect, and by his steady nerve and accurate aim Dr. Penrose had saved his own life. Had the beast lasted another half minute the doctor would have been with his fathers, and the little cub's death would have been avenged. But the heroic mother had fought to the last, and now, with her dead baby, lay quiet and still forever.

Recovering sufficiently, the bleeding man sat up and began to take stock. As he meditated thus, there came a new adversary. In actual fact, or in the suffering man's delirious fancy — I have never known which — a third bear bounded out of the brush from another direction. The doctor's heart sank; he could make no resistance now; he hoped that death might come quickly. The new enemy approached to close quarters, and, walking around, snarled and growled savagely, yet was evidently undecided what to do. Then, with a cry of mingled rage and fright, it dashed off down the gulch and was lost in the forest.

The journey back to camp was difficult and dangerous, but the suffering doctor, who now began to realize his frightful condition, was bearing up bravely. Wrapping my big cow-boy slicker around him, I managed to get him on my horse, and we turned back to the camp, where we had left the Penrose party. My faithful horse did his duty nobly, as we climbed and stumbled along for two hours without a trail, at last reaching the teepees at nightfall. The unexpected sight of the wounded and bleeding doctor somewhat demoralized the group of waiting men, and after some delay a pine-knot camp-fire was made for light, and with the patient lying at full length on the ground I began my surgical operations, assisted by such much-needed instruction as the doctor, in his awful pain, could give me while the work progressed. I applied antiseptics and placed bandages, all of which happily he had with him in a small emergency case. Finally the broken wrist was reached. It was agreed that I should remove the protruding bones, the nervy patient thinking he could endure the pain of the operation without anesthetics. I disinfected the little knives and appliances and the last operation began. The pain was awful. With one agonized groan the man gave up for the first time. We held a hurried conference. The wrist would have to be left as it was, and we bound it up once more in signal cloth. It was one o'clock in the morning when I finished my amateur surgery. Thoroughly distracted by the sight of their brother's suffering, Senator Penrose and Spencer withdrew to another tent, and I lay down near Dr. Penrose to wait for dawn.

My life on the frontier has been full of trying episodes, but oh, that night! How would we get Dr. Penrose out of the mountains? I dare not guess how many times I asked myself that question. As the gloomy hours dragged by I listened to the heavy breathing of the man whose nerve and fortitude I had already come to admire, now asleep and groggy with the morphine injected to stop his unbearable suffering.

To go back the way we came up would mean two days and a 600-foot climb on foot. He could not last. By the second day we would be packing out a dead body. Yet there was no other route. The situation was desperate. In the lonely flickering of that camp-fire I meditated, and my sympathies went out to that wounded man. As the case presented itself at that moment success in guiding the party to the railroad meant the doctor's life, if not his comfort; failure meant death, simply. Before that welcome dawn had come I decided to run a hazard. We would take Dr. Penrose to the railroad by an unheard of route. Providence might point the way.

At dawn the little caravan started. Again the big black horse carried the almost helpless doctor, Senator Penrose and Spencer walking on either side to steady their brother through the tight places. The faithful guide, Bill Hague, lead the extra "packs," and two young men from the Survey party, Malcolm Force, of Montclair, New Jersey, and Billy Kemeys, of Washington, D. C., worked as axemen. Thus, for eleven hours, we climbed down, down, down, five miles through the forest and jungle, cutting our way as we went. At dark we dropped through to the railroad, completely exhausted, but safe. Our route had proved successful. I could not have cut another tree or broken another brush, and my two Survey boys had stood by me like men.

Quickly we conducted Dr. Penrose to a lonely section-house two miles down the track, where the Great Northern Limited was flagged, and he was taken away to Minnesota, where, three days later, he was operated upon by the surgeons at the Mayo Hospital. Since then he has retired to his country home near Philadelphia. Though his recovery is not yet complete, his progress has been very remarkable.

As a memento of the encounter with the bear, Dr. Penrose has presented the writer with a beautiful Mauser rifle, imported from the Krupp works at Essen, Germany. In the stock of the rifle is set a little silver nameplate which bears the simple inscription: "Arthur Stiles, from C. B. Penrose."

The Cabin Where Terror Came Calling

KEITH McCAFFERTY

A man, knowing what damage a grizzly can do, and knowing that one grizzly in particular means to do him harm, knows fear.

The grizzly bear is believed to be among the few mammals besides man which commonly dies in its sleep. Winter takes it in the end, although its fate is not that of deer shrunk to skeletons by March, nor of bighorns drowned by avalanche. It may be that a bear nearing the end of life takes to its den early one fall, and pulling up winter for its funeral shroud, lies entombed there forever.

In the Rocky Mountain West, the grizzly has made its final stand in a handful of retreats: in Yellowstone National Park, in a slender finger of Canada's Selkirk Range that juts into Washington, and in the high country of northwestern Montana, principally Glacier National Park and the Bob Marshall Wilderness. Some grizzly researchers believe the last bear to grace this country will leave its skull in a den in the Bob Marshall Wilderness, and that its bones will be finished by rodents in time for our generation to be the voice of its history.

In the Bob Marshall Wilderness, native trout teem in three forks of the Flathead River; green, transparent races of water that vein a vast roll of mountains where every other feature of land has been named for its bears: Silvertip Mountain, White Bear Creek, Grizzly Gulch.

This area used to be a favored hunting ground of timber wolves. A few can still be heard in its forests. It also was the winter haunt of pine marten trappers, just a few of whom remain.

The marten trappers were a colorful lot who defended individual creek drainages as vigorously as did the old, boar grizzlies that ransacked their camps. Like the bears they were victims of progress, finished four decades ago by Russian sable farms that exported domestic furs thickened in Siberia. Blackened scars where traps were notched into the trunks of trees blemish the older stands of lodgepole pine in the Bob Marshall to this day. Tiny log cabins the trappers built are less noticeable. Most have returned to the forest floor, although a scattering still stand, banked back into the sides of ridges for insulation. These "cabins" were little larger than coffins, and the trappers heated them with body heat. They remain as testament to a hard way of life that has all but disappeared from this country.

This is a story told by one of the last marten trappers. He is my age, thirty, but already an old hand in the wilderness. He has run a trapline up the headwater tributaries of the South Fork of the Flathead River since he was seventeen years old.

Shortly before I met him, the trapper had the misfortune of stepping on one of the decaying, nail-quilled bear doors that are strewn about various cabins constructed by the Forest Service for backcountry rangers. I had come into the Bob Marshall with a party of three to measure the spring snowpack for government records. We had traveled 90 miles by snow cat to the wilderness boundary, and gone on skis from there. The last 2 miles of the 20 we skied trailed the lopsided dinosaur waddle of snowshoe tracks. I knew whoever was up ahead had a bad left foot.

The trapper, hunched under the bulk of his pack, looked like he had journeyed to this place from somewhere considerably farther north. He had tangled hair down to his coat collar, a winter's growth of thin beard, a hawk nose. He was not a big man, yet his handshake brought blood to the tips of my fingers. His eyes, clear and green, moved as deliberately and as carefully as his speech, which sounded like that of an older man.

"I don't want to make trouble for you," he said. But he said he had been on the bad foot for a week, and the pain which radiated from the deep puncture the nail made grew worse by the hour. The nearest passable road was still on the far side of a broad belt of mountains that avalanched frequently this time of year. This was no small predicament, and the trapper well knew it.

Our party had the key to an outpost ranger cabin that sat over the river on a bench of timber, near the junction of the South Fork with Big Salmon Creek. We had to dig out the door through 3 feet of snow. The mattresses hung up under the ceiling in looping hammocks of rope. On the slab pine floor the mousetraps were all long sprung and the mice collected in them had rotted away, leaving miniscule skeletons, puffs of fur, and threads of tails.

We walked around inside like crabs on blistered feet, banging the pots for our supper. The trapper sat beside a big barrel wood heater, his boots and stag shirt dripping off 60-penny nails driven into the log center beam, his foot soaking in a dishpan of melted snow.

There is an unspoken code in the backcountry that no one broaches the subject of grizzly bears until a suitable interval has passed. To speak of the grizzly too soon is a sign of insecurity. We had pumped up a lantern going into that night. But the circle of light dimmed considerably before we heard the trapper's story.

He said that years ago, a grizzly bear stole an elk he had shot for winter meat. That fall he was guiding elk hunters for an outfitter who took a string of mules up the South Fork of the Flathead. The outfitter packed out Thanksgiving week, hurrying to beat the snow out of the mountains. He left the guide his best wishes. For the trapper it would be his first winter alone in the wilderness.

The bear raided the trapper's camp the following week. It took a beaver he'd left lying on top of a skinning table; stuck its head inside the tent flap to get it. It jerked the elk out of the tree where it hung nose up with a rope around its antlers. The trapper had slept through the night; he read the story in the snow in the morning. He followed bear tracks to the river. It was a grizzly all right, its long claws biting into the snow inches from the impressions of the feet. Under a heaping of branches the trapper found the torn, bloodied carcass of the spike bull elk. He caught himself staring at a heap of dung that spread a brown pillow in a pool of water isolated from the current of the river.

But he wanted revenge, and took up the track again, crossing the river and climbing the slope on the far side. As he climbed, smelling the rank odor the grizzly left in its wake, the fear began crowding into his mind, and the cold desire to even his score began to dissolve in sweat and dread. At the top of the ridge he turned to look down at the ruin of his camp. He saw the sagging tent and the reddened trough in the snow the bear had made dragging the elk to the river. He thought: *no more.*

In that moment the bear, which must have been lying in the shintangle, rose to its height. The trapper later recalled that when the bear put its nose on man scent the hair of its thick neck rose like a cat's. And he had heard the hissing of his own hair as it stood against the crown of his hat.

Then in an instant the bear was down on fours, bulling through the matchstick lodgepole and gone out of sight over the ridge. The trapper never hesitated. He turned and ran, dodging through the close trees in the thicket, coming off the mountain in a flood of adrenalin to lurch against the river and stagger to the giddy safety on the opposite bank. He sat down, sucking air. His Springfield rifle was held in gripped fists, at the ready, forgotten at his moment of opportunity.

With little forethought and no real experience the trapper had set out to kill a grizzly bear. "It was the rug," he would say. "I'd always wanted a grizzly bear rug." And a little of the morning's instant courage lingered even after retreat, a thrilling, insane urge to bend once more to the tracks.

But it had been foolhardy to take a bear to task in such tough country. The trapper knew it. He faced the fact that whatever return of confidence he enjoyed with the sun up and the bear gone would desert him utterly at the close of day.

Downriver an old plank shed had weathered the snows of too many winters. There were the remnants of a corral; a few crossed logs deteriorating over the cleared ground. The trapper had this shed in mind as he heaved at the corpse of the elk. Even with its hindquarters eaten the elk was a burdensome animal which hugged the snow as the trapper worked. It took hours to move it to the higher ground. He finally dropped it outside the shed's solitary window, a black, square hole that had been crudely barred with twisted strands of barbed wire in an attempt to keep out the bears of a former era.

Quickly the trapper retraced his steps to the tent. He packed his backpack with food, sleeping bag, lantern. He had a side of bacon for cooking grease and he packed it. Upon his return to the shed he pried a nail from a plank of wood, and stepping on top of his elk for height, nailed the bacon outside and just over the top of the window.

He figured to fire on the bear soon as it stood up to take down the bacon.

It was either a brave or foolish thing to have done. But at the time the trapper felt certain the bear would return, if not that night the next, and it would keep returning until one of them was dead. He dreaded this uncertainty as much as he feared the bear.

The shed itself offered little protection against a grizzly bear. The trapper had to prop the door with axed sections of a lodge-pole snag just to keep it from falling in the wind. Inside, he sat on a cut stump, facing the door. He drank coffee he made over a fire built on earth exposed by some charred floorboards. There were blackened rings where others had built fires inside this tinderbox. It was not something to make a practice of, but the trapper knew how desperate men could be in this country.

The stars came out; they shone through the window and separations in the shed walls. He thought the stars were peculiarly beautiful; remembered precisely how they had appeared to him. He fell asleep looking at them.

When he woke up the stars were gone. The night was black and the river which murmured him to sleep, despite the coffee, had a new cadence he sought to place. The window over his head was a solid square. It was blacker than the room. The trapper did not move once his eyes opened; nor did he take his eyes from the window. Breath, not wind, blew in through the window, and the trapper, wide awake, felt his body break into sweat.

He had fallen asleep with his hand on his rifle but the trapper did not dare lift it. He feared that the slightest movement on his part would trigger the bear, there all along, so close he could have touched it with an outstretched arm.

Many minutes passed. Then abruptly the tiny shed flooded with starlight and the trapper heard a heavy dragging noise as the bear moved the elk away from the window. A bone cracked outside the shed door. The grizzly began to eat, 6 feet of air and 1 inch of wood from the ridiculously small hole at the muzzle of the rifle which now swung like a compass needle to every snuffing grunt, every underwater rumbling of the bear's great belly.

Now the trapper only wanted it to be over. He pointed his rifle at the window during maddening periods of silence. Hours passed; the trapper wondered if the bear had forgotten the bacon. Then there was lingering quiet. The trapper heard the bear's heavy tread. The light went out of the window.

In the confined quarters of the shed, the report of the rifle was deafening. The trapper threw the bolt of the Springfield, his finger on the trigger. But there were no clues at all. The sky framed the window as it had before. The river murmured through the vast emptiness of the night, smothering all sounds from the forest.

At dawn the trapper removed the braces from the door. Out on the snow was his elk, a torn drag of spine with mangled flaps of skin fanned over its bones like a wedding train. Even the head was missing. (The trapper found it later in a clump of aspen saplings, tossed many feet apparently, for no tracks approached the trees.) A riot of snow showed the path the bear had taken to the river after his shot. Above the window the slab of bacon was still nailed to the shed. Below it the huge tracks of the hind feet cut deeply and the snow had iced under them.

The trapper didn't have to look far to see what happened. The bullet had cut a hole in the braided strands of wire crossing the window. He looked for cut hair, speckles of blood, and found nothing to indicate that the bear had been hit. The trapper imagined his bullet must have deflected enough to miss it entirely.

Once again he found himself standing at the river. On the far bank he could see where the bear had shaken itself before entering the forest. This time the trapper allowed himself no illusions of following.

The bear never returned. The trapper stayed the winter, but moved back into his tent only when he felt sure that the grizzly had gone to its den. The trapper caught beaver until the river froze in its backwaters. He continued to take marten in the creek bottoms through March, when their lustrous chocolate fur began to thin and lose its value. Then he wrapped his Springfield in the fabric of his tent and pitched it high in a tree, where it would stay safe until his return. Like many trappers, he would not be burdened with a 10-pound rifle. His pack weighed 90 pounds, and he had no fear of the woods, even unarmed.

Ten years passed. The trapper never did get his rug. In fact, he said he didn't see much sign of grizzly bears anymore. He said he wouldn't shoot one now if he had the chance.

"But that was a real silvertip," he said, "a really big bear. I'll never forget him."

So that was the story.

Like the best of stories it had been unexpected, and I don't believe there was a man among us who did not wish it was his story to tell, who was not reminded of probings into wilderness which paled in comparison. No doubt we all seek places where the air is sounded by bears and trees grow too close together.

In the morning we saw the trapper off. He said he could make it back downriver to the wilderness boundary on snow-shoes. We'd catch up in a day or two, then we'd all ride the snow cat to Hungry Horse where a doctor could attend to his foot.

In the interim there was our work, my part of it being to ski to the inlet of Big Salmon Lake where I hoped to find open water and perhaps a cutthroat trout or two for our supper. Part of the trail wound up from the river passing through a thicket of lodgepole pine. In the thicket, shafts of light escaped through the tree trunks, striping the snow abstractly.

"Trees no bigger around that that," the trapper had said, making a circle with his thumb and finger to describe a country where his hair stood on end. Now, it seemed to me a measure of grizzly bears that you felt their presence even when snow covered the dens, their graves in a foretold future.

I cast out, and while the fly settled and the rings spread from the center of the pool to the ice at its edges, I searched among the trees on the shoreline for any sign of movement.

A Grizzly Chase

WINNIFRED WEIR

Not all those who venture into wild country are looking for bears, but bears may find them, just the same.

The hills and trails of the Windermere Valley, part of the longer Columbia River Valley in the Rocky Mountain Trench, were familiar territory to Hal and Helen Bavin. And they were never happier than when they were roaming the wilderness.

Last August, Helen, recently widowed, was reliving a trip into the Upper Palliser River country that she and her husband had taken three years before. The weather was sunny and warm when, accompanied by her son, John, 37, and his wife, Brenda, 31, she set off on what she anticipated to be a five-day camping trip.

The trio packed two tents and ample food for themselves and the three dogs. The dogs carried their own packs of food, and the three shared the rest of the gear. Their destination was another river valley, the Middle White.

They drove up Settlers' Road in Kootenay National Park for about 25 kilometres, then followed on foot a horse trail to a mountain meadow used by big-game guides to field their horses. Here, they camped for the night.

The dogs were as accustomed as their owners to life in the wilds, and they revelled in the freedom of the camp. Toby, a 10-year-old border collie, and Rascal, a 10-year-old basenji hound, belonged to John and Brenda. Honey Bear, so named because of her silky, golden coat, was Helen's 10-month-old sheltie-collie cross.

Up at 6:30 next morning, they savored the crisp mountain air. Bright sunshine filtered through the heavy timber surrounding the meadow onto alpine flowers, and there was a feeling of approaching autumn.

After packing, they started up a trail made by hunting parties through the years, then turned to follow Joffre Creek, the dogs running ahead. They had hiked along the trail about an hour-and-a-half through heavy timber when they spotted a slide area ahead.

Describing the incidents that followed, Helen, experienced in the wilderness, recalls that they should have stopped to scan the slide. They all knew that grizzlies like slide areas and the huckleberries and saskatoon berries that were then abundant. They also knew that they should have been carrying a bell or other noisemakers. John had a whistle but didn't think to use it as a precaution. In fact, they were all so absorbed in the beauty of the wilderness that they made barely a sound.

The dogs were about 50 metres ahead, followed by John, Helen, then Brenda. Suddenly, the dogs began barking. Helen called to John to blow his whistle to call the dogs. Before he had a chance, they heard a roar and the dogs ran back down the trail, followed at full speed by a grizzly sow and her yearling cub.

"Each of us responded as instinct dictated as the bears, at breakneck speed, piled onto the three dogs," Helen explained. Brenda dropped her pack and ran for a tree. John stood his ground, immobile, and Helen dropped on the trail putting her arms around her head and curling under her pack as best she could.

The sow ran over her twice in a frenzy to attack the dogs. Then it sidetracked to attack Brenda, embedding its claws in her thigh as she fell. The grizzly paused momentarily to put its cub up a tree, which gave Brenda breath to yell, "I'm okay. I'm okay."

Focusing its aggression on the barking dogs, the grizzly reared on its hind legs and John was eyeball to eyeball with the huge creature. He yelled as loudly as he could. It worked.

The cub had descended from the tree, and the sow, roaring her disapproval, leapt over deadfalls after it. But the cub had attacked Honey Bear.

Toby had hidden behind a log and the sow didn't see her, so it roared down the trail after Rascal.

Helen thought the cub would kill Honey Bear.

John carefully made his way to Brenda; then suddenly the roaring and barking ceased. There was an eerie silence and the three hikers drew relieved breaths. The bears had gone.

First, they had to dress Brenda's mangled thigh. Their first-aid kit, adequate for small mishaps, was hardly sufficient for the torn and bleeding flesh. They had alcohol pads, bandages, tapes and a tensile bandage. Helen remembered the elastic stocking she had packed, and it helped to keep the makeshift dressings in place.

They were terrified that the bears might return. Toby had appeared from her hiding place, but they could only guess at the fate of Rascal and Honey Bear. They left as quickly as they could, but because of her wounds, Brenda set the pace. It was slow and agonizing, and they were all in shock.

About one-and-a-half hours down the trail, they found Rascal, ecstatic at the reunion. Then at last they reached their vehicle and hurried to Radium Hot Springs where they telephoned the hospital at Invermere, 20 kilometres away, to advise that emergency patients were on their way. A doctor, nurse and wheelchair were waiting at the door when they arrived. Brenda required 18 stitches in her thigh. One talon had missed an artery by only an inch. The doctor commended them on their emergency first aid, especially the use of the elastic stocking.

On the way out, Helen had discussed getting a guide friend to return the next day to search for Honey Bear. The guide was pessimistic. "You must accept it," he sympathized. "There's no hope for your pet."

Grieving for her little dog, which had been both company and comfort since her husband died, Helen lay awake at night, reliving the terror of those moments in the wilderness. She tried to reconcile herself, saying, "I must accept that this is the end."

But it wasn't the end. Fifteen days later, two young campers, Ronnie and Leslie Ede, camped in the Albert River country nearly 50 kilometres from the scene of the grizzly incident. They were amazed to see a small honey-colored dog cowering at the edge of their campsite. The pup seemed terrified and unapproachable until hunger overcame her fears, and she let them pick her up and feed her. Then Honey Bear slept for hours in the security of their camper.

The next day, the Edes tried to find out if anyone had lost a small, bewildered dog. No one claimed her, so they took her home to Invermere and phoned the veterinarian to see if he could identify the owner by the dog's tag. The doctor was about to discard the dog's file on which he had recorded "killed by a grizzly."

The Edes took the dog to Bonnie Bavin, Helen's daughter-in-law. She was so excited that she ran down the street to the bank where her husband was in the lineup at the teller's cage. She burst in the door with the dog in her arms to the astonishment of the staff and customers. The local paper had carried the story of the grizzly attack, and everyone in town knew about Honey Bear.

But that was nothing to the reunion with Helen shortly after. She had been out of town, and when she returned, she found her family gathered on the lawn. Their beaming faces told her something was afoot. "Come into the house," they called. "We have a surprise for you".

Helen thought to herself, "They have a puppy for me. They know how I miss Honey Bear." She opened the door and a flash of honey-colored fur and wagging tail raced to her feet. Tears of joy flowed down everyone's cheeks.

Examining the dog later, the vet found two healing talon wounds in Honey Bear's hind legs. Her near starvation and exhaustion were evident. It was incredible, he said, that she had found her way through the wilderness.

In retrospect, Helen says that if the dogs had not been with them to distract the bears, the outcome might have been far worse. "As experienced woodsmen," she says, "I don't know how we could have been so dumb as not to make a noise in grizzly country. We don't blame the bears. We blame ourselves. The dogs saved us."

Her hands rest lovingly on Honey Bear as she speaks. "It's incredible."

The Dentist and the Bear

MICHAEL V. DICKINSON

Does a member of the jogging generation stand a better chance in an encounter with a bear than his predecessors? Maybe . . .

Bears: the majestic grizzly with its great shoulder hump, the slow padding of the huge polar, and the ubiquitous black bear in a variety of shapes and sizes. Chasing game, rooting in garbage dumps, pacing zoo cages, scooping salmon out of streams, ripping campsites asunder, their power is evident. Bears are strong. Bears are quick and agile. Their hearing and smell are acute. Bears can run, swim, and climb far faster than most men. Bears are terrifying when aroused, standing on hind legs, roaring and slashing with long claws, sniffing out the transgressor before the deadly charge.

Dentists: middle-aged, bespectacled men with hairy fingers, potbellies, and grey coats. Dentists root in mouths, pace golf courses, and scoop instruments from trays. Dentists hang mobiles and cute animal posters from the ceiling. Their power consists solely of the ability to shock patients with the bill. A dentist without a drill or needle is not apt to terrify, even when aroused.

In a contest of speed, strength, and stamina, bears have all the advantages over dentists. Should such a contest be arranged, however unwittingly, the outcome is certain. The mauling so often used to describe sporting events would in this case be literal.

Floyd Jones is a dentist. He practises in the town of Cadomin, nestled in the foothills of the Canadian Rockies near Banff National Park. He is also a runner of modest ability, being a middle-of-the-pack marathoner and a sub-seven minute miler in shorter events. Hardly champion material, but he is not a great dentist either.

Jones is running along the Spray Lakes Road, a narrow track fringed by dense forest. He likes running. He is enjoying himself. He is not thinking of bears or competition, only the pleasure of stretching his legs and feeling the miles roll beneath him. His dog Topper accompanies him, examining every bush and tree in sight, a job to drive a thorough dog like herself to distraction, but she maintains the pace without difficulty.

Near the crest of a hill, Topper disappears on one of her occasional forays further afield. Moments later she raises a great clamour. Jones turns into the forest to investigate. He finds Topper trying to climb a tree, up which two bear cubs have climbed. He has scarcely registered this fact and the danger it represents before his attention is drawn to a loud crashing in the nearby undergrowth. A large black bear bursts through a thicket and barrels toward him, obviously intent on the rescue of her young.

Jones is in a quandry. To lie down and play dead here is to suffer a certain mauling. To attempt escape by climbing a tree or fleeing would be futile. He is, after all, a dentist, albeit a running dentist, and he is well aware of the odds against him. With his options diminishing as rapidly as the gap between himself and the bear, Jones accepts the challenge. He turns and runs.

Jones breaks from the trees and bounds down the hill. Frightened yelps and fierce bellowing assure him that the dog and bear are close behind. Jones runs as he never has before, knowing that this is one race he must not lose. Fuelled by fear, adrenalin surging, arms and legs pumping, lungs gasping, footfalls jolting, blood roaring in his ears, he sprints away like an Olympian.

But the contest is not one-sided. The bear has no intention of conceding the race. Jones risks a glance backward, wondering why Topper has not passed him. She is ten yards behind him, fleeing with all her considerable speed. Half that distance behind her, the bear lumbers forward, rolling from hind legs to front, grunting, swaying, yet gaining visibly. This is one competitive bear. Jones faces front again, resolving not to look behind until Topper catches him. With nothing between him and the bear, the incentive provided by a second glance might be needed.

The race seems endless to Jones. He feels he has been running for hours. His breathing is laboured. His knees are weak. His heart may burst from his chest. His mouth has never been so dry. The hoarse grunts from behind are nearer. He fancies he can smell the beast and hear her claws on the tarmac. A small corner of his mind has already accepted the inevitable: dentists cannot outrun bears.

Topper pulls abreast. Jones wonders what has taken her so long. Her flanks are heaving and her tongue is almost dragging on the ground. "Damned dog," thinks Jones, "I hope you get out of this anyway."

Topper has no intention of deserting her master, however. She demonstrates her loyalty by trying to leap into his arms. Jones fends her off, but not easily dismayed by this rebuff, Topper tries to slip between his rapidly moving legs. Stumbling, he looks behind, already sensing the fetid breath and yellow fangs of the victor on his neck.

The bear is ambling back up the hill, defeated, having decided that she is no match for this particular dentist. Jones stands trembling. He glances at his watch and estimates that he has run almost a mile in less than four minutes, world calibre speed, aided by a downward slope and the most intense adrenalin rush of his life. He turns and leaves the arena, walking slowly, savouring a precious trophy: his intact skin. He might even be a better dentist after this.

How to Cope in Bear Country

STEPHEN FRELIGH

*Most bears are faster than most men. But if it's not often possible
to outrun an angry bear, it may still be possible to survive the
chase.*

"Few backcountry campers have ever seen a bear. Far fewer
have been injured by one," says Stephen Herrero, a wildlife
biologist with the University of Calgary. "But encounters do
occur, and sometimes people get hurt." For several years now,
Herrero has been studying the outcome of such encounters.
After conferring with National Park Service officials and experienced campers, Herrero and other concerned experts have
come to some sharp conclusions about why bears attack humans, and how campers can avoid problems with the creatures.

"There are no absolute formulas," says the biologist, "because the characteristics of individual bears vary as much as do
the characteristics of individual people." As many seasoned
backpackers have already learned, anyone who travels in bear
country should expect the unexpected, and being prepared for
an encounter with one of the animals may be the most valuable
ingredient to a safe, accident-free outdoor experience.

The first recorded human injury inflicted by a bear in a national park took place around 1900, when a Yellowstone tourist
ignorantly chased a grizzly cub up a tree. The cub's mother

attacked the man, ripping out his breastbone and one lung. He survived five days in emergency care and then died. In the years since, reports of bear maulings have sporadically appeared in newspapers and magazines across the country. Yet while news of such tragedies make for sensational headlines, surprisingly little research has been done on what actually causes such incidents and how to anticipate them. One reason: bears are predictably unpredictable.

Last summer, for instance, a grizzly that biologists considered a "good" bear tore into a tent at Montana's Hebgen Lake campground and dragged a man in his sleeping bag to the woods — a fatal attack that researchers still cannot explain.

Usually bears are shy animals, and if given a choice will run rather than challenge an intruder. But if they are surprised or are defending cubs they may stand their ground. Rearing back on hind legs to inspect their surroundings, they will grunt, woof and snap their jaws as they determine the threat of danger nearby. "Sometimes a bear will charge toward a hiker at full speed for a short distance and then retreat," explains Kevin Rhoades, one of two Montana State University graduate students working with the Interagency Grizzly Bear Study Team, which has been researching bears in western parks.

Rhoades and fellow graduate scholar, Bart Schleyer, suggest remaining calm as the first step to avoiding trouble — even if that seems impossible. "Running or shouting could encourage an attack," says Schleyer. Both biologists recommend retracing your path on the trail each time the bear retreats, slowly working your way toward a tree of sufficient size to carry your weight and tall enough to be out of reach from below. "Stay in the tree until you're sure the bear is gone — even if that means roosting all night."

If an attack seems unavoidable and there is no tree in sight or not enough time to climb it, playing dead could save your life. Some experts suggest playing opossum, lying limply on the ground as if you were dead. Others advise kneeling on the ground, pressing your head between your knees and clasping your hands behind your neck — forming a tight, well-protected ball while shielding your face, neck and chest areas.

Encounters with bears are not limited to the West and its grizzlies. Bill Cook, a wildlife biologist at the Great Smoky Mountains National Park in North Carolina remembers one summer when two Japanese tourists stormed into his office with an unusual complaint. "They were hiking a safe, well-travelled trail when they came across a large female black bear," recalls Cook. "Both hikers were carrying day-packs, and following the advice we give all our visitors, they placed one of their packs on the ground in the middle of the trail and carefully sidestepped their way to nearby trees. In most cases the bears will just move on, totally ignoring the pack. But in this instance, she picked up the sack and quietly disappeared down the trail." Unfortunately, the pack contained camera equipment and the outraged men expected $7,500 compensation from the U.S. government for stolen property.

That same year, 1979, 16 people in California's Yosemite National Park were injured by black bears. The summer before, a Teton Park employee was severely mauled by a grizzly sow in Yellowstone's Heart Lake district. "She was hiking alone when she met the sow and two cubs walking toward her on the trail," says Stephen Kemp, a close friend of the victim. "The sow immediately charged and attacked her."

Although the woman never lost consciousness, the grizzly was actually eating her alive when an approaching group of hikers frightened the bear away. After three years of treatment the woman's life has returned to normal, but her story is a reminder that hikers should not travel alone. Some biologists even recommend hiking in groups of six or more people making noise by singing or talking as they walk.

Being familiar with an area and selecting a proper campsite is also an important factor. Avoid camping near game trails — bears often use the same paths every night. Schleyer and Rhoades sometimes sleep in "pocket hammocks" suspended at least ten feet off the ground in areas where there may be problems with bears. "They may not be the easiest beds to climb into, nor the most comfortable," says Schleyer, "but in bear country they're probably the safest." One night a sow grizzly with one cub walked underneath them, stopping only to inspect the human scent on the ground below.

If you prefer sleeping with Mother Earth solidly beneath you, set your tent near a tree that you know you can climb in case you have to escape from a midnight intruder.

Keeping a clean camp is also advised. "Many campers leave scraps of food lying around their site after eating," complains Kemp. "No hungry bear would pass up such an open invitation." If there are fishermen in your party, remind them to prepare their catches at least 100 yards from camp and to carefully store their clothes overnight in plastic, airtight sacks to prevent the odor of fresh fish from attracting dangerous company.

"I never discourage novice backpackers from hiking into wilderness areas," says Rhoades, "but if they are not careful their inexperience could put them in the hospital — or worse! If you know what you're doing, it can be a thrill to see a bear in the wild — even finding foot prints or discovering a scat can be exciting."

The Grizzly and the Golden Rule

JAMES OLIVER CURWOOD

A theme that occurs repeatedly in bear stories is the hunter's obsession with his quarry. In these two excerpts from his book, God's Country, *the writer describes first, his fascination for the great bear he calls Thor, and second, the moment of illumination that occurs when he recognizes the bear's equal claim to liberty and life.*

Ahead of me, on the edge of a little wallow of mud, stood Thor. He had smelled me, and, I believe it was the first time he had ever smelled the scent of man. Waiting for this new mystery in the air, he had reared himself up until the whole nine feet of him rested on his haunches, and he sat like a trained dog, with his great forefeet, heavy with mud, drooping in front of his chest. He was a monster in size, and his new June coat shone a golden brown in the sun. His forearms were almost as large as a man's body, and the three largest of his five knifelike claws were five and a half inches long. He was fat, and sleek, and powerful. His upper fangs, sharp as stiletto-points, were as long as a man's thumb, and between his great jaws he could have crushed the neck of a caribou. I did not take in all these details in the first startling moments; one by one they came to me later. But I had never looked upon anything in life quite so magnificent. Yet did I have no thought of sparing that splendid life. My rifle was at my saddlehorn in its buckskin jacket. I fumbled it in getting into action, and in those precious moments Thor lowered himself slowly and ambled away. I fired twice,

and would have staked my life that I had missed both times.
Not until later did I discover that one of my bullets had opened
a furrow two inches deep and a foot long in the flesh of Thor's
shoulder. Yet I did not see him flinch. He did not turn back,
but went his way.

Shame burns within me as I write of the days that followed;
and yet, with that shame, there is a deep and abiding joy, for
they were also the days of my regeneration. Day and night,
my one thought was to destroy the big grizzly. We never left
his trail. The dogs followed him like demons. Five times in the
first week we came within long shooting-range, and twice we
hit him. But still he did not wait for us or attack us. He wanted
to be left alone. In that week he killed four of the dogs, and
the others we tied up to save them. We trailed him with horses
and afoot, and never did the spoor of other game lure me aside.
The desire to kill him became a passion in me. He outgeneraled
me. He beat all our games of trickery. But I knew that we were
bound to win — that he was slowly weakening because of exhaustion, and the sickness of his wounds. We loosed the dogs
again and another was killed.

I came to a sheer wall of rock that rose hundreds of feet above
me. Along this ran a narrow ledge, and I followed it. The
passage became craggy and difficult, and in climbing over a
broken mass of rock I slipped and fell. I had brought a light
mountain-gun with me, and in trying to recover myself I swung
it about with such force that the stock struck a sharp edge of
rock and broke clean off. But I had saved myself from possible
death and was in a frame of mind to congratulate myself rather
than curse my luck. Fifty feet farther on I came to a "pocket"
in the cliff, where the ledge widened until, at this particular
place, it was like a flat table twenty feet square. Here I sat down,
with my back to the precipitous wall, and began to examine
my broken rifle.

I laid it beside me, useless. Straight up at my back rose the
sheer face of the mountain; in front of me, had I leapt from the
ledge, my body would have hurtled through empty air for a
thousand feet.

And then, suddenly, there came a sound to my ears that seemed to stop the beating of my heart. I had not heard it until it was very near — approaching along the narrow ledge. It was the click — click — click of claws rattling on rock!

I did not move, I hardly breathed. And out from the ledge I had followed came a monster bear!

With the swiftness of lightning I recognized him. It was Thor! And, in the same instant, the great bear saw me.

In thirty seconds I lived a lifetime, and in those thirty seconds what passed through my mind was a thousand times swifter than spoken word. A great fear rooted me, and yet in that fear I saw everything to the minutest detail. Thor's massive head and shoulders were fronting me. I saw the long naked scar where my bullet had plowed through his shoulder; I saw another wound in his fore leg, still ragged and painful, where another of my soft-nosed bullets had torn like an explosion of dynamite. The giant grizzly was no longer fat and sleek as I had first seem him ten days ago. All that time he had been fighting for his life; he was thinner; his eyes were red; his coat was dull and unkempt from lack of food and strength. But at that distance, less than ten feet from me, he seemed still a mighty brother of the mountains themselves. As I sat stupidly, stunned to the immobility of a rock in my hour of doom, I felt the overwhelming conviction of what had happened. Thor had followed me along the ledge, and in this hour of vengeance and triumph, it was I, and not the great beast, who was about to die.

It seemed to me that an eternity passed in these moments. And Thor, mighty in his strength, looked at me and did not move. And this thing he was looking at — shrinking against the rock — was the creature that had hunted him; this was the creature that had hurt him, and it was so near that he could reach out with his paw and crush it! And how weak and white and helpless it looked now! What a pitiful, insignificant thing it was! Where was its strange thunder? Where was its burning lightning? Why did it make no sound?

Slowly Thor's giant head began swinging from side to side;

then he advanced—just one step—and in a slow, graceful movement reared himself to his full, magnificent height. For me, it was the beginning of the end. And in that moment, doomed as I was, I found no pity for myself. Here, at last, was justice! I was about to die. I, who had destroyed so much of life, found how helpless I was when I faced life with my naked hands. *And it was justice!* I had robbed the earth of more life than would fill the bodies of a thousand men, and now my own life was to follow that which I had destroyed. Suddenly fear left me. I wanted to cry out to that splendid creature that I was sorry, and could my dry lips have framed the words, it would not have been cowardice—but truth.

For Thor knew me. That I know. He knew me as the deadliest of all his enemies on the face of the earth. Yet until I die will I believe that, in my helplessness, he no longer hated me or wanted my life. For slowly he came down upon all fours again, and, limping as he went, he continued along the ledge—*and left me to live!*

I am not, in these days, sacrilegious enough to think that the Supreme Power picked my poor insignificant self from among a billion and a half other humans especially to preach a sermon to that glorious Sunday on the mountainside. Possibly it was all mere chance. It may be that another day Thor would have killed me in my helplessness. It may all have been a lucky accident for me. Personally, I do not believe it, for I have found that the soul of the average beast is cleaner of hate and of malice than that of the average man. But whether one believes with me or not does not matter, so far as the point I want to make is concerned—that from this hour began the great change in me, which has finally admitted me into the peace and joy of universal brotherhood with Life.

I returned down the mountain, carrying my broken gun with me. And everywhere I saw that things were different. The fat whistlers, big as woodchucks, were no longer so many targets, watching me cautiously from the rock-tops; the gophers, sunning themselves on their mounds, meant more to me now than a few hours ago. I looked off to a distant slide on another mountain and made out the half-dozen sheep I had studied through my glasses earlier in the day. But my desire to kill was gone. I did not realize the fulness of the change that was upon me then. In a dull sort of way I accepted it as an effect of shock, perhaps as a passing moment of repentance and gratitude because of my escape. I did not tell myself that I would never kill sheep again except when mutton was necessary to my campfire. I did not promise the whistlers long lives. And yet the change was on me, and growing stronger in my blood with every breath I drew. The valley was different. Its air was sweeter. Its low song of life and running waters and velvety winds whispering between the mountains was new inspiration to me. The grass was softer under my feet; the flowers were more beautiful; the earth itself held a new thrill for me.

The Bargain Trap

ANDY RUSSELL

There are new elements in bear stories of more recent vintage: a greater respect for the bear, perhaps, and a recognition that he is one of an endangered breed. The conflict between man and bear reflects these changes. It is less of a sport—more like a lingering war.

It has often been said that to know a man well, study his friends. It might also be well to take a long thoughtful look at his enemies. The same thing can be said of the grizzly, for if one is to reach a fuller understanding of the great bear, then it becomes necessary to know and understand something of his only real enemy—man.

Many frontiersmen have shared my campfires with me: fishermen out on the Pacific coast, professional guides of the west and north, prospectors searching for the pot of gold at the end of the rainbow, trappers of the wilderness country, and my neighbours the ranchers. Tough, sometimes generous to a fault, quick to laugh, and courageous, such men are the kind who help carve out empires. Almost to the last man they have a queer blind spot when it comes to bears, and their favorite view of the grizzly is the one seen over the shining blue barrel of a rifle. Many times over the years I have known of grizzlies being killed and left to rot for no other reason than their presence. To suggest to these men that most grizzlies are not trouble hunters and ordinarily are not destructive is to receive a long, silent, quizzical look, perhaps momentarily generous of your opinion but still only veiling the thought that you have lost your marbles.

Yet strangely enough these are the men who get the greatest kick out of recounting their experiences in bear country. If all the bears were suddenly gone, most of these men would sorely miss them; for they enjoy the presence of the grizzly and take a certain satisfaction in their association with the big bear.

However inclined towards such single track thinking, my outspoken, hard-working neighbours the ranchers are noted for their thrift. This is an admirable kind of thrift for the most part—a necessary characteristic for the sake of their continuance. They have to be thrifty to exist. But sometimes, if overworked, the exercise of thrift can backfire with disastrous results. One group of ranchers making up the membership of a local stock association and representing enough collective wealth to buy out the nearest town, lock, stock and barrel, niggardly decided to purchase a cheap black bear trap instead of a much more expensive one adequate for grizzlies. Thus for the sake of a few dollars they lost the price of a foundry equal to producing all the bear traps the world would likely ever see, much less need.

Following this thrifty purchase, decided upon at a meeting with sage and solemn nods of heads, a small, somewhat nondescript mother grizzly with two small cubs came out of her den one spring. She was likely somewhat depressed by a shortage of feed and the burgeoning responsibilities of her new family, for she proceeded to kill a cow in an unfortunately conspicuous place. Consequently the new trap was set for her, and shortly thereafter the mother grizzly unwisely put her foot in it.

As is often evident among men, size is not always a measure of strength, sagacity, and determination. Following her first flurry of disorganized bawling and fighting, she got down to serious business and pulled out of the trap. Undoubtedly her foot was sore. Perhaps she blamed the discomfort on the dead cow, for she promptly went on a cattle-killing spree as though she had invented the pastime. Through experience, she was now very careful and wary, avoiding any further contact with the trap, which followed her hopefully around the hills from one kill to another. When fall arrived, she returned to her high denning ground in the mountains, leaving the ranchers to tally their losses and blame everything but the trap.

The following spring she came back with her cubs, now rollicking yearlings, and promptly opened a spring festival in bear country by killing another cow. Once more the trap was set for her. She must have been a bit fuzzy in her mind after the long winter's sleep, for she walked into it a second time.

Once more she fought it and successfully escaped, although this time she injured her paw in the process — a lingering hurt that honed her cunning day and night. Thus a killer of true psychopathic proportion was developed by a misdirection of thrift and further cultivated to new heights of bovine murder by the very men who wished to destroy her.

Her kills were easily recognized by a missing ear. Probably because of her injured foot she developed a unique method of killing cattle. Instead of striking them down in the usual fashion with simultaneous blows over the head and spine at the top of the shoulders, she ran up beside her quarry, grabbed it by an ear, and threw it end-over-end. Then she fell on it to worry the unfortunate beast to death. In due course her cubs joined in this mayhem, and so two more killers were well on the way.

This she-grizzly had developed into a habitual killer as wary and cunning as a three-toed wolf. To set a trap for her was an open invitation for her to kill again. In fact she would immediately abandon a fresh kill if a man so much as handled a twig within a hundred yards of it. One rancher lost sixteen head to her in one summer, removed his cattle from the Forest Reserve summer ranges, and to this day has never put another animal to graze there.

Finally a heavy bounty was placed on her head. This had the advantage of bringing her to the attention of the best trappers and hunters in the country, but it also had the disadvantage of attracting sufficient inexperienced ones to spoil the chances of the others. I briefly joined the hunt for her, but I quit after a few days in a split frame of mind, divided between admiration for this bear's wonderful cunning intelligence and complete frustration at interference from other hunters. About all that happened to the bear was that she was kept continually on the move, so that she rarely fed on any kill twice and was thus elevated to a new crescendo of killing.

Jim Riviere, a keen-eyed, rawhide-tough trapper of real wilderness stamp, took up her trail with an adequate trap; but as he admitted, his medicine was no good on this one. He found a fresh kill one day and set a carefully concealed trap by it. When he came next morning, a grizzly was caught in it—but the wrong bear as it turned out.

Jim approached the set through a thick stand of aspens on horseback, and on coming within easy range of the grizzly in the trap, he stepped down from his saddle to shoot it. As he reached for his rifle hanging in its scabbard, a big boar, likely the mate of the sow in the trap, came boiling out of a clump of alders in a roaring charge. The horse pulled back, taking the rifle out of Jim's reach, but fortunately he had a short hold on the bridle reins with the other hand. As his mount whirled and plunged past him, he grasped the pommel and vaulted into the saddle. The horse shot back through the aspens, knocking him on trees as it went, but Jim managed to stay with him. When he pulled the wild eyed animal to a stop on the far side of an open bench to look back, the grizzly had vanished. It had been a close shave, for the horse had long scratches from grizzly claws down its haunch.

In this way other bears paid the price for the killer's work. As her second year of terror among the herds came to a close, she once more headed back up among the high peaks, a smouldering promise of more hell to come. By this time the bargain bear trap had become a most valuable piece of equipment, its price reaching a substantial five figures, somewhere in excess of $10,000. Though adequate traps were now being used, no one but the most reckless gambler would have risked a well-worn dollar bill on their success.

There came another spring and with it came the bear—hungry for beef as usual. In the meantime the stock association had hired Roy Marshall, an old hand of about sixty years who had spent all his life in this country since he left Texas as a boy.

He was the kind who did not wait for trouble to come hunting him without making some preparations for its proper welcome. When the grizzly made her first kill down on the Carpentier Creek flats, he was ready. He had worked out a plan that was about as cunning as anything the grizzly had improvised in her most inspired moments. Furthermore fate took a hand, and the kill was ideally located for his plan to be carried out.

Fate and human ingenuity had conspired, for in the late weeks of winter Roy had taken a grizzly trap and sundry other gear and boiled the lot in a strong solution of wood ashes. After a thorough scrubbing to remove any dirt, rust and clinging man smell, he boiled everything again for hours in a soup made of willow and aspen bark along with a handful or two of bunch grass. When this was done, the trap was not only completely cleaned but also smelled of odors blending into the country in which it would be used. He hung his entire trapping outfit in a tree to weather and mellow until needed.

Now he loaded it into his wagon and drove his team toward the kill. He did not go to it but swung wide and went to an old kill made the previous summer by the wanted bear. It was located beneath a big aspen, and there Roy made his medicine to cure the country of its most notorious murderer of cows.

Standing in the wagon box, he threw out a canvas tarpaulin and then stepped down onto one corner of it to arrange it as a sort of platform from which to work. He took a shovel and dug a shallow hole in the midst of old hair and bones piling the dirt on another bit of canvas. From this he dug a shallow trench around the tree to conceal the logging chain that was to hold the trap. When this was ready, he set the trap and cunningly hid it in the hole with the chain looped around the tree. Using carefully cleansed canvas gloves, he touched nothing with his bare hands, nor did he set foot upon the ground. When he finished he stood up to survey his work with a critical gaze. Not even the most practiced eye could tell where the trap was hidden.

Fate chuckled softly — and directed his eye to a triangular

piece of old weathered hide lying a bit to one side. With a touch of pure genius he picked it up and nailed it as high as he could reach on the tree, where the breeze made it flop like the wing of a wounded bird. When he left he took everything with him including the unused dirt rolled in the canvas. That evening a heavy shower fell and washed away any possible trace of man-smell that might have lingered.

The grizzly returned to her kill that night, hungry but wary as usual. Wise to the ways of her enemy, she circled slowly, testing the wind and the whole flat with her nose for any tiny tell-tale smells of danger. Finding none, she went to the carcass and fed heavily. When she struck out for the slopes of the mountains at the first waking squeaks of dawn, her path took her past the old kill.

Perhaps old memory of it drew her close without her being entirely aware. Maybe fate was singing its siren song, for the she-grizzly saw the piece of hide flapping lazily against the trunk of the tree. She forgot everything of her usual caution, drawing closer and closer to it, filled with a consuming curiosity. She looked at it and smelled of it. She wanted to feel of it too. So she reared and took a staggery step forward to mouth it. But it eluded her momentarily, and as she reached, the ground sagged beneath a hind foot and there was an upheaval followed by the metallic clank of the closing trap. The soft quiet of the morning was torn to shivering shreds by her high, wild bawl of rage and pain.

Nothing fights like a grizzly in a trap. It is the greatest power of the wild and the wild free-roaming spirit of the mountains ignominiously shackled in steel, fighting in almost maniacal rage and mercilessly flogged by the need for freedom. It is a kind of desecration — an obscenity. There is a lurching and a stench that does not fit the dignity of this animal. No matter the need, it does not fit the principle of a true hunter.

This one fought even harder than most, her will steeled by former experience. She plunged against the chain over and over until her breath came in great sobbing gasps. She bit savagely at the trap until the slobber fell in bloody ropes from between her splintered teeth. Her coat was full of dirt and filth. She pulled and clawed and heaved until the tree stood in the centre of a mound of torn up earth.

Then she saw him coming astride his horse, black against the reddening sunrise. She checked her wild plunging to stand as still as her favorite mountain, as though listening to that last verse of the song fate was singing far away. She did not cower or cringe but stood her ground. And when the man got down from his saddle and walked toward her with something shining in his hands, she eased back, throwing slack in the chain. Then she roared and lunged straight at him. There was a flat, cracking whiplash of sound and everything was still.

That fall there was much less red ink in the ledgers, and the market for cheap bear traps was at an all-time low.

Now You Take Bear

RUSSELL ANNABEL

These recollections have the air of tales told beside the campfire, but the writer drew on years of wilderness experience when he wrote them. He knew bears as few others have known them.

One of the reasons why bear hunting is a great and fascinating sport is that it is full of surprises. For instance, you never can tell how bear—any kind of bear—will react to a set of circumstances. Three times out of five, they will do something you would have bet they wouldn't do. And the remaining two times, the country they inhabit will deal you a surprise.

Take an experience Tex Cobb and I had in the Yanert Basin. We were snowshoeing along the river bars in the early glow of a bright, golden May morning. Halting to scan the range ahead with his binoculars, Tex sighted a bear coming down the face of a ragged mountain that separates the Yanert and Wood River headwaters. It was a glacier bear, a fairly large one, with a pelt as blue as a pair of overalls.

Now, plenty of so-called glacier bears are taken each year in the Territory, but most of them are either brown or yellow, and I suspect that examination of their skulls would reveal the greater number to be grizzlies. The real article, the little blue bear of the moraine hills, is the rarest of Alaskan trophies, and in my opinion the most beautiful. This one was a sure-enough glacier bear.

"If we can beat him to brush-line," I said with optimism that hope gives a man in such cases, "his pelt is as good as on a frame."

Tex shook his head. "Those blue beggars are hoodoo bear. I've hunted in Alaska for forty years, and I ain't killed one of 'em yet. Betcha we don't kill that one either."

Snow lay from two to five feet deep on the mountain-side, and it was so wet that our webs dragged as if they were weighted with lead. But we sweated up through the timber, taking turns breaking a switchback trail, and managed to reach the last scattered ranks of spruce with plenty of time to spare. The bear was still a good six hundred yards above us, plowing down the middle of a long, shimmering slope.

I was certain we were going to make a kill. The set-up was perfect. All we had to do was wait. I remember I even felt through my pockets for my whetstone, thinking I would have to touch my knife up before we began the job of skinning.

At this juncture the bear gave us a demonstration of temperament. For no good reason that I have ever been able to figure out, he turned and started back up the mountain. It was impossible that he could have seen, heard or winded us. Rather, the impression I got was that he had simply decided he didn't like the looks of the Yanert valley, and so was going elsewhere.

We knelt on our webs and opened fire. But the steep angle of elevation, the long range and the raw brilliance of the sun on the snow made him an extremely difficult target.

Finally I stopped shooting and put my glasses on the bear in an attempt to call Tex's shots. The slugs ripping into the snow around the animal had caused him to leave his trail and slant up across the head of a funnel-shaped draw. Suddenly, as he wallowed through a corniced drift, I saw the snow below him begin to slip. It was only a miniature slide at first, so small you could have stopped it with your hands — just a couple of cubic feet of snow he had dislodged from the top of the drift. But it grew, and gathered speed, and other small slides came into it from either side. Presently the draw was filled to the brim by a roaring, heaving cascade of snow. I saw the bear look down at it, and then make a scrambling rush for the safety of a shale rim.

"Get going!" Tex yelled at me, and kicked his webs around.

Behind us, as we headed across the slope at a right angle to the path of the slide, the sound of the down-rushing mass of snow burst the decibels of a roar and became a sort of rising earth-shaking shriek, comparable only to the racket a fast train makes when coming through a cut on icy rails. It passed us and hit the timber.

There was an instant of quiet. Then in the language of the Western thrillers, all hell busted loose. A cyclonic wind, the backwash of the slide, screamed through the spruces, whirling branches, splintered tops, slabs of ice and tons of loose snow high into the air, which all rained back down on the mountainside like debris falling after a dynamite blast.

We were blown off our feet and half buried by the lashing sheets of snow, but fortunately nothing heavy landed on us. When the wind had died away to a mere gale, we stood up and, moved by a common curiosity, looked up the mountain. Dimly, through a swirling, rainbowed cloud of snow, we could see the glacier bear, an ant-sized dot climbing steadily toward the jagged, sunlit spires above.

"Some bear!" I said.

"I knew dag-goned well we wouldn't get the blue son-of-calamity," Tex declared, digging snow out of his ear with a horny forefinger. "I had sort of a pre-admonition."

Maybe I had better explain here that snowslides are not a serious menace in the spring bear ranges. You will see plenty of them in late May and early June, but nearly all of them will be bad among the higher peaks, where the bear aren't ranging anyway, and your guide will know how to keep out of the way of the others. As a matter of fact, it has been at least ten years since a non-resident hunter was injured by a slide in the Alaskan mountains. Which makes your chance of being caught by one approximately minus zero.

Doc Lane and I received a hair-raising surprise a couple of years ago during a jaunt we made through the Crystal Creek bear country, over in the jumbled foot-slopes of the Alaska Range. We were casting flies one morning over a school of fat grayling that we had located in a beaver pond. Suddenly we heard Doc's dog sound off back at camp.

The dog was a rattle-brained cross between an Airedale and a Kaiyuh husky, whose chief ambition in life was to find a porcupine he could whip. Not only had we de-quilled him on an average of three times a day since we left the railroad, but often it had been necessary to get up at night and yank anywhere from a dozen to a hundred of the barbed spikes out of him. Most of the time he went around with his eyes swelled shut and his nose looking like a chunk of raw steak. His name was Bucko. I don't know why we brought him along.

"Sounds as if the ineffable cuss has tangled with another one." Doc said, closing his fly book and reaching automatically into his hip pocket for a pair of pliers, which had become an indispensable item of his equipment. "Give me a hand with him, will you?"

We hurried down the creek. Doc was ahead of me when we barged around the corner of the cook tent. He took one look, and halted so abruptly that I ran into him and nearly knocked him down. The scene before us was a remarkable one. Instead of a porcupine, Bucko had bayed three grizzlies — an outsized female, a spring cub and a husky mustard-colored yearling. Manifestly, the bears had been in the act of looting our commissary when the dog surprised them; grub was scattered all over the flat. To complete the picture, the spring cub had his head caught in a jam can, and was running in tight circles, snarling wearily.

As we stood there, gaping, Bucko flashed in and grabbed the she bear by a hind leg. His determination to defend the camp was commendable, but he certainly didn't know how to tackle a grizzly. She spun like a huge top, kicking out as she did so, with the result that Bucko sailed a dozen feet through the air, landing on his head in a wild-rose clump.

"Pick your tree!" I yelled.

The she bear had swung around to glare at us, foam spotting her flews, her little pig eyes glinting wickedly. Neither of us was carrying a gun; and even if we had been, we wouldn't have shot her except as a last, desperate resort. Well, I reached up in full flight and caught hold of a cottonwood limb, and didn't stop climbing until I was a safe twenty feet above the ground.

I supposed, of course, that Doc had sought a similar refuge. But when I looked around for him, I was amaged to see he was running down toward the creek. Bucko, a sadder and wiser dog, was at his heels, and the she bear was bringing up the rear, gaining at every bound. Apparently Doc hadn't had time to climb a tree.

He didn't hesitate when he came to the creek, but plunged in and struck out for the farther bank, using a ponderous breast stroke that I could see was going to be inadequate when he got into the swift mid-stream current. Bucko, after a wistful glance at his floundering master, must have decided he would rather take his chances on dry land. At any rate, he whirled, dodged a sledge-hammer blow from the bear, and fled back toward camp — only to collide with the cubs at the top of the bank. Probably feeling they were more in his class, he grabbed one of them — the yearling — by the rump. The animal was nearly as large as a grown black bear, but it lay down, took hold of a tree with both front legs, and squalled loudly for help.

That was what saved the day. The she bear turned back from the water and galloped to the rescue, bawling hoarsely. Bucko saw her coming, and for once in his life displayed some sense. Giving the uninjured but badly scared yearling a last shake, he sidestepped the old lady's rush and retreated up the creek, barking at her to decoy her in that direction. She followed a hundred yards or so, then swung off into the alders, with the two cubs at her side.

At some point during the final phase of the mêlée the spring cub had succeeded in getting the jam can off his head. I didn't happen to see him do it; so I can't report what means he used.

Probably the can got caught in the brush, giving him the opportunity to jerk his head out of it.

I waited to make certain they weren't going to return, then slid out of the tree and went down the bank to find out what had happened to Doc. He had grounded on a sand-bar a short distance below. When he saw me, he laughed and extended his hands.

"Look," he said. "No wonder I couldn't swim!"

In one hand he still clutched his fly book, in the other the pair of pliers.

Next to running foul of a female with cubs, the easiest way to get yourself crossed up on a bear hunt is to follow a wounded Kodiak or grizzly into thick cover. An excellent example of this occurred three years ago during a spring hunt I made in the Tahnita country with a band of Tyone Indians. While we were eating breakfast one morning the ace hunter of the band, a young sub-chief named Chilligan Redshirt, spotted a grizzly on a brush mountain above camp.

I put my glasses on the animal and saw that it was a fine big bear for this part of the country: light yellow in color, with black feet and a white face — the kind of bear the old-timers call a silvertip. Chilligan belted on his knife and picked up his rifle. The gun was a relic, an ancient remodeled .40-82, its forearm held to the barrel by a seizing of snow-shoe babiche and its stock covered with Shamanistic designs, outlined with brass-headed tacks that were supposed to insure Chilligan against being mauled by bear.

"I'm goin' to go up and kill that grizzly," he told me. "You want to come?"

He made a good stalk. He was fast, he had an uncanny ability to find holes through the endless maze of alders, and he managed to choose a course that gave him a look at the bear every few minutes — something that is very hard to do in brushy country. When we reached the top of the mountain, I sat down to watch him make his kill.

The bear was now about two hundred yards below us, in a point of brush at the lip of a long grassy chute that went down steeply to a huddle of junipers. He had bent over a bush and was eating the buds. Taking his time, Chilligan approached within a stone's throw before he knelt and raised the rifle. At the bellow of the shot, the grizzly reared straight up, pawing the air, then fell forward and rolled into the alders.

As there was a dense stand of winter gray grass under the brush, I was unable, even with my glasses, to see the animal after it dropped. It was a situation that called for plenty of discretion. Chilligan, however, didn't show any.

Running down the slope, he shouldered confidently into the brush, worked through it to the farther rim and was standing there, looking around in a puzzled manner when the bear rose up behind him, roaring. The ambush couldn't have been more cleverly executed. Chilligan ducked and jumped to one side, firing from the hip. But the bear was too close. A front paw caught him on the shoulder and belted him backward a half-dozen feet. He landed on his back in the open and rolled, and had wits enough to keep himself rolling. This last, together with the steepness of the pitch, was all that saved him.

The bear followed, striking savagely, but was unable to land a solid blow. Partway down the incline, the two bullets the animal was carrying began to take effect. It halted, biting at its side, and presently lay down. When I reached it, it was dead.

Chilligan had rolled all the way down to the junipers, and was sitting with his back against a boulder, sick, dizzy and humiliated. He had a torn shoulder, some cracked ribs, and a wonderful assortment of bruises. His rifle, lying in the grass beside him, was ruined, probably as few rifles have ever been ruined: one of the bear's pile-driver wallops had put a two-inch bend in the long, tapered barrel.

When I asked Chilligan why he had been such an utter fool as to go into the brush after the bear, he said it had never occurred to him that the animal wasn't dead. He had held on its head, and had supposed that was where the bullet had struck. Actually, the slug had gone low, passing through the bear's throat. The second shot had hit the animal in the chest, coming out its side.

"Well, anyhow," I said, "you can trade the hide to some Indian for another rifle."

"No, I can't do that," Chilligan said regretfully, wincing as a spasm of pain from his cracked ribs caught him. "I've got to give the hide to the medicine man. I ain't paid him yet for those charms he put on the gun."

Then there was something that happened in the course of a camera hunt that Larry Benson and I made in the Big River region. We had been trying to get some close-up shots of brown bear fishing salmon, but hadn't had any luck. Every stalk we had made went haywire. The wind would change, or the light would fail, or the bear would wander out of camera range.

After a week of this, Larry decided the only way to score was to rig up a set camera. So he drove a post into a mud bar beside a spawning riffle and lashed his new rapid-action camera to the top of it, with the telephoto lens focused on the middle of the stream. Then he ran a fish line from the release mechanism of the camera to a hillside thicket a hundred yards distant.

"Now, by jeepers creepers," he said with satisfaction, "I'd like to see a bear catch a fish in that riffle without getting photographed!"

We sat on the hillside for two days without seeing a bear. But on the morning of the third day a big fellow came across the flat from the mouth of the river. He was a rough-looking customer, mud-plastered and gaunt, with a yellow blaze on his forehead and a lot of unshed winter hair still clinging to his neck and shoulders. He slid down the bank and started into the riffle, but halted when he saw an empty cardboard film container that Larry had unwisely left on the bar. Going over to the box, he smelled of it, then took it in his mouth and shook it viciously.

Suddenly the camera caught his eye. We had camouflaged it with grass, but, of course, the lens was visible, and he could also see the fish line. He shuffled closer to it and half reared, one paw raised. Larry jumped up, waving his arms.

"Hey! For the love of Mike," he shouted in anguished tones, "don't hit that camera!"

But he had realized too late what the bear was going to do. The big paw came down in a tremendous roundhouse slap that tore the camera off the post and sent it flying out into the riffle. Then, whuffing and grunting, the bear fled up the bank and headed for the timber. Larry pulled the fish line in. The camera was still attached to it, but the lens was the only part worth salvaging. The rest of it looked as if it had been run over by a truck.

"It's cost me two hundred dollars," Larry said ruefully, "to find out that what a guy needs for this work is three or four of those buck-and-a-half mail-order box cameras. Set 'em up in a battery, and while the bear is wrecking one take his picture with another."

One of the most dramatic and memorable incidents I have ever witnessed in the Northern gamelands took place during a grizzly hunt that Bob Neil and I made back among the ice-ribbed peaks above the head of the Knik. While we were following a sheep trail along the flank of a glacier one afternoon we saw a grizzly on a cliff-hung mountain a quarter of a mile up the valley. We climbed for him and, after some tricky rock work, came out on the brink of a graywacke precipice almost directly under the animal. It was feeding in a saskatoon thicket that grew at the base of the next cliff above us, pulling the branches down with its paws and stripping off big mouthfuls of the purple frost-sweetened berries. A typical mountain grizzly, it was very dark in color, nearly black, with high shoulders, a short neck and a broad hog-snouted head.

"The trouble with this," I said, "is that if anything goes wrong we'll be in a tough spot here on the edge of this drop-off. I like more room to move around in."

But Bob was afraid, with good reason, that the bear would see us if we tried to flank it. So he rested his rifle over a boulder top and fired. As the report flatted along the cliffs the bear sagged, its legs buckling; but it recovered and lurched out of the thicket, swinging its shaggy head from side to side, trying to locate us. Bob fired again, and this time I saw the bullet smoke off a rock slab an inch above the bear's ears.

I think the battering echoes confused the animal and caused it to think we were above it. Anyhow, it came galloping down the pitch, and had covered about half the distance to our position when it saw us. At once it laid its ears back, let out a bawl and charged with everything it had, coming down the boulder-strewn slant in a series of diving bounds.

Bob fired again, and I heard the softnose smash home. But the bear kept coming. I knew Bob wasn't going to stop the animal before it got to us; a machine gun wouldn't have stopped it in that short distance on that slope. So I took hold of his belt and pulled him back behind the boulder over which he had rested his rifle. My intention was to try for the bear's head when it turned to come around the rock after us. But it didn't turn.

Without slackening its pace, it slammed past us and went over the cliff. Its legs were still working like pistons as it plunged into the dizzy 300-foot drop between us and the moraines. I saw it turn over twice in the air before it crashed into an icy trough below the sheep trail. I glanced at Bob, and his face was the color of a dirty sheet. I guess mine was about the same.

When we opened the carcass, we found that one of the bullets had struck the bear's heart, cutting it nearly in half. The animal had made at least a third of its wild, spectacular charge while literally dead on its feet.

"When you've seen something like that," Bob said, "it's easy to understand why the grizzly is the top American game animal. In fact, for my money he'll stack up with the best any game range in the world has to offer."

For mine, too.

Guaranteed Unpredictable

RALPH W. YOUNG

Those who spend time in bear country are more aware than others of their own mortality. The writer was pretty sure that somewhere there was a bear that had his number . . .

The great bears of the Admiralty Island country of southeast Alaska have drawn hunters and, to a lesser extent, photographers since the end of World War II when big game hunting took its first upward swing. Many were the stories that came back about these brown bears, or coastal grizzlies, as some people call them. What was this hunting *really* like? I was a guide in this area for thirty years, specializing in bears, and some of what I saw and learned may surprise you.

My attitude toward Alaskan brown bears is one of tremendous respect and admiration. I base my opinion on the thousands of brownies I have seen and the hundreds of kills in which I have participated. Frequently I have gone out alone on Admiralty Island and lived with the bears. I ate the same food, slept in bear beds (but not when the owner was there), and tried to think and act as a bear. As a result of my experience and close observation of bear behavior, I believe no animal is more dangerous to hunt or to photograph under conditions of fair chase.

To begin with, this mighty monarch of the northern wilderness has tremendous size, strength, and tenacity of life. Although these bears attain about twice the size of a tiger or an African lion, they are just as quick and agile as either. A brownie in full possession of all its faculties and making a determined attack can cover 100 feet in something like 10 seconds. This statement sounds a bit fantastic, but I believe it's true.

An attacking Alaskan bear is as chilling and awesome a spectacle as nature has to offer. Once I witnessed a bear attacking a deer. It leaped out of the forest like a huge cat, seized the deer in its jaws, and tore the animal's head off! As often as not, these bears start their attacks with no warning and at close range. If the man isn't ready to shoot — and shoot straight — he's a goner. Nor do bruins charge in the classic storybook manner — erect on their hind legs, paws extended to engulf the hapless victim in a bear hug.

Actually, a bear standing on its hind legs is as harmless as a man doing a handstand. The animal charges on all four feet in great leaping bounds, very reminiscent of a huge, eager dog chasing a cat. When an Admiralty bear charges, the beast kills you, or you kill it. On the several occasions I have faced charging brownies, I have rarely been able to get in more than one hastily aimed shot, and the only thing I've seen through my sights was blurred hair.

The single factor that makes the big Alaskan coastal bear so dangerous to hunt is the complete unpredictability of its behavior. No one, no matter how much he may think he knows about bears, can always correctly predict how one will react to any situation. Each bear is an individualist. Some are cowardly; some are brave. There are foolish ones and smart ones, just like people. Most panic at the scent of man. A few are indifferent and even contemptuous of man's close presence. Most unpredictable and volatile are sows with cubs. Through the years I have seen so many bears do so many things that I take nothing for granted when hunting them. That's one reason I have beaten the longevity statistics so long.

Many years ago, one of my dudes, whose name I have long since forgotten, shot a brownie late in the evening at the head of a timbered cove. I sent the hunter down the creek to watch our skiff while I skinned out the trophy. Halfway through the operation, I looked up and spotted a small male bear watching me from the edge of the forest about 100 yards away. Sitting on his broad rump, he was evidently an interested observer. While I worked, I kept close watch on my uninvited visitor.

After completing the skinning, I had to walk to within 30 yards or so of the bear to wash my hands and clean my knife. The animal made no move to give ground. Since I had sent my rifle back with the dude, I was a bit uneasy. After I lashed the hide to my packboard and was ready to move along, the bear was still watching from its original position. Down the creek a couple of hundred yards I looked back.

The brownie had walked to the still-warm carcass, had picked it up in its mouth, and was carrying it into the woods. The whole area must have reeked with man scent, yet this brute was indifferent.

Do Alaskan brown bears attack? Of course they do. I'll go so far as to say that nearly all of the wounded ones I have encountered have attacked if they had the opportunity and were physically able to do so. Every year I guided hunters, I used to trail two or three or several wounded bears. It was a disagreeable job, and if I wasn't getting paid to do it, I doubt that I would have trailed up any bear I didn't personally wound. Some people seem to enjoy living dangerously. I just don't happen to be one of them.

Although following a wounded brownie in thick cover is certainly hazardous, it isn't precisely suicidal, provided the tracker knows his business and maintains control of the situation. The tracker has one tremendous advantage — the bear doesn't know it is being followed. I knew that so long as I kept this advantage, the odds were overwhelmingly on my side. Always, however, I knew that if the bear located me before I found it, and if the range was short, it was a toss-up as to who would come out of the fracas alive. That was why I always preferred to go after a bear alone. If I saw any movement in the cover, I knew it would be the wounded bear I was trailing and not my partner blundering about.

In any situation, Alaskan brown bears are impressive animals. Meeting a thoroughly aroused one in the gloom of the southeastern Alaska rain forest is an unforgettable experience. The bear always looks twice its size and has the nightmarish, malevolent appearance of some prehistoric creature. Each time I finished the job of trailing and killing a wounded bear, I would feel weak and limp. Sometimes the reaction would be so strong that I'd vomit. I guess I'm no hero.

Will a brownie attack without apparent provocation? My answer is an unequivocal yes. At least three times I have been charged with no provocation except that we happened to be in the same area at the same time. In none of these cases were we hunting the particular bears that attacked us.

The first positively unprovoked attack I experienced occurred in the summer of 1950. I was guiding the late Dr. Sterling Bunnel of San Francisco on a photography trip. One fine bright day we set up cameras on a salmon stream on Admiralty Island and sat to wait for a bear to stroll along. In due time, a medium-sized brownie came down the creek, looking for salmon. It picked up a dead fish, ate part of it, and moved farther down the creek and out of sight. I thought we had seen the last of this bear. However, in their usual unpredictable manner, this one, unknown to us, had turned into the thick brush bordering the stream and had traveled back in our direction. Next time we saw the animal it was coming out of the woods directly opposite our blind and hardly 60 feet away. It was a rare chance to get some good closeup footage. As the doctor swung his camera around to get the picture, I automatically covered the bear with my .375 Magnum. The brownie saw our movements and although it was only a few feet from cover and safety, the beast chose instead to attack. In two mighty bounds it had covered half the distance toward us when I dropped it with a chest shot.

In September 1957, I was guiding Lee Doerr of Milwaukee. Lee had made it plain on this and previous hunts that he wanted a 9-foot bear or nothing. The first day we went afield, we tried one of my favorite spots — a salmon stream on the south shore of Admiralty Island. Conditions were just right, and from the start we began seeing small and medium-size bears, but nothing that interested us. The farther upstream we went, the more numerous were the bears. Finally we came to a mean stretch of water where the creek broke into a series of rivulets. Hundreds of salmon were stranded in the shallows, and the area was laced with big trees that had blown down in a recent storm.

It was just the kind of place in which bears love to feed and precisely where an experienced hunter dreads to meet one. We moved through the jungle with the most extreme caution.

When we were nearly in the clear, we heard a tremendous splashing to our left, and out of a hidden wash came three bears — a sow and her two cubs. They all ran up the far bank, and the two cubs jumped over a log into the woods. The female looked as though she were going to follow them, then suddenly turned around.

Uttering a series of coughing roars, she came straight at us from about 100 feet. So unexpected was the attack and so rapid the action, that I think she might have reached us if she hadn't been forced to cover part of the distance through 2 feet of water. Lee and I both hit her in the chest, and she dropped about 35 feet away.

If ever there was an unprovoked attack, this was it. The bear had no broken teeth that might have pained her, she was unwounded, her cubs weren't threatened, and the avenue of escape was clear. And for our part, with a limit of one brownie to the license, we had no desire to kill her. Yet we had no choice. This sow meant business.

A year later almost to the day, I had another bad experience — this time a near fatal one. I was hunting with Jerry Kron of Mount Kisco, New York. Again, this occurrence was on Admiralty Island. We really shouldn't have been hunting that day. It had been raining hard for thirty-six hours, and all the salmon streams were flooding. The creek we were on was so high that we could wade it on only a few of the shallower riffles. So we spent most of our time struggling through the almost impenetrable thickets and alders that line the banks of any Admiralty Island salmon stream. Fish were scarce, and during our slow progress up the creek we never saw a track or other fresh bear sign. Finally we decided there was no point going farther upstream, and started across a point of land to strike another creek, which we intended to follow to tidewater.

Very soon after, we found ourselves in the midst of one of the worst jungles I've ever seen. The brush was higher than our heads, and we actually had to force our way through it. Visibility was practically zero in any direction.

Presently I saw a raven fly out of the jungle ahead, perch in a dead hemlock, and begin croaking dismally. Ravens acting this way often indicate the presence of a bear. I had a sense of foreboding and heartily wished we were out of that place. I climbed onto a spruce log several feet in diameter to look around. I huffed and snorted, trying to get any nearby bear to answer me. Nothing happened. The only sound or movement in that dismal, dripping, sodden jungle came from the raven still perched in the tree. I checked my rifle to be sure the sights were clear and jumped off the log. Jerry was behind me. I had taken perhaps six steps when I heard something come crashing through the brush in our direction.

It had to be a bear. As soon as I saw the brute, I pressed the trigger. That was the luckiest shot of my career. The 270-grain bullet passed through the neck and lodged in the spine for an instant kill. The bear died just 9 measured feet from where I stood.

We carefully examined this bear for signs of old or fresh wounds but found none. It was a perfectly healthy specimen. The only possible reason it could have had for attacking was that we happened to be in the same patch of brush. Furthermore, it must have charged without knowing what manner of creature it was attacking.

It's always startling to meet a brownie at such close range in thick cover. Years ago I guided a well-nourished gentleman from a small country in central Europe. All of the bears we had seen until one eventful day were mild-mannered, inoffensive, and small. My client wasn't impressed with these bears.

One afternoon toward the end of our hunt, after another unsuccessful day afield, we were wading down a salmon stream. We came to a large spruce that had fallen across the creek and were about to crawl over it when a really big fellow rose on the other side of the log. Never in my life have I been so close to a live wild brown bear. I believe I could have touched it. I remember looking right into the brute's eyes.

Both my client and I had our rifles slung on our backs and were absolutely at the mercy of the bear. In a crisp, commanding voice, my companion said, "ATTENTION!" I have never been able to figure whether he was talking to the bear, to me, or to himself.

The big bear glared at us for what seemed a long while. Then it snapped its jaws, making a sound like a trap springing shut. It roared once, leaped onto the creek bank, and disappeared into the cover.

It took my dude awhile to recover from the experience. He was visibly shaken and had some trouble lighting a cigarette. Finally he remarked, "I zink zome day one of zese bears kill you, no?"

Any person who has hunted Alaskan brown bears for any considerable number of years must surely have had experiences such as mine. I was acquainted with four guides who were seriously mauled.

Allen Hasselborg, who lived alone on Admiralty Island for fifty years and did some guiding for bear hunters, told me he had been charged no less than twenty times. His crippled right arm was a reminder of one encounter that had a near tragic finale.

Hardy Trefzger, who guided with me on several trips, had his arm nearly bitten off and was partially scalped by a bear that he had been photographing. The beast attacked Hardy the moment it saw him and without the least provocation.

Then there was the classic case of Frank Barnes. He was a guide and the mayor of Wrangell, one of the largest towns in south-eastern Alaska. Thus, he was well known and respected locally. One fall he took a party of sportsmen up a river to hunt wa-terfowl. They left their cabin one morning and were hiking toward a lake where they hoped to enjoy a good day's sport when one of the party discovered that he had forgotten an essential piece of equipment. Barnes volunteered to go back for it. Shortly afterward, a single shot was heard from the direction Frank had taken. His companions waited a reasonable time, then went back to investigate.

They found the guide wedged so tightly in the crotch of a tree that he had to be chopped out. He had been fearfully mauled. Incredibly Barnes was still alive and rational. He kept repeating, "She got me! She got me!" He died four hours later.

I sincerely hope no one gets the impression that I have been trying to build a case against the bears. The only reason I lived all those years in Alaska was that brown bears were there. I consider them the grandest and most interesting animals on earth. I have always been dedicated to their preservation and still am. So long as they roam the Alaskan wilderness, there will be at least one creature in North America that cannot be tagged, branded, taxed, or deprived of life, liberty, and the pursuit of happiness without a fight.

During all the years I hunted, I always had a premonition that somewhere out on Admiralty or Baranof or Chicagof Is-land there was a bear that had my number. Someday we would meet, and it would be too bad for me. It never happened. I quit the guiding profession and haven't hunted bears for several years. Now I find myself dreaming of returning for just one final bear hunt. If I do, I may meet that brownie that has my number. But it isn't a thing I worry about. The bears have to win one once in a while, don't they?

Yukon and the Bear

R.D. LAWRENCE

A powerful and savage dog is befriended by a man who has made a homestead in the wilds of northern British Columbia. The dog is called Yukon. At his master's bidding, he joins the battle with the bears.

Then, in the second week of June, Yukon had a fight with a bear. It happened at twilight.

I was sitting at the typewriter. Yukon was lying on his back against the kitchen door, his legs sticking out at odd angles. Suddenly he sprang to his feet, thumped the door with one paw, whined, and looked at me. Because I knew him so well by now, I understood from his behavior that something unusual was going on outside, an event that he felt must be investigated. It wasn't a visitor, for he faced differently in such cases; it was not the need to void bladder or bowels, for he asked for this by standing near me and whoofing softly. No, this, he was telling me, was something of importance.

I rose, walked over to him, and took hold of his collar, and opened the door, whereupon he immediately dragged me outside, leading the way toward the pigpen I had built near the barn. Within an enclosure made of two-inch spruce saplings, I had constructed a small, low house of logs roofed with rough lumber and made waterproof with tar paper.

On top of the lean-to roof stood a large bear. It was tearing off the tar paper, obviously trying to get at the hoglets that had been locked in for the night. The neighbors had warned about this predilection that bears have for tender pork.

Without stopping to think, I released the eager dog and urged him to "go get it!"

The bear heard us. It stood upright, the way bears do when they want to check a doubtful situation, then it whirled around and scrambled off the roof almost at the same time that the streaking dog reached the rail fence.

Yukon swerved away from the pigpen, caught up to the bear, and charged into it. That's all I had time to observe, because I realized belatedly that the dog was in danger and I turned and ran back into the house to get the rifle.

By the time I had taken the rifle down from its rack, inserted the loaded magazine, and worked a shell into the breech as I ran outside again, the two had disappeared. The crashing sounds of their going were audible, coming from the northwest.

No dog is a match for an adult bear. Even timber wolves avoid the large and powerful animal unless it is threatening their young, when, by combined attack, they usually manage to drive it away, although one or more of their number may be killed or injured during the battle, while the bear, made almost bite-proof by its thick coat and tough hide, usually escapes unscathed.

As I ran toward the fast-fading sounds of the chase, I hoped that Yukon would either make the bear take to a tree or break off the encounter quickly; otherwise, he could be seriously injured, perhaps killed. But I tried not to think of this as I entered the darkening forest.

The idea of Yukon lying somewhere out there bleeding was unthinkable. He *had* to be all right. I willed him to turn away, to come home, all the time knowing that he would not, that he would chase the marauding bear until it either treed or turned at bay, knowing also that I stood little chance of finding the two animals unless the bear stopped quickly.

I was too worried about Yukon to consider what my own danger might be if I did catch up with him and the bear. In daylight a Lee-Enfield bullet will stop a bear clean in its tracks if the rifleman knows how to handle the gun. But inside a nearly darkened wilderness the rifle sights are invisible. One must shoot almost by instinct then, either by using the dark outline of the barrel and swinging it more or less on target, when the equally dark shape of the quarry blots out the vague silhouette of the gun, or by shooting from the hip, John Wayne stuff, keeping the body lined up on the animal.

I preferred the latter method, but in either case, accuracy is lost. A miss at short range will almost certainly make a bear run; a lucky shot may kill it. But a wounding shot might make it charge, maddened by pain, seeking to claw and bite; then only some fast, chancy shooting and plenty of luck can settle matters finally. But I wasn't debating these things as I stumbled through the gloomy forest, calling Yukon's name and whistling intermittently.

When it was too dark to search without light, I returned home, planning my next moves. I didn't intend to give up the search.

At home I exchanged the rifle for the 12-gauge shotgun, loaded this with 00 buckshot, and fastened the flashlight clamp on top of the barrel just forward of the trigger. I had made a holder for the light to fit either rifle or shotgun after I had experienced some difficulties tracking, and eventually killing a deer wounded by a snap shot in early evening. The animal staggered into the heavy bush, and when I put the gun up the second time, it was too dark to see the sights. At some fifty paces I missed clean with the first five shots, finishing the deer off with the sixth by pure luck. Because the thought of an animal wandering wounded through the wilderness, dying miserably perhaps days later, was abhorrent, I determined that I would not hunt after sundown again, but to be on the safe side, in case an animal wounded in daylight eluded me until it was dark, I made the flashlight holder. Now I put the five-cell light into it, got a lead for Rocky, and set out anew, taking the malamute with me in the hope that he would be able to pick up Yukon's trail and feeling personally more secure with the shotgun instead of the rifle. Loaded with heavy buckshot, a 12-gauge at short range is a devastating weapon capable of stopping the heaviest game. With 00 shot, at eight lead balls .33 of an inch in diameter in each shell, it is just about impossible to miss; and even if the gun is a somewhat cumbersome bolt-action three-shot weapon, as mine was, it is yet able to outclass a rifle during close shooting at night.

I didn't really believe I would have a confrontation with the bear at this late stage, but by then I had learned that caution equates with survival in the wilderness; taking the gun was instinctive. I didn't give the matter much thought. My one and only concern was for Yukon's safety.

As Rocky and I moved through the darkened forest, I kept repeating Yukon's name aloud, coaxing the malamute to "seek." As a result, though I could not know whether he understood or even if he was, indeed, following his leader's spoor, I was forced to give the dog his head, hoping he was on track.

As may be imagined, when a chase takes place in heavily timbered country, the escaping animal does not stick to well-defined pathways but charges pell-mell into brush, jumps dead-falls, and squeezes under obstructions that are almost impassable to an upright human. Through such obstacles did Rocky lead me, pulling eagerly.

It was a grim course over which I was dragged that night, a black marathon during the running of which I was scratched and buffeted by branches and shrubs, my clothes were torn, and my right eye was almost put out by a needle-sharp spruce twig. But it was not the physical discomfort that caused my mood to match the darkness; only later did I notice the cuts and scratches. I cannot fully express the state of my emotions during that seemingly endless night except to say that I alternated between hope and despair, that I blamed myself for allowing Yukon to race after the bear, and that my love for that dog can really be understood only by those who have had the good fortune to love a dog of their own.

Adrenaline kept me going long past the point of exhaustion, but there were times when I was forced to stop, to pull Rocky close to my side, while tortured lungs gasped air. During the first two or three hours I whistled almost continuously; then my lips couldn't obey anymore, and I called until my voice gave out; periodically I fired the shotgun, hoping that the irresistible sound would bring Yukon back if he was able to travel. And then it was dawn.

Orienting ourselves by the sun, I realized we had traveled a circular course; we were now moving toward the glowing east.

After such a wild journey I should have been hopelessly lost, but the forest in which we now found ourselves was familiar; a number of its trees carried blaze marks I had made more than a year earlier, when I was exploring the wilderness adjacent to the farm. We were about two miles from home.

I didn't want to, but it was necessary to go back. In my haste and anxiety last night I had neglected to feed the dogs; worry killed my own appetite, but Rocky and the others would by now be starving. In any event, I needed a rest.

I started to pull Rocky off the trail, but he fought the lead anxiously, wanting to continue in an easterly direction. My hope was forlorn, but I decided to let him go on for another half hour.

A few minutes later we emerged into a fairly open grassy area. At one end of this Rocky found the place where Yukon and the bear had fought. A section possibly ten yards square had been beaten down by the action; there were tufts of shaggy black fur scattered around, bear fur. And there was blood; in some places just a few drops, in others big smears, as if a wounded body had rolled, rubbing its gore on the grasses. After fastening Rocky to a tree, I search for tracks on my hands and knees and in this way learned that the fight had broken off and that the bear had run again, pursued by Yukon. Who had lost the blood? Once more Rocky was put on the tracks.

The trail led to a small beaver pond. In the mud at the edge of the dam there were footprints, Yukon's and the bear's. The right-front-paw impressions left by the bear were bloody.

There were spots of dark blood on some bushes, but it was impossible to determine which animal had left these. The trail ended, and Rocky, despite frantic casting about could not pick it up again. It seemed that the bear had taken to the water and Yukon had followed.

The bent grasses at the scene of the scuffle were beginning to straighten and the blood was coagulated, the lighter spills a rusty brown color. These things told me that the fight must have taken place during the night, probably not long after the chase began. Where was Yukon now?

For three days Rocky and I searched the forests. On the evening of the third day I gave up; either Yukon had been killed by the bear, or he had followed it so far into the wilderness that he would not now return. Yukon was gone.

At fourteen, when the civil war in Spain came to upset the tenor of my youth, I somehow learned to cope with the emotions engendered by the loss of relatives and friends. In my late teens and twenties, during World War II, this emotional shield was made stronger, perfected to a point where, by my early thirties, I rather boasted that death could not affect me; I was no longer vulnerable because I thought I knew how to live within myself. Friends were enjoyed in the present and dismissed in the past; romance was an interesting exercise of the moment, real enough while it lasted, quickly disposed of when it ended. In a vague sort of way I knew I had become incapable of really caring for others; it didn't bother me. Indeed, I preferred it that way.

More recently, living in the northern wilderness, subtle, disturbing changes in my emotions made me occasionally uneasy, but except for some momentary spells when I silently wondered about the cause of this new concern I was beginning to feel, I devoted little time to the matter, putting it down to the circumstances of my present life and believing that as usual, it would leave me unscathed in the end. When the morality of trapping became a question, I realized that here was something different, but I concluded vaguely that what upset me was the carnage that went with the job, the blood and the smell of death that were too vivid reminders of the old days.

Sitting in the living room thinking about Yukon, I became fully aware that a great change had come over me. I discovered to my dismay that I had become deeply and emotionally involved for the first time in my adult life — with a dog! I immediately rejected the concept. It was nonsense. I was tired from the days of frantic search, out of sorts; I'd feel differently tomorrow. I got up and found the remains of the New Year's bottle of whiskey; there was about a third left. I drank. Two hours later the bottle was empty and I was angry, terribly angry. I wanted to do violence, to smash things. I paced about the house, kicking at anything that got in the way. As I was passing the kitchen door, I punched the unyielding wood, hurting my knuckles and enjoying the pain because it gave me something tangible upon which to vent my temper. I knew I was drunk, yet I was sober. My body was drunk, my mind clear. I stopped, rubbed the swollen knuckles, heard the dogs howling in the barn, and rushed outside to stand spread-legged and to yell, telling them to shut up. I had not done that before. The dogs were silent.

Back in the house I stumbled upstairs and went to bed fully clothed. Without knowing why, feeling utterly unmanned and ashamed, I cried.

When I woke up next morning nursing a deserved headache, I realized almost immediately that I could not escape reality. Yukon was gone, but I could not dismiss the hurt of his going. I cared. And somehow this made me feel better. It did not minimize the grief, but it allowed me to accept it.

The dogs greeted me effusively when I took them their breakfast, but although I patted each for a moment or two, I could not stay to play with them; I was too depressed.

Thinking to take my mind off my problems, I made a shopping list and drove to town, changed my mind about shopping in Ontario and drove across to Minnesota to visit Old Alec, as he was universally called, an octogenarian whom I had accidentally met after arriving in the backwoods and who had become a good friend. Sitting in his small, neat log cabin, playing chess, and drinking the aquavit his Swedish palate was so fond of, we talked between moves, and I told him about Yukon, and about my grief. In the end, looking at me intently with his rheumy blue eyes, he summed up my problem.

"You are in love, Ron. Not yust wit' a dog, wit' life. Yesuss Christ, tho'! You sure did take a long time to love! Yah, Yessus Christ, you shore took a long time . . . You're lucky, tho'. Yust so you love somethin' beside yourself, that's good, ver' good. Yah. . . . "

He poured me another measure of aquavit, filled his own glass, and started to set up the chess pieces.

"Now ve play. Yust one more, yah?"

Old Alec lived eighty miles south of the homestead. I spent the two-hour return drive examining the state of my emotions. When I got home at dusk, I knew that the wilderness and especially Yukon had combined to make a considerable breach in my old defenses. I wasn't sure whether I liked this greatly, but there seemed to be nothing that could be done about it. I had become emotionally involved with a life other than my own in a lasting manner for the first time since infantile dependency had bound me to my parents. Recognizing these things, I knew I would never forget Yukon, but I hoped that the sadness, the depression, generated by his disappearance would not take too long to become dulled and bearable.

After the other dogs had finished their suppers that night, I led them all to the house, feeling somewhat guilty that I had neglected them. During the play that followed I discovered that I cared for all of them to a degree greater than I would have admitted to myself a few days before, but not in the same way that I cared for Yukon. No other dog would ever replace him in my affections.

Afterward, the dogs back in the barn, I stood outside for a while and watched the moon come up. Inside, I found my copy of Steinbeck's *Sweet Thursday* and began to read it once more, knowing it almost by heart, but never tiring of it, and finding that, as always, Steinbeck's sensitive feelings for his subject and his marvelous storytelling abilities were able to assuage my troubles.

When something scratched against the south window of the living room, I was so engrossed that I almost didn't bother to glance up, but when I saw what was out there, the sudden rush of gladness that filled me was beyond description.

Standing with both front paws on the windowsill, his face blurred in the yellow light of the kerosene lantern, was Yukon. But even as I jumped to my feet and started moving toward the doorway, the gladness changed to deep concern as I saw the bloody look of him.

His entire face and head seemed to be plastered in old gore and one corner of his mouth sagged dreadfully; his lips, on the left side, were slit beyond his jawbone, their edges tinged the dirty white that is characteristic of an unhealed wound.

It didn't take but a second or two to reach the door and open it, but he was already there. He rushed at me, whining his gladness, pushing against me, his matted tail wagging furiously. I wanted desperately to examine his wounds, but I couldn't help hugging him, and it seemed that he was just as determined to make a fuss over me.

He was filthy and bedraggled, his coat was filled with wood ticks; they were big on his skin. He was thin and starved. But he was back!

I knew that his stamina and my care would return him to health; nothing else mattered. As we were telling each other how glad we were to be reunited, the other dogs greeted their returned leader in their own characteristic way; they howled as I had never heard them howl before. A pack of wolves baying at the moon, the primordial song of the ageless wild.

The War in the Woods

EDWARD HOAGLAND

The bear is "the forest's reason for being," writes Edward Hoagland. But forests and bears are both rapidly disappearing.

Even in the present day there are a few individuals scattered about the world who have a power of communicating with animals that corresponds, perhaps, to ESP. It is more easily believable, however, since we can see that animals themselves, both wild and domestic, communicate with each other across the barriers of species and of habitat. Bits of filler about these people appear occasionally in the understrata of the news: some herdsman or charcoal burner in a corner of Afghanistan, a leopard hunter, an elephant driver, a racetrack groom. The best animal trainers undoubtedly have had this special capacity along with their daring and verve, but more often it seems to be a man who does not put the gift to any especially profitable use, who lives humbly, as snake charmers and village madmen do, and whose insights bring him as much sadness as gaiety — whose allegiances are torn. I've known trainers who at least were acquainted with the Berlitz equivalent of animal talk, the phrase-book forms — how to arrest the attention of a wildebeest or comfort a whistling swan — and once I heard a firsthand description of the real article, a wandering fellow who appeared,

Pied Piper-fashion, at a zoo animal dealer's and asked for a job as a cage hand. He went into all the cages and soothed the pandas who were just off the boat, encouraged the toucans, and babbled softly to the llamas, gesturing, mumbling, making small sounds. He lived in the sheds with the animals for as long as he stayed, and was a queer, inoffensive, skinny person of no recognizable age, with a timid, energetic stoop like Danny Kaye's. Animals of every type hurried sociably to meet him at the bars when he drew near, following him as far as their cages allowed: an immediate reaction from the first day. He was invaluable as an employee. The creatures who were on hunger strikes took food, and none of them injured themselves in struggling to escape while they were being crated. And yet the prisonlike routine saddened him—being warden, and then shipping them off when telegrams from around the country arrived. Soon he was on the road again, with his suitcase.

This was thirty or forty years ago. The chance for such a singular changeling to spring out of the throng has lessened as the rest of us see fewer animals, have less to do with animals —even a farm boy is becoming quite a rarity. The animals we do know something about are manufactured as commodities: our million steers like cardboard cutouts and our frenetic, force-fed hens. Most of the dogs in the pet shops come out of virtual factories now, and dogs are notable because they go three-fourths of the way in preserving a semblance of an interchange between animal and man. They go so far as to learn English, they cringe on cue and look laudatory. For reasons that are as intense as they are inexplicable, dogs really want to reach us, and when they do, our kindness or our wizardry, our amazing *imaginations*, bring them joy.

Interestingly, though, some of the wild animals make advances to us too, like porpoises and the primates and certain birds. Campers often have a camp weasel or mouse hanging about, and mountain lions on many occasions have poked their heads into a tent and sniffed the sleeper in his sleeping bag, peaceably and curious—the big tracks came and went—or bounded invitingly around, while he pulled the eiderdown over his head. Both the Indian tribes and early settlers developed legends of the friendliness of mountain lions to travelers and children which, if exaggerated, must still have contained a core of truth. In the southwestern U.S., Indians even revered them—it was believed that their urine, in drying, hardened into a precious stone—and in Argentina they were known as "the Christian's friend." Wolves did not establish such a reputation for curiosity about human beings, but wolves are related to dogs and the ferocious Russian wolf is outvoted in folklore by numerous Mowgli-prototype stories of wolves on the Indian subcontinent, in Rome and Italy, and even in Vermont. (In 1780 Ethan Allen, leading a search party, found two lost little girls, aged five and seven, who after forty-eight hours were in the company of a timber wolf.) Of course, among the duchies of the animal kingdom there are plenty of creatures who feel no affinity for man at all, or for kinkajous either. Still if they have backbones, they do perhaps feel an affiliation with the pulse of life itself. Reptiles eat with great relish, preferring twisting, living prey, the livelier the better; and recently a small boy, washed overboard in the Atlantic, was rescued hours later clinging to a large sea turtle which was swimming on the surface at a stately, level pace. Presumably this act of keeping him afloat was not an act of mercy on the turtle's part (though some turtles do know about "drowning"—they drown ducks, catching them from below by the feet and pulling them underwater). The turtle probably just felt comfortable with the boy, animal-to-animal, felt a sort of rudimentary comradeship, so that it made no objection to being utilized as a life ring.

Bears are not as chummy, however; hence our word "bearish." They are exorbitant eaters. They must sleep for six months at a stretch and they must eat enormously in order to be able to sleep, so their main connection with people is that they like most of the foods that people do. The strangely delicate or lonely accord a puma gives evidence of feeling as it touches the nose of a man lying sleeping, having circled a deserted lake to reach his camp, or when it follows him for half a dozen miles, placing each foot exactly in his footprints and playing hopscotchlike games — this is not the style of a bluff bruiser like a bear. Bears are lugs, and they have dim eyesight but superb ears and a superlative nose, maybe the best on earth. They're brainy too, and they've distinguished between their front and hind limbs so long and diligently that the paws have acquired different shapes. They really do love food, eating ingeniously, omnivorously, such items as horse plums, wild apples, parsnips, shadberries, lupine, Solomon's seal, Epilobiums, chipmunks, beetles, rhubarb, and watercress and spawning fish and carrion meat. Zoos feed them loaves of whole-grained bread baked with molasses and supplements. Naturally they're broader-beamed in the rear than in the front, though since they don't often kill game (polar bears are an exception), their mouths are modest in dimension. They have a good set of teeth tucked inside but the mouth isn't sharklike, isn't proportioned like cleavers and axes, and they don't eat desperately, the way shrews do; their timetable is leisurely, they fatten like a woodchuck, moving from feast to feast as between cheerful surprises, scooping fruit, pruning the branches with their paws. They like our leavings too, if they can find a dump, and people who eat bears report that their meat tastes much the same as our meat used to taste to cannibals, or like the other famous omnivore, the pig. Bears may be tall and rangily built or stocky, squat, and with a pot, the short bear perhaps heavier than the large-looking fellow, just like the many varieties of man; and with their overall man-shape and size, their spirited minds, their manlike wails and grunts, they have intrigued people for centuries. In societies where they didn't serve as a manhood test, they were captured alive and employed as crude gladiators in underground arenas, fighting dogs and bulls. The gypsies made them dance for coins, training them by torturing their feet with heated irons. Grizzly Adams, the mountain man, slept with his bears on cold nights (as some of the gypsies must have), and bear rugs were standard bedding throughout the northern hemisphere at times — they're still *de rigueur* for "dens."

Bears are fairly casual about how they pass the winter. Protected from the snow by their warm coats, they just roll in under a fallen spruce when food gets short, pulling a few boughs over themselves, as often as they take the trouble to search out a cave. They choose the north side of a mountain so that the sun won't melt them out, but don't necessarily trek back to the same area year after year. They hibernate singly; cubs are born to a mother every other winter while she lies in a cave, waking only to bite the umbilical cords. Sometimes a woodsman on snowshoes will notice a rhythmic succession of puffs of steam rising from a tiny hole in the cover of snow and know that he's passing a sleeping bear. It's as personal as an experience I once had, of finding in mud alongside the Bowron River a grizzly's tracks so fresh the water was still trickling into them.

Bears are a kind of shadow of man, a tracery or etching of him, as mutes and schizophrenics and idiots sometimes are — a view of him if he'd stayed in the woods, among the rocks, instead of becoming community-minded. The "wild-man-of-the-woods" whom northwestern Indians fear wears a bear's shape, though he is humanoid in his sexual proclivities — he catches Indian girls; his face and his coat are a mask. Even a real bear's face is quite a mask, from the standpoint of an animal trainer. The stolid, terse muzzle, the small, practically hidden eyes, the thick short fur overgrowing the features, give the trainer no window to the bear's emotions such as he has in a lion's great eyes. A tiger's white whiskers, as flexile as they are, are worth a good deal toward saving the trainer from harm, and the expressive lip, the subtle, definitive index of roars are worth much more — not to mention the tail and the curl of the toes. By comparison, a bear's lips hardly move, he has no whiskers to mention, no particular tail, and blocks for toes, and though he may occasionally chop his jaws before attacking, emitting a low breathy growl, often he won't. His hasty antics when he meets you on the road and prepares to make good his escape cause you to wonder which way he actually intends to go; and a trained bear, losing the restraining element of fear, becomes even more bouncy, cryptic, and clownish.

Grizzlies do roar and *waw* and make all the faces of Baal, but grizzlies have not been trained in recent times and they can pretty well be written off, relegated to the paleontologist. In a few spots they are managing to make a stand, feeding on the moose that hunters wound—inland grizzlies with bush to roam. The polar bears—"sea bears"—are in a worse predicament, being hunted with airplanes. Part of the bears' plight may be our own, although they need so much more space that they are being squeezed off the earth sooner than we. The black bears are more apropos, being gerrymandering scroungers who manage to fit into any dab of forest that presents itself; in any few square miles of tangled growth they can set up house, eating beechnuts and leopard frogs, and render themselves almost indiscernible. But in those woods, that concealed bear is like the mercury in a thermometer or the bean in a jumping bean. He moves so fast (when once he moves) when you come upon him that you know he's the forest's reason for being, or the nearest thing to a reason for being that you will ever see.

I talked to a man who had lain helplessly under a grizzly. He was living in Manson Creek, a settlement of twenty citizens in north-central British Columbia where the mail was delivered every second week. He was a clear-faced, well-built, balding man in his late thirties, and a disaffected philosopher, a man who had read mightily on his own but had no one to talk to, who had left Indiana University, estranged from his wife. He read half the night by the light of a Coleman lamp and wrote during the day, hoping to finish a book; but he liked the rough life, skiing out to look at wolf kills, and though he worried about his marriage, so far as I could tell he was holding up sturdily under the pressures of isolation, except that he needed to air his thoughts.

The encounter occurred when he was driving along a dirt road that wound for a couple of hundred miles to a mining camp. He'd stopped his car and climbed down a bank, aiming for a promontory where he hoped to see into a valley. Instead he blundered into a bowl-like depression a dozen yards wide in which a grizzly, waxing fat with the hunting season, was feeding on a moose carcass. The moose had gone there to die and the grizzly's quick nose had found it. The brush was wet, the wind blew loudly in the fellow's face, so that the bear may not have scented him, or may have scented him and waited. At nearly the same instant they saw each other, close-up — the bear's head lifting, bloody and aswarm with flies. This shocking sight, really before he could take it in, was followed by the impact of the bear bashing him over. Flung as if hit by a bus, he was not immediately reactive, yet the bear seemed loath to bite him. It lurched and bunched its neck, he said, and swatted at him, raging. Lying on his back, he drew up his feet as a buffer. It was so big he saw it as a shape then, without color, but in the same factual detail as if he were a third party observing. And though its charge had knocked him sprawling, a sort of disgust or revulsion, apparently, a wish not to contact him with its mouth, kept it from grappling him more closely. Reaching around his legs, it raked and gashed him, roaring with fury but reluctant to use its mouth.

He said he'd had no nightmares to confuse his memory of the accident (he thought of it as that); nor did he expect any. And he was not a sentimental man who would falsely anthropomorphize the bear's behavior; he was living in the bush to write a philosophical study and take a breather, not in order to feed the finches. The bear started leaving, but bumped against the moose, lunged over it, then paused, unable to pull itself away, as if the outrage of being interrupted when eating was too obnoxious for it just to be able to back away from him and leave. It seemed "torn," he said — wanting to rush for cover and yet standing in the middle of their little amphitheater, boiling with insult.

When a grizzly mauls a man the real destruction it does is with its mouth: in bedside interviews, people who have been bitten have described the cumulatively catastrophic damage inflicted on them by a series of chomps. Even so, in most cases the man survives; the bear bites near his neck but doesn't quite get there, and runs off, leaving him mauled but alive. This bear, likewise, torn between its obvious abhorrence of approaching my informant and the urge to wreak havoc on him, hesitated, bawling and swaying, chopping its jaws. Finally it attacked again, lacerating his sides, pummeling his arms when they were interposed, reaching around his boots as he lay balled-up on his back and kicked and, deaf to himself, probably shrieked. Outweighing him by several hundred pounds, it growled like a bass banshee, but it was so absolutely aghast at their proximity — holding its face away as if at the stench of him — that its blows were just tentative. The doctor found dozens of scratches on him afterwards but not many substantial hurts, though one claw had cut through his wallet and through the money in the wallet. And for my friend, as well, once the first terrible glimpse and charge were over, the really ghastly horror of the experience was the matter of scent. He could avoid watching the bear but he couldn't escape its smell. And, as soberly, methodically as he was speaking to me, he couldn't describe it either, except as odious suffocation — violent, vile aversion. It was not like pyorrhea, nor like a garbage pit; it was everything fetid and scarifying and strangling rolled into one disgusting cloud which was more frightening than all the injuries and pain. Hunters call the smell cabbagy and go wild with excitement when they catch a whiff, but he was lying right underneath the mouth, which was its source.

If bears usually go to such considerable lengths to avoid our company, why do we search out theirs? It seems to be in order to count coup. Even at the taxidermist's, where the bears arrive daily in trucks, you notice that the youngster who is in charge of rugged work, like sawing off their heads, does it with an Homeric zest. "You see how we treat you?" he tells them, rolling their corpses and slapping the contorted mouths. A hunter after grizzly must spend a thousand dollars or more in transportation costs simply to get to grizzly country, and in New England bear hunters are usually bear hunters by chance, the bears are so wary and shy. Only about 3 per cent of those killed in Vermont, for instance, have been inveigled to their deaths with bait. Ten per cent have been tracked down with hounds, and the rest fall prize to hunters who "stand and stalk," in the official Fish and Wildlife phrase — they're out in the woods carrying a gun, maybe after deer, when they happen to pitch upon a bear.

I've gone on several hound hunts, as well as stand-and-stalk hunts and ambushes. But hound hunts are the realistic ones; also, the hounds, being agents, interest me. Grizzlies have seldom been hunted with hounds (though some of the Indians did, adding themselves to the pack to give it extra authority); and even in running down black bears, which are neither so dangerous nor the size of a King Kong, the first problem is finding dogs gritty enough to hold the bear—make him come to bay. The smell is strong, goodness knows, and the bear, though big and vital and thick-skinned, cannot run faster than a dog, especially in the fall when he is necessarily fattening himself (very old bears die during hibernation because they haven't been able to fatten up enough). Therefore if a bear is lurking around, no worthy hunting dog will have much difficulty scenting him or catching up; the feat is to conquer him and send him scrambling up a tree. When they contact the bear, most dogs stop dead a moment, then promptly swing around and dash for home. Some sportsmen call a bear hunt successful if they can only catch their hounds by the end of the day. On Monday mornings, the local radio stations broadcast appeals for "a Walker hound lost on the Long Trail under Hazen's Notch."

Besides the Walker breed, others that can be worked on bear are the Blueticks, the Black-and-tans, Redbones, and Plotts; and Airedale blood is sometimes bred into a pack for extra grit. Basically, there are two jobs—the strike dog's and the hold dog's. Working alone, the strike dog finds a cold trail and works at it till he approaches the bear and makes him feel uneasy enough to get up out of his noon bed. He needs to have an excellent nose and an instructive voice which carries well, and to be a dog of self-sufficient sense but not too fast, since the rest of the pack is not released until he is full-out on a fresh track. The hold dogs, fast as fickle lightning in a scrimmage, specialists at "pulling fur," are the fighters who will risk their skins. The bear may run for twenty miles altogether, fighting wherever he can set his back against a ledge or a big tree and only running on again when the hunters draw near. States like New York and Pennsylvania have outlawed trailing bears with hounds because they think the animals have a hard enough time as it is; and the contest does include a quite peculiar proxy element. Besides the metaphorically turncoat nature of the dog's role — who leads his master to any creature, to a woodcock or a slew of truffles — there is a mameluke-style madness too. The dog is kept chained the whole year to focus all his personality on his brief spurts of work, then let loose for a few weekends in the fall to run and run and run, trying to crowd in a lifetime's excitement before he's chained up for another year. Dogs are very much like other animals (watch a mother training her pups), except for the one central dislocation that they are no longer able to collect their food. Even hunting dogs, when lost and starving in the woods, can't, and so with this linchpin removed, they're like a Chinese girl hobbling on bound feet for her husband's accommodation, or like the birds which feudal young ladies kept, which didn't require caging because the front of their bill was broken off — they couldn't pick up their own food from the ground and only ate from their possessor's hand.

A bear's about the biggest game. Foxes are for horsemen in open country, and coon hunting is not much of a sport; it boils down to just watching the dogs do a job. The raccoon doesn't run very far before climbing a tree once he is chased in earnest; the dogs only have to unravel the evidence of where he is. Bobcats are a better quarry because the chase is more complex. The cat has a poor nose but compensates for the handicap with his eyes and ears and will slip through the boondocks for many miles, using marsh ice and deadfalls to confuse the scent — the females are said to be harder to tree, as if they valued their lives more hotly. Bears, being so large, so manlike anatomically and yet lusciously furred, wily and yet raunchy, "understandable" but possessing a beast's stamina, are way ahead of the other North American game animals as prospective adversaries. They can kill dogs — they're brutes — but since their pleasures, their sense of play and diet, their cast of instincts, their strategy or reasoning, are within a realm which we can reach by an effort of empathy, we can pretend that we're Jack-and-the Beanstalk and they're a personal sort of Goliath, which is both fun and very bolstering.

The Vermont season extends three months, starting September 1. During September a bear's coat is so flimsily rooted and thin that you can see right through it, so a scrupulous hunter doesn't shoot the bears he runs across but restricts himself to training and conditioning his dogs for the grueling, more businesslike pursuits of October, when the woods still belong to him. In November the deer hunters are everywhere and any hound is shot on sight. This bloodless September stuff suits me fine, however. My companion is Paul Doyle, a gentlemanly, diffidently chatty insurance man in the town of Orleans, Vt., whose engrossing hobby is chasing bears. As a hunter he is compelling and leaderly, and young men gather about him; he's in his forties and has a family of four daughters but no sons. He's a good-humored, resourceful talker, making it all as individualized as he can. He talks about the game as though they were a bunch of comic understudies for mankind, a shrewd and shadowy tribe whose delight is playing jokes and tricks: if the bugger outsmarts him and the dogs, that day he gets away. Doyle is dry, doubting, but rather fond when mentioning the residents of the many farms we pass as we roar around by truck on the dirt roads toward various hunting grounds. He receives frequent calls from people who think that a coon is threatening their chickens or their corn, or who claim they've seen a bobcat's track. The tracks are often illusory and the wind may have blown down the corn, but it gives him a chance to chat awhile and maybe write some insurance. For eighteen years he himself farmed, and he grew up on one. Besides, he enjoys people and is a man whose hunting is primarily combative, the dogs being deputies and proxies. He's not the type of hunter who prefers the company of animals and who would just as soon sneak across somebody's woodlot on the way to a kill as first go to the house and get acquainted with the owner.

Here are three hunts. Doyle and I and his three dogs, which are a Plott-and-Bluetick cross, rode in an International Scout, a jeeplike truck, and Bob Cody and Eric Gilfallen, sidekicks of his, rode in their own vehicles behind, each with a pair of dogs. Eric, who brought along his little son, is a trainee for IBM, a sloping-nosed, blue-eyed fellow just growing out of being callow, a modernized young man whom I tended to like better each time we met. Bob Cody, a bus driver in Burlington, puts up a tent on Doyle's lawn on weekends for the sake of these hunts. He's a kidder, a stanch-looking, husky person who tilts and fusses with his square-billed cap like a coach giving signals.

On the first hunt, we went to the Duck Pond Road in the township of Glover, a defunct jigsaw road, scarcely navigable, that twists past abandoned farmsteads and log houses for a dozen miles. Tuffy, Doyle's strike dog, trotted ahead, urinating repeatedly as he warmed to the occasion. He was butter-footed in the beginning, as stiff as if he were walking on ice, having hunted in Holland, Vt., the day before and treed a yearling, which the hosts and landowners there shot. He has grasshopper legs, a long gazelle waist, and a broad face for a dog, providing plenty of space for his teeth and for his smelling-chambers inside. He's even blacker than a bear, and he doesn't lope or pace the way a wolf does, for instance; his gait is gimpier, pointier, pumpier, dancier; his legs seem to dangle — long girlish legs — and there's a trotting-horse quality to him — he has a thin tail and shaky, mule-jigging legs. His ears flop incongruously, like a cartoon puppy's, and yet he sniffed like a jackhammer as he started hunting more smoothly, after relieving his bowels and getting the excess of high spirits out of his system. The stark, gaunt persona of a working dog, whether a sled, hound, or attack dog, emerged — the scarred face flattening like a Janissary's, the eyes going gaily daft. His tail swung with the degree of interest the smells he encountered aroused. Checking the sides of the road, he knew that we were after bear, not the raccoons of August, when he had first been exercised, and so he only honored coon signs with a moment or two. When he found a bobcat's trail he "opened up," as the saying is, his voice falsetto when he first used it, but Doyle went into the woods and led him back.

The chokecherry bushes along our course were fully fruited, and we found clumps where a bear must have rummaged, stripping leaves off the branches and treading down the surrounding brush. But this was action of a week before, there was no scent for Tuffy, and though we generals could see the score, the soldiers who would have to fix on the bear and fight him for us had nothing to go on. We poked around an old millrace and an old house site, where a porcupine as round as a turtle was lurking down among the salty timbers. We looked into a pond, looked at the crumpled barns and farm layouts — eighteen abandoned farms, they said. It was all lovely and elegiac — the farms where nobody lived anymore and the dense second-growth wilderness which is slated to be leveled again eventually for a superhighway.

A heavy dew had made scenting ideal but there was no bear scent. We drove over to Barton Mountain in the next town and, leaving the dogs in their boxes, searched for some traces of bear in a neglected orchard grown up with spruce and scrub maple, a place where once in a long while a bear is seen in the daylight sitting on its ample rump and raking apples up. Doyle walked ahead of me, conversing softly, hardly audible. We found a deer skeleton, well picked and scattered, and loads of deer droppings, which, although pellety ordinarily, soften up in September when the deer eat apples. No bear turds, however. Then Bob Cody came across a smudged bear print beside a stream, too old for Tuffy to get going on, but since the stream chattered appealingly, we had lunch, let Eric's son, who had been cooped up in the jeep, climb some rocks and stretch his legs, and freed the dogs from their boxes to drink.

Bob seemed to grow beefier and more phlegmatic as the heat increased and as our schemes were disappointed. Eric became less adenoidal and adolescent, more like somebody's husband, more grown-up, agreeable, and witty. Old man Doyle, whose hair is gray, was wearing his farmer's chore-face — lumpy and tough, his big jaw masticating gum, his eyes narrowed and inaccessible. It was a first lieutenant's face (though he has never been in the service) and a face such as full-time big-game guides wear. His enthusiasm for hunting developed late; if it had seized him as a youngster he might have gone out West to where the wildlife was still large. He trapped bears before he hunted them — this while he was milking cows for a living — baiting them with spoiled fruit in a ravine. The first he caught was a three-legged bear which lay low when he came to check the trap — he was also patrolling his electric fence for a branch that was grounding the wire. He wouldn't have noticed he had a bear except that the trees were peeled completely white for yards around, where it had suffered. Bear traps, teethed medievally, are the cruelest of tools. Eventually Vermont outlawed them, but before that Doyle and many another farmer had stored theirs away in souvenir status, after a private discovery.

Doyle used to be rougher on bears that bayed than he is now. He still carries a slingshot to sting them with, but, if nobody along wanted a trophy, he used to put the animal through an ordeal of three or four hours anyway, running it up a tree and forcing it down to the ground again, he and the gang of kids with him firing bullets into the trunk next to its head. It would have to fight the dogs for the movie cameras, and "tree," then scramble down and "tree" again, being hit with stones in its rear end all the while, and run for its life as a finale. If it injured a dog or if anything in the scenario went wrong, of course it was a dead bear. He sold a few bears that he shot to unsuccessful hunters from the city. But all that was in the savagery of his thirties. Now, he lets the animal off with a warning if no one along "needs a bear," as he puts it — that is, someone who hasn't already at some point shot a bear. And sometimes he reminisces sympathetically about how the whole world must have seemed to fall in on a bear he caught last week, being chased so far and suddenly finding itself surrounded by more dogs and human beings than it had seen in a lifetime.

Almost every young man needs to bathe in blood at least once, if only his own. The problem is that nobody else can do it for him beforehand, and there are many more young men than bears nowadays; automobile accidents take the place of bears. Bear is a big word; Doyle uses it as much as he can; it makes for a better hunt. By now he's such an old hand that he orchestrates the hunts, overseeing the sequence of excitements as well as the hounds and the bear. In preparation for our next trip he'd checked all week for tracks as he drove from town to town making his rounds, and the next Saturday we went out to Brownington Pond and let Tuffy loose in the labyrinthine cedar swamp which stretches behind it. Tuffy peed on fifteen trees, and so did we, and Doyle and the two younger hunters, as part of the gearing-up process, imprinted bears' feet in the mud by thrusting their bunched knuckles in to represent the toes. (In contrast to the black bears, a grizzly has claw tips marked way out in front, which you may miss at first, like a delayed explosion.)

The clover and chokecherry bushes were trampled, the thorn apples, crab apples, and cranberries had been sampled, and there were scatterings of real tracks too, scuffed and undiagrammatic. Tuffy mouthed a dried bear stool aggressively. Though he is tarpaulin-black, his two partners, Jeff and Zeke, are a pretty brindled brown, with reddish eyes, Jeff ash-faced. Weighing sixty pounds, they stand thigh-high to a man and, like Tuffy, have a fanatic, glassy, vacuous look, an hysteric look, like slaves from the world of Buck Rogers. They were rattling their tails against the panels of the truck, whimpering to go, fighting each other in their impatience. Jeff is the fastest dog — if he jumps a bear he can get half a mile ahead of the pack, although he hasn't quite as fine a voice or nose as Tuffy. Zeke ranks as the second most useful dog because his nose is best, but he is not as tough or bear-minded as Tuff; he'll tie himself up trailing a coon. Tuffy is worth maybe $400 and was bought from a famous string of dogs in Olympia, Washington, that destroys a hundred or more bears a year in some of the seed-woods of Weyerhaeuser.

This second hunt turned into the classic variety. As it grew plain that at last they all were going to be given something to do, the crated dogs howled pathetically to be let loose. Tuffy had struck a fresh track, voicing the news with abrupt, hornlike barks in monotone at fifteen-second intervals. Guessing that it might be a sow bear with cubs who would therefore only circle within a mile or two when she was pursued, Doyle released Zeke to help Tuffy, thinking he'd put in the other dogs later. But the bear, a young male, streaked straight to the east instead, through the township of Brownington toward Charleston, territory which no doubt was familiar to him from his nightly meanderings. With Zeke and Tuffy ragging him, he followed a series of nearly impenetrable swamps that Doyle calls Bear Alley and that connect in a seven-mile rectangle bordered by hard-top roads and other barriers. Neil, Eric's little son, had been left in the truck with the main radio, and he saw the top of the bear's head rushing through the grass, aiming for a sag between ridges of high land, with both dogs hard after him. Since Neil couldn't manage to operate the radio, however, we tramped through tamarack, cedar, and pine, jumping brooks and stumbling through the muddy sloughs, because in order to hunt bear on foot you really have to outbear the bear — go where he goes. The red shirts with buckskin vests looked like a combat uniform and the men in them slogged about in confusion and listened painfully.

At last, hearing the dogs' mournful-sounding, hectic barks above us in the cut on the ridge, we ran for the three vehicles to try to head the creature off at one of the old logging roads which intersect Bear Alley. A bear's a beast, but once he has been treed and let go he will tree the more readily on the next hunt because of the experience. It doesn't induce him to become fiercer; like the dogs, he is being trained for the later time when you decide to kill him. The bears fare best who take a risk, such as swimming a lake or plunging through a populated area where the dogs are seduced and bewildered. Otherwise the bear had better simply stay on the ground and battle grimly, taking the gumption out of each hound individually, until they drift home one by one and he is left in silence to go his way. Of course for the bear the paradox is that such a truculent nature will get him into trouble in other situations in a settled region like New England, and furthermore he doesn't know until late in the game that the dogs after him aren't just an unusually pertinacious gang of farm collies and are being followed by hunters.

Finally, we all raced for a notable big pine on the crossroad that severs Bear Alley from farmland and from higher, open ground at its east end. Sure enough, just as we got there we heard Tuffy and Zeke arrive, hectoring the bear in the tangle of brush and trees. The bear stayed out of sight so Doyle let loose Jeff, who was frantic, and Bob added his two mature dogs, Belle and Duke, and Eric his two pups. We could hear the ki-yiing when the bear clipped somebody; with so many in the fight he didn't have time to take hold and chew. Smelling us, he didn't come in our direction, and as soon as we moved toward the sounds of scrapping, he started right back toward Brownington Pond again, since there were no rough mountains at hand for him to turn into. "He won't stop to eat cherries!" Doyle shouted, laughing. He said the dogs don't know enough to stop and listen for each other, they only hear their own yelping, but now that they were in a tight pack none of them was going to lose its bearings.

Paralleling the swamp, swinging into it from time to time on the gridwork of lumbering roads, we could interpret the noises of the chase and see tracks spattered here and there. The bear treed about quarter-to-ten, after some final sparring, having run five miles on this, his second lap. He was in a jungly patch of marsh next to a pasture filled with Guernseys and junk autos. The cows seemed to be curious more than upset.

We got the farmer's permission to drive as close as we could. Doyle put some bullets in his revolver in case of an emergency; cameras and rifles were unlimbered too. The bear was seventy feet off the ground, in the crotch of a tall poplar, the only impressive tree around. A woodpecker was pecking a rotted spar nearby, and the bear himself, perhaps because he was so high, apparently did not recognize that this was a life-and-death meeting, or else he was maintaining his dignity. He seemed as removed from our mundane glory-whoops and the dogs' inane tromboning as a bear in a zoo; or maybe every wild animal by now has come to look like an animal in a zoo. He twitched his nose, lifted his head to see if there weren't a branch higher still, and opened his mouth a little, like a gorilla yawning, playing it close to the vest, not wanting to draw attention to himself in case we were ready to go away. He licked his paws for the moisture on them, because he must have been very thirsty. He was resting. Doyle guessed that he was three or four years old and weighed upwards of two hundred pounds, though he was a bit thin for this time of year. He had large, lengthy arms, a handsome, straight, substantial head and did not appear panicky, just uncomfortable and uneasy. In the beginning he pushed his tongue out of his mouth because he was thirsty and hot, but later he did it as a signal of pugnacity, looking down at the dogs and tilting his head slightly, as if he didn't wish to show us he was looking down. Animals are alert to note where another animal is looking, and many of them — from bighorn sheep to wolves — scrape their tongues in and out through their teeth to indicate a willingness to fight.

Throughout, Bob Cody shrieked and yelled, at a pitch; Eric crowed and thumped the tree trunk with a post. They encouraged the dogs to yelp and leap as high against the tree as a man could have, and they excited them so much that Duke and Jeff began to tussle uproariously. The bear was so high up that I had to walk away a hundred feet to see him. He leaned back on his rump above us, looking at the tops of other trees and at the branches of the poplar above him, as if for an avenue higher and higher. As he became increasingly unhappy, he moved his gray muzzle in confidential ruminations like a traveler who finds that the traveling companions with whom he's penned are in fact renegades. Eventually, while the dogs were being disciplined and the cameras were clicking, while we were festively busy at the base of the tree, he began coming down. Altogether he'd had nearly an hour's rest. His long, relaxed, powerful, gorilla-type arms grasping the trunk slung him upwards or downwards or around the tree with very little effort.

Much hollering on our part, guns were grabbed again. He paused, however, halfway down, hanging in place like a telephone lineman and watching us and looking off. His life hung in the balance, although he didn't know that. The hunters really didn't know that his life hung in the balance either; they knew they'd shoot him to save the dogs but they didn't really comprehend that he'd be dead. Which is the trouble with most hunters, and why when one of them shoots another, the shooter generally collapses, vomits, has to have his rifle taken away immediately, has to have his remaining companions sleep beside him, hold and comfort and reassure and protect him, even keep him from doing violence to himself. Suddenly the man realizes that he has been dealing with the miracle of death.

But after considering, the bear climbed back up. Doyle cut a twig for a toothpick and told the dogs, "You beat the son-of-a-gun! That's all we wanted." Between the dogs' baying, the Choctaw yells, and Bob's banging a pole against the tree for the last footage in the camera, there was a terrific racket. I noticed that although I couldn't smell the bear himself, I could smell uprooted grass and bark torn off the tree. He was extremely discomposed by now, stirring up there. After ten more minutes, he came almost all the way down, making no fuss when he started, just swinging down feet first in silence, with his long forearms clutching the trunk, his vigorous body like some ancestral figure's. He seemed to be hoping that we were prepared to call it a day if he simply came down, uncontentious and nonchalant. It's hard to keep a good bear up a tree, as Doyle had said, but we didn't give in to him and he hung overhead for a long while, chopping his jaws softly and snarling — a fluffing, breathy sound. Then he climbed clear up again. The noble dimensions of the tree and the bear's moxie were making it a perfect treeing.

Since the cameras were empty and this was only supposed to be an exercise, Doyle and the others caught their dogs. Immediately, even before they'd leashed them, the bear came skidding down, hasty as a fireman. When he was six feet from the ground he leaped straight out for cover. One of the hounds got loose, unfortunately, so that they all had to be released so the single dog would not come to grief. They ran the bear for two or three more miles, back east toward Charleston and the notable big pine. Eric and Bob in the two jeeps, knowledgeably speeding around to an intersection, contrived to meet the bear just as he emerged in a clearing. Letting him go by, they intercepted the dogs while he was still tiredly breaking brush within their hearing.

A week later, we attempted somewhat wistfully to recapitulate these triumphs by taking the dogs to Brownington swamp at dawn again. Lakes of fog lay between the hills; frost tufted the goldenrod, the fields of hardhack, and the evergreens. We listened to a farm boy shouting at cows in the distance. The scenting conditions were ideal: no rain to wash the traces away but a dousing of dew to spice and accentuate whatever there was. We led the dogs on leashes into the brush to get a fast jump on the bear if Tuffy, who was out ahead, found one. Slogging through the mud, the streams, and over deadfalls, we saw an osprey's nest and paths of coons and porcupines. Deep in the swamp there was a tin shanty where several lumberjacks had lived. There was plenty of bear sign too, though nothing recent. Tuffy was puzzling along an unproductive trail; we listened to him respectfully, wading in tangents whenever he turned. We climbed a sunny knoll and waited. He was on a beechnut ridge to the south, croaking like a chicken; then he entered a sugar orchard. Eric and Bob went off to listening posts on crowns of hills around the countryside. "The needle in the haystack," said Doyle.

Getting tired of waiting for Tuffy to strike something hot, we drove around to a crossroads and caught him and drove to the town of Westmore, checking in various orchards, finding deer beds and bushes that the bucks had stripped when rubbing velvet off their antlers. At midmorning we went to look at a cow carcass which a woman had buried a week before, using her tractor, and which she said a bear was digging up. Unlike so many tips, however, her report turned out to be true. The evidence of digging and chewing at the black remains was plain; also the tack which he had taken through a hemlock woods toward the hiding place where he lay up during the day. Spirits surged, and though the scent was dry, for his sins we tromped round and about for another hour or two with all due military drama, generating in ourselves the sensation that the war in the woods hadn't actually been won a century ago—that we were needed, that this bear exhuming the week-old carcass of a cow was a real emergency.

We drove back to the notable white pine at the end of Bear Alley, where we had listened to the dogs ki-yiing in the screen of trees. It wasn't far; and here too we found tracks—faint, hand-sized imprints in the road, like Sanskrit underlying the language of the many tire and boot marks. This may have been the bear whose endeavors we had just been inspecting at the cow's grave, or even the same bear we had treed in the poplar. He had to eat something, after all, and bears aren't overly plentiful today. Necessarily, there will be more and more of this business of letting the bear go after treeing him; bears will be run up a tree quite regularly; it will be a kind of bearbaiting. Bears may be one of the group of animals whose welfare will become associated with the paper industry, since they hide in the pulp woods. I think that Doyle probably would spare all those his dogs tree except that earning the $100 guiding fee pleases him. It's not the sum of money, which doesn't seem as much to a busy insurance agent as it might to a man who was still milking cows for a living, but rather the role in which he earns it: professionally guiding hunters. A hundred dollars is little enough to pay for a bear in the 1970s and enormous numbers of hunters in Massachusetts and New York are eager to pay it. Sight unseen, they call him up and say flatly that if he can find them a bear—if he knows where one is holing out—they will be up in four hours, right then and there, any time, any day. It puts him in a quandary.

I stopped at the taxidermist's next day. By coincidence, a bear had just been brought in, lying in a pickup truck. It had been shot in Franconia, New Hampshire, and was a male of seven or eight (the sex organs had been removed by the game warden), weighing perhaps three hundred pounds. The hunter, a wiry long-haired man from Hollywood, Florida, was inside the shop consulting about prices. He had a sharp and knowing tipster's face, clever and gay. His wife had come along for the ride. She was pregnant and pleasant-looking, wearing white lipstick, her hair rinsed a white-blond. He was as short as she, and they appeared to have achieved the marriage-of-friends that most of us seem to be heading for. The bear lay on its back, its legs extended upwards, each one bent differently, so that its posture was like a man lying *in extremis* next to the site of a catastrophe. In height it might have compared to a fourteen-year-old boy, but it was built like a barrel. After its head had been sawed off, what remained looked as a prisoner must look after visiting the guillotine, a circle of vital red stuff jamming its neck. It looked truncated and shortened and uncompleted, like an uncolored figure in a coloring book. The paws also were cut off to be mounted and all the rest of the bear, in its ragged September coat, was thrown away. After asking whether they ought to cut off "steaks," the Floridians tooled out of town in search of a covert where they could dispose of the trunk and legs. They were flirting and celebrating because, as the fellow said, this was a big event. Thousands and thousands of guys are out in the woods and in a lifetime of hunting you may only manage to see one bear.

The Rubber Bear

RAY W. LANE

Bears, by all accounts, are among the most intelligent of mammals. They are also inclined to be contrary, however. This is the tale of a bear who agreed neither with man-made rules nor, finally, with the writer's digestion.

It was 1939. The Great Depression, which had lasted for almost a decade, was soon to come to an end with World War Two. However, it was only spring, and the employment boom of the war years still lay ahead. Both the federal and provincial governments anxiously sought answers to the growing problem of unemployed youth — the Lost Generation.

The answer had been suggested earlier in the United States, where Roosevelt's "New Deal" initiated a number of make-work programs. One of these was called the C.C.C. (Don't ask me what those letters stood for.) C.C.C. camps sprang up all over America. They provided young men with a wilderness experience, work to do, money in the pocket, and food in the stomach. In return, the country gained park and recreational facilities that were second to none.

Following the American example, in the spring of 1939, Canada set up a combined Dominion-Provincial program for youth across the country. I applied to the program, was accepted and sent, along with about thirty others, to a camp in the Banff park. We ranged in age from about 18 to 28. We were given work uniforms and paid thirty dollars a month each.

One of the jobs at which we took turns was that of "bull cook," or cook's helper. There were two of us at a time, one on days and one on nights. We chopped wood, did the dishes, and kept all the fires going. We were even given some minor cooking chores.

It was while I was on this job that we had an interesting visitor to our camp. One morning, while washing up for breakfast, we heard an awful bellow from the cook — or "Cookie", as we affectionately called him. We looked up in amazement to see Cookie, brandishing a large cast-iron frying pan, in hot pursuit of a full grown black bear. Mr. Bear, with great loping strides, made it to the nearest Lodgepole pine and climbed to the very top.

One of the fellows, waving a double-bitted axe, shouted, "Come on! Let's get him!" We all grabbed our axes, headed for the tree, and commenced chopping it down. It was an enormously high tree. Mr. Bear seemed to get the message from each blow of the axe and inched himself ever higher. The top of the tree swayed back and forth. Then there was a great cracking sound, and someone shouted, "Timber!"

The mighty tree crashed in slow motion through the other pines. I was sure Mr. Bear would break every bone in his body — but no! With unbelievable agility for such a large creature, he scrambled from the falling tree across to another.

I had never seen anything so big move so fast. Half climbing down, half sliding, he reached the bottom before you could say "black bear" and then ran for the mountains nearby.

We all thought that was the last we would see of Mr. Bear for sure, but — lo and behold! Within a week or so he was to return. A bit humiliated, he was ready to forgive us for his ordeal in the tree and seemed only to want to make friends. He tried hard to be a good bear in the days that followed, but he had a few falls from grace.

For example, he could not resist our slop pit. It was, because of the flies and the odor, located some distance from our camp. I found him there one day on one of my many visits with a pail of slop. He was having a glorious time wallowing in the slop and slurping up the maggots that floated on the surface.

Bears, like dogs, it seems, love to roll in anything that stinks. He didn't think he was being bad—just having harmless fun!

Then there was the time I almost literally bumped into him. I had been sent to the meat house to fetch a slab of bacon. I stood rooted to the ground as he rushed by me with a guilty look on his face. When I recovered, I went on to discover the meat house door had been torn off its hinges. A quarter of beef, still hanging on its hook, was badly mauled and chewed. "There but for the grace of God go I," I said to myself.

Only once during all this time did he ever show hostility. But in a way, this was my fault. I had not seen him for a day or two, so I set out some fresh pies to cool on the shady side of the dining tent. I suppose it was the delicate aroma of pies fresh out of the oven that brought him on the run. Mr. Bear found them at once and proceeded to have hot apple pie for lunch.

I was astonished. He must have had a cast iron stomach to down that stuff right out of the oven. Believe me—it was hot! I put on my gloves to rescue what I could. I had one of the pies in my hand, when someone saw what was going on and burst out, "Well, I'll be damned!" I think it was this sudden exclamation that frightened the bear.

Let me tell you—there is nothing to compare to the sight of a bear with hair bristling and teeth bared, nor to the angry guttural noises half growl and half roar that escaped from between those rows of horrible yellow teeth. He had bad breath, too. I dropped my pie and ran, just checking to see if my arm was coming with me. Mr. Bear finished off the pies, grunting a few warnings now and then while he ate.

Apart from that one incident, he tried his best to be a good, friendly bear. During the night shift, he followed me about from tent to tent. He stayed respectfully outside the door of each tent until I had stoked the fire, then followed me to the next tent. I was delighted one morning on my rounds to see our friendly black bear licking Cookie's bare feet which stuck out from under the flap of his tent. Cookie was an enormous man. He had once been a professional wrestler and was much too big for the pup tent. When Cookie slept no power in heaven or earth could wake him. Nevertheless, he did stir in his sleep and moved his feet, subconsciously trying to avoid the tickles.

Mr. Bear, however, thought this was a game of some kind and jumped about like a puppy with a new toy. I thought the sight was hilarious, but I didn't dare to laugh. I had already discovered how a bear reacts to a sudden burst of sound, and I didn't want it to happen again.

For many weeks the bear stayed away from our cooking and dining tents. He was often seen sniffing the air, but always at a respectful distance. When Cookie decided, however, that the isolation of our camp was too much to bear — funny that I should use that word — things came to a head.

Right under our noses Cookie had built and cleverly concealed a most effective still. After the day's work was done, the cook tent was transformed into a distillery. Everyone else was suffering from the effects of a dry spell, but Cookie was toasting himself every night. No wonder he slept so well.

None of us suspected anything, but Mr. Bear's nose was keener than ours. He said to himself, "Enough is enough!" So one morning there was a deafening clatter, and the cook tent and its contents came apart. The noise was appalling. It was hard to distinguish the roars of the bear from the bellows of Cookie. When it was all over the shambles was unbelievable. That did it! Mr. Bear had to go.

In those days no one had thought of trapping and transporting bears to remote areas by helicopter. There were no helicopters for one thing. So after much soul-searching by park authorities, permission was given to shoot the bear. A park warden was sent to our camp and waited for the bear's return. It was not a long wait. He dispatched the bear with three shots from an ancient Ross rifle.

We all gathered around to view the remains. The occasion was like a wake. Soon we got talking about eating our friend. When it came to eating the exotic or bizarre, in those days I was never one to back away. Would I eat bear meat? Well sure! Why not?

The cook, who had experience in these things, said it was not the right time of year; the bear was still thin from his long winter's nap. He would likely be quite tough. "We can give it a try," he said reluctantly, and cut off a large piece of tenderloin.

Did I say tenderloin? What a misnomer! There was nothing Cookie could do to make *that* loin tender. He tried aging it. He tried pounding the daylights out of it. He tried long, slow cooking over low heat. But the best Cookie could do was to change the texture of Mr. Bear from leather to rubber.

THREE

CAPTIVE AND DOMESTICATED BEARS

A Dirge for the Polar Bear

ANONYMOUS

*The zoo is a half-way house. Its prisoners are neither wild,
exactly, nor pets. This unsigned article, taken from the
Spectator of 1894, describes the character of one bear, long a
captive in the London Zoo, with earnest sympathy.*

The belief in animal portents, which was never lost by the
practical Roman mind, no longer survives in our century, or
some omen would be drawn from the mortal sickness of the
great white bear in the Zoological Gardens, following the in-
ternment of the "Great White Czar" in the capital of the Caesars
of the North. For the Arctic bear is the appropriate emblem of
the Russian Emperors, a creature which, in the fancy of poets
and painters, is always tragic, and never ludicrous like the brown
bear, and which British humour, half-grudging, half contemptuous, has made symbolical of the Muscovite in the caricatures
of half a century. The old polar-bear, which has lived for close
on a quarter of a century in Regent's Park, is dying. For the
last fortnight it has wasted rapidly, and refused all food, though
it seems to feel no pain, but lies all day extended upon the
ground, with its limbs spread out exactly in the position of a
semi-stuffed skin prepared for a hearth-rug.

Except the Arctic foxes (three of which have this year already
assumed the pure white colour of winter), the two polar-bears
are the only purely Arctic animals in the Society's Gardens.

Though the sick bear is the elder by some eighteen years, the pair are excellent friends, and when standing face to face in their den, looked like the originals of the portraits of *ursa major* and *ursa minor* on the old-fashioned celestial globes, in which the northern constellations were always conscientiously represented as polar-bears.

In all stories of Arctic travel, the extreme of cold appeals so strongly to the imagination, that the heat of the nightless summer, in which the Eskimoes strip themselves naked in their snow-houses, is often forgotten. The good health and long life of the polar-bears in confinement in this country is less surprising than it at first appears, when this extraordinary range of Arctic temperature is remembered. Moreover, the white bears are absolutely indifferent to fog and wet. Creatures that live and thrive on islands like Nova Zembla, where half their life is spent in frozen fog and semi-darkness, are little troubled by the London fog and damp of Regent's Park. Mr. Weller's remark that it "was pleasant weather for those as were well wropped up, as the polar-bear remarked ven he was apractising his skating," applies to damp and wet, as well as cold, in the case of these semi-aquatic bears. They will plunge and roll in their bath with as much pleasure in pouring rain, or when the tank is full of clinking ice, as on a hot summer day, and the only weather which seems to cause them discomfort is a hot August afternoon, when they pant and loll out their tongues like Newfoundland dogs. The predecessor of the "big bear" at the Zoo lived thirty-six years in Regent's Park, an age which is very seldom reached by any creature in captivity, except the half-domesticated elephant and the Indian rhinoceros. Size and longevity seem closely related in the conditions of animal existence; and the polar-bear is far the largest of the great carnivora, and by consequence lives to a much greater age than the lion or tiger. When in its prime, the *Ursa major* of the Zoo must have weighed at least three-quarters of a ton, and its companion, though a female, grows at a rate which promises before long to bring it to nearly the same bulk. This is about the weight of a large English drayhorse. Possibly the regular food-supply and warm climate which the captive bears enjoy may increase their size; but Captain Lyon mentions that he shot one which measured 8 ft. 7 in. in length, and weighed no less than 1,650 lb.

The body of this bear, unlike the *felidae*, is rounded like a barrel, and though its limbs are long, and it stands high, its bulk is more in proportion to that of the ox or the elephant than to the more slender forms of the true carnivora. As the average weight of a large lion is 500 lb., and of a large tiger 450 lb., the offensive power of the polar-bear must greatly exceed that of either, if its muscular strength and activity are in proportion to its size. In some respects, its powers of movement exceed those of the great cats. It can maintain a gallop at a pace equal to that of a fast horse, leap wide gulfs with ease, swim fast enough to catch a salmon, and dive like a seal or an otter. The old bear at the Zoo has for some time rarely entered its bath; but the aquatic feats of its younger partner are thus described in a chapter on "London Bears," in Mr. C.J. Cornish's recently published work, "Life at the Zoo." "Fresh water is let into their bath two or three times a week, and as soon as the bottom is covered, the younger bear rolls in and "cuts capers," to use the keeper's phrase. She always prefers to take a "header," but not after the orthodox fashion; for when her nose touches the bottom, she turns a somersault slowly, and then floats to the surface on her back. Then she climbs out, shakes herself, and gallops round the edge of the bath. In spite of her bulk, this bear is as active as a cat, and can go at speed round the circle without pausing or missing a step. Her next object is to find something to play with in the water. Anything will do, but if nothing else is handy, she usually produces a nasty bit of stale fish, which she seems to keep hidden in some handy place, and dives for it, coming up to the surface with the fish balanced on her nose, or on all four paws. If the water is still running in, she will lie under the spout and let it run through her jaws. But the most amusing game which the writer has seen, was played with a large round stone. After knocking it into the water, and jumping in to fish it out, she took it in her mouth, and tried to push it into the hole from which the water was still running. This was a difficult matter, for the stone was as large as a tennis-ball, and the pipe was not much wider. Several times the stone dropped out, though the bear held it delicately between her lips, and tried to push it in with her tongue. At last she sat up, and holding the stone between her fore-paws, put it up to the pipe, and pushed it in with her nose. This was a great triumph, and she retired and contemplated the result with much satisfaction. Later, being apparently tired of this achievement, she threw water at it with her head, and failing to wash it down, picked it out with her claws, and went on diving for it in the bath.''

For all this hearty enjoyment of play, the Arctic bears of the Zoo are dangerous animals. No creatures are more carefully kept at arm's length by their keepers. Men who will rub their hands over a lion's face and eyes, or pat the neck of a tiger, shift a bison-bull across its stall like a bullock, or handle a python like a length of rope, would think it rash to put hand or limb within reach of these bears. Their outdoor den is partly cut away from a mound at the back, and at the top of the scarp a railing runs, behind which is a path. This railing had to be double-barred with steel wire, because the younger bear had discovered that by hiding below the wall, and then suddenly springing up, there was just a chance of clawing a visitor's legs. Yet she has a boisterous sense of humour, and will not only splash visitors on purpose by sousing herself into her bath, but has often been seen to get up, and dash the water at them with her broad paws. The fierceness of the polar-bear is probably due to its enforced carnivorous diet. Every other bear is largely a fruit, vegetable, and insect feeder. But in the frozen north the polar-bear lives by necessity mainly on fish, carrion, seals, walruses, and birds. Its notion of an "egg for breakfast" is rather amusing. It will clear an islet of eider-ducks' eggs in a few hours. It not only plays in the water, but is so fine a swimmer that it deserves the name of sea-bear, or water-bear. To judge by the performances of the different animals in their bath in the Zoo, it swims faster than a seal, and almost as fast as the sea-lion. It regularly stalks basking seals from the water, swimming below the surface, and only just rising to breathe and note the right direction. Not unnaturally it sometimes mistakes the sealskin-clad Eskimo, watching motionless beside the seals' blowhole, for a seal. "I have known several men," writes Dr. R. Brown, in "The Arctic Manual," "who have had its rough hand laid on their shoulder while sitting watching or skinning seals. Their only chance then has been to feign being dead, and to shoot it while the bear was sitting at a distance to which it had retired to watch its intended victim." Yet even in lands where man is never or rarely seen, curiosity rather than aggression seems the first impulse of the polar-bear. Herr Nordenskiold found himself unarmed face to face with one on Scoresby Island. It came up and inspected the explorer, until he drove it away by hitting it on the paw with a stone. Another bear, which ransacked a boat full of stores, took fright at the sound of a pile of biscuits falling from a bag it had opened, and ran off in a panic.

Polar-bears do not seem to breed in captivity, and there is no male successor waiting to take the place of the veteran now *in extremis*. But it is remembered that a cross-bred cub between a polar and an American black bear was once born in the Gardens. The sight of a polar-bear with her cub taking a bath would be one of the greatest attractions ever provided at the Zoo.

The Bear That Came for Supper

ROBERT FRANKLIN LESLIE

This is the remarkable story of an understanding that developed between a man and a bear in the Canadian wilderness.

I met Bosco in the remote wilderness north of Mt. Robson in the Canadian Rockies. At the end of a long day of backpacking I had made a lean-to in a clearing beside a stream and was preparing to catch supper. Then I looked up — and there he was: an enormous boar black bear, slowly circling the clearing within 30 yards.

He wasn't Bosco to me yet, and I viewed his presence with trepidation. My provisions were vulnerable if he was in a piratical mood, since I was unarmed. However, I decided to go about my fishing. The bear came along.

A lifelong outdoorsman, I've lived with wild creatures for 30 years, respecting their first fear — fast movements — and now I let him see the reason and the beginning in every slow, deliberate move I made. Soon he was sitting on his haunches less than five feet away, intensely interested in my activity. When I landed a 14-inch Loch Levin, I tossed it to him. He gulped it without bothering to chew. And when I flipped out the fly again he moved closer, planted his well-upholstered fanny on the turf beside my boot, and leaned half his 500 pounds against my right leg!

I plied the gray hackle along the riffles and got another strike. Before reeling in, I eased over a yard, convinced the bear would grab fish, line, rod — and maybe me. But he didn't. His patience and dignity were regal as he sat rocking back and forth, watching carefully. When I released the trout from the hook, he bawled a long-drawn-out "Maw!" I held the wriggling fish high, stepped over to my "guest," and shakily dropped the prize into his carvernous, red mouth.

When drizzly darkness set in, I was still fishing for that bear, fascinated as much by his gentle manners as by his insatiable capacity. I began to think of him in a friendly way as Big Bosco, and I didn't mind when he followed me back to camp.

After supper I built up the fire, sat on the sleeping bag under the lean-to and lit my pipe. All this time Bosco had sat just outside the heat perimeter of the fire, but the moment I was comfortably settled he walked over and sat down beside me. Overlooking the stench of wet fur, I rather enjoyed his warmth as we sat on the sleeping bag under the shelter. I listened to the rain thumping on the tarp in time with the steady, powerful *cur-rump, cur-rump* of the heartbeat beneath his thick coat. When smoke blew our way, he snorted and sneezed, and I imitated most of his body movements, even the sneezing and snorting, swaying my head in every direction, sniffing the air as he did.

Then Bosco began licking my hands. Guessing what he wanted, I got him a handful of salt. Bosco enthusiastically nailed my hand to the ground with eight four-inch claws — claws capable of peeling the bark from a full-grown cedar, claws that could carry his 500-odd pounds at full gallop to the top of the tallest tree, claws that could rip a man's body like a bandsaw.

Finally the last grain of salt was gone and again we sat together. I wondered if this could be for real. I recalled Sam Ottley, trail foreman on the King's River in the Sierra Nevada, whom I had seen sharing tent and rations with a bear; but Sam's creature was old and toothless, no longer able to live off the country; this monster was the finest prime specimen I had ever seen.

Bosco stood up on all fours, burped a long, fishy belch, and stepped out into the rainy blackness. But he soon was back — with a message. He sat down near the sleeping bag and attempted to scratch that area of his rump just above his tail; he couldn't reach it. Again and again he nudged me and growled savagely at the itch. Finally I got the message and laid a light hand on his back. He flattened out to occupy the total seven feet of the lean-to as I began to scratch through the dense, oily hair.

Then the full significance of his visit hit me. Just above his stubby tail several gorged ticks were dangerously embedded in swollen flesh. Little by little I proved that the flashlight would not burn, so he allowed me to focus it on his body. When I twisted out the first parasite, I thought I was in for a mauling. His roar shook the forest. But I wanted to finish the job. Each time I removed a tick I showed it to him for a sniff before dropping it on the fire, and by the last one he was affably licking my hand.

A cold, sniffing nose awakened me several times during the night as the bear came and went. He left the sleeping bag wetter and muddier each time he crawled around over me, but he never put his full weight down when he touched any part of my body.

The next day I set off again, over a ridge, down through a chilly river, up the next crest, through thickets of birch and alder and down a wide river canyon. To my surprise, Bosco followed like a faithful dog, digging grubs or bulbs when I stopped to rest. That evening I fished for Bosco's supper.

As the days passed and I hiked north, I used a system of trout, salt and scratch rewards to teach the bear to respond to the call, "Bosco!" Despite his perpetual devotion to food, he never lagged far behind. One evening he walked over to the log where I was enjoying my pipe and began to dig at my boots. When I stood up he led me straight to a dead, hollow bee tree at which he clawed vigorously but unsuccessfully. Returning to camp, I covered my head with mosquito netting, tied shirt, pants, and glove openings, and got the hatchet. I built a smoke fire near the base of the tree and hacked away until the hollow shell crashed to earth, split wide open, and exposed the hive's total summer production. For my understanding and efforts I received three stinging welts. Bosco ate 20 pounds of honeycomb, beebread, and hundreds of bees. He snored most of that night at the foot of the sleeping bag.

At campsites Bosco never tolerated long periods of relaxation and reflection; and, true to my sucker form where animals are concerned, I babied his every whim. When he wanted his back scratched, I scratched; when he wanted a fish dinner, I fished; when he wanted to romp and roll with me in a meadow, I romped and rolled — and still wear scars to prove that he played games consummately out of my league.

During one particularly rough session, I tackled his right front leg, bowling him over on his back. As I sat there on his belly regaining wind, he retaliated with a left hook that not only opened a two-inch gash down the front of my chin but spun me across the meadow. When I woke up, Bosco was licking my wound. His shame and remorse were inconsolable. He bawled like a whipped pup when I was able to put my arm around his neck and repeat all the soft, ursine vocabulary he had taught me.

After that experience I let Bosco roll me around when he had to play, but I never raised another finger toward originality. If he got too rough, I played dead. Invariably he would turn me over, lick my face and whine.

There were times when he spent his excess energy racing around in 100-yard circles, building up speed to gallop to the top of the tallest fir. When he returned to camp immediately afterward, I could detect no increase above his normal breathing rate. He panted only when we walked for long periods in full sun and he got thirsty.

It is not my intention either to attribute character traits to the bear which he could not possess or to exaggerate those he had. I simply studied him for what he was, and saw him manifest only the normal qualities of his species, which were formidable enough without exaggeration. Other than calling him Bosco, I never attempted human training upon him; conversely, I did everything possible to train myself to become a brother bear.

Like all sensitive mammals, Bosco had his full complement of moods. When serious, he was dead earnest; when exuberant, a volcano. Being a bear, he was by nature uninhibited; so I never expressed even a shade of the word "no." The affection we developed for each other was spontaneous, genuine brotherly bear; when it occurred to him to waddle over my way on his hind legs, grab me up in a smothering bear hug, and express an overflowing emotion with a face licking. I went along with it for two reasons: first, I was crazy about that varmint; second, I had a healthy respect for what one swat from the ambidextrous giant could do.

Although he was undisputed monarch of all his domain, I think Bosco considered me his mental equal in most respects. It wasn't long before he taught me to expand communication through a language of the eyes. How a bear can look you in the eye! Terrifying at first — it grows into the most satisfactory medium of all. Bosco and I would sit by the campfire, studying each other's thoughts. Once in a while he'd reach some sort of conclusion and hang a heavy paw on my shoulder. And I'd do the same. It would have made an odd picture, but many times as I looked into those big yellowish-brown eyes, I felt an awed humility as if the Deity Himself were about to effect a revelation through this, another of His children.

Although his size and strength made Bosco almost invulnerable to attack by other animals, he had his own collection of phobias. Thunder and lightning made him cringe. When whiskey jacks (Clark's nutcrackers) flew into camp looking for food, he fled in terror, the cacophonic birds power-diving and pecking him out of sight.

Bosco's phenomenal sense of smell amazed me. Trudging along behind me, he would suddenly stop, sniff the air, and make a beeline for a big, succulent mushroom 200 yards away, to a flat rock across the river under which chipmunks had warehoused their winter seed supply, to a berry patch two ridges over.

One afternoon when we were crossing a heath where dwarf willows grew in scattered hedgelike clumps, Bosco suddenly reared up and let out a "Maw!" I could detect no reason for alarm, but Bosco stood erect and forbade me to move. He advanced, began to snarl and pandemonium broke out. Every clump of willows sprouted an upright bear! Black bear, brown bear, cinnamon bear, and one champagne (all subdivisions of the same species).

But these were young bears, two-year-olds, and no match for Bosco. He charged his closest contestant with the fury of a Sherman tank, and before the two-year-old could pick himself up he dispatched a second bear and tore into a thicket to dislodge a third. At the end of the circuit my gladiator friend remembered me and scoured back, unscathed and still champion.

That night we sat longer than usual by the campfire. Bosco nudged, pawed, talked at great length, and looked me long in the eye before allowing me to retire. In my ignorance I assumed it was a rehash of that afternoon's battle. He was gone most of the night.

Along toward next midafternoon I sensed something wrong. Bosco didn't forage, but clung to my heels. I was looking over a streamside campsite when the big bear about-faced and broke into a headlong, swinging lope up the hill we had just descended. I did not call to him as he went over the crest without once looking back.

That evening, I cooked supper with one eye on the hillside, then lay awake for hours waiting for the familiar nudge. By morning I was desolated; I knew I should never again see big brother Bosco. He left behind a relationship I shall treasure.

Memories of Mooween

H. MORTIMER BATTEN

The writer was a naturalist, with a happy knack for telling stories. His brief cohabitation with a bear cub named Mooween ends with a bang — but not a fatal one.

The great forest fire had scourged the north country, leaving behind it a belt of charred and blackened desolation, stretching from Alaska to Hudson's Bay. For all its tragedy and its destruction, forest fire is in two ways a friend to the prospector after it has passed. For months he lives in dread of it, of being caught in waterless country — but once the fire is over it opens up the forests for those who hunt for mineral wealth, and for a time, at any rate, it kills off the blackfly and the mosquito pest.

Joe and I were camped at the edge of the fire belt — near enough to the unburnt country to obtain firewood, yet just far enough out of it to be reasonably free from flies. That evening Joe was frying the flapjacks, and a pleasant aroma from the cooking mingled with the tang of burnt timber and the fresher scents of the unburnt forest just across the creek. Then suddenly he laughed, and called me from the tent. "Here's a young fellow out of a circus," he shouted. "Come and look at the animated windmill!"

Raising the tent flap I beheld a blackbear cub, about the size of a Rugby football, seated on the opposite side of the fire and begging in the most approved fashion. Not only was he begging, but he was also saluting most skilfully with both arms, dragging each paw in turn quickly over his ears, and creating curious sucking noises, his small pink tongue outstretched towards the frying-pan. This habit of saluting is, I have found, quite common among bear cubs when they scent something very appetizing, and it may possibly be an instinctive movement, designed to keep the bees out of their ears should the tempting food be honey!

"Poor little fellow," said I. "He's evidently lost his mother!"

Joe nodded. "A good many of them do," he observed, for the fact of the matter is that when forest fire comes, the she-bear with small cubs has to choose between water deep enough to cover her and the chance of her cubs drowning, or the shallow water for the cubs and a roasting for herself. I have seen a good many she-bears going about with their backs terribly burnt during the fire season, and after a bad fire the woods are full of little orphan cubs. "At all events," Joe added, "we shan't get rid of him now he's smelt the grub till we've given him a good feed."

Out in the woods food of the kind one cannot catch or shoot is precious, and we had no thought of feeding this little woodland tramp on our flapjacks and maple syrup. The poor little bloke was obviously weak from hunger, and as I approached he came ambling up to me, and standing with his hindpaws on the toes of my moccasins, and his forepaws on my knees, he looked up into my face with pleading whimpers. It was an appeal no man could resist, though at the moment it struck me as strange that this little creature, who had never seen a human being before, should know at which end of the body the face would be.

"Don't pick him up," warned Joe. "They can bite like mischief!" But something prompted me to ignore the warning, and, possibly out of bravado, I did pick him up, and certainly he had not the faintest idea of biting. "We've plenty of rice," I pointed out; "why not a boiling of rice and a spot of maple syrup?"

We were hungry, but we simply had not the heart to sit down to our own food with that child-like little creature looking on, so Joe made up a good mess of rice and boiled it well, saying that uncooked rice would "do in the little beggar, sure as little apples".

On later experiences, in view of the stones, leather goods, bits of cloth, and large pieces of wood which Mooween — that was what we named him — ate daily while he was with us, I rather doubt whether we need have cooked the rice at all; but, having boiled and chilled it, we added a little maple syrup and put it down for Mooween. There was about as much as a couple of lusty men could have eaten, but Mooween went straight through it, and even then, while we ate our own supper, he scrambled all over us, trying to grab the food from our hands.

We expected him to amble off when the food was out of sight, but nothing of the kind. He was still young enough to follow anything he saw moving, and all that evening he was under our feet, causing a good deal of merriment by his clumsy antics.

"We shall have to get rid of him," said Joe. "He'll steal all the grub in the camp." We had already hung our food packs from a branch.

So we took him down to the creek, and having given him something to chew we slipped out of sight and ran, making a detour back to camp, where we promptly turned in. Even full-grown blackbears are very short-sighted, and there was no difficulty in giving Mooween the slip, but scarcely were we asleep on our brushwood mattresses when I was awakened by an exclamation from Joe. Mooween had "come home", and so great was his delight that he scrambled all over us just like a friendly little puppy.

So there was nothing for it but to induce Mooween to quieten down and go to sleep. He took his place between the two of us, and thus started our strange friendship.

Mooween slept like a log, contributing at least his warmth to the small of our backs, till the daybreak brought the thin, plaintive call of the little brown bird of the thickets, and somehow the idea of trying to give him the slip never again occurred to us. Why we christened him Mooween I cannot now recall, but if memory serves me rightly it is the Chippusay Indian for blackbear; nor can I clearly recollect the sequence of the next few weeks. Certain incidents stand out very clearly in my mind—namely that Mooween was the silliest well-meaning lump of an animal I ever knew. There were not many ways in which he could cause offence out there in the woods, but he, of course, suffered from an entire lack of inherited knowledge as to the ways of man and the affairs thereof. Since man fed him, he was endowed with the idea that everything we owned was good to eat!

There is one small luxury of life which, no matter how stony and remote the corner of God's earth, I have always refused to forgo—a sponge! I used to hang my sponge to air from the ridge cord of the tent, much to Joe's disgust. Joe was ashamed of my sponge. He hated other prospectors to see it. "Who ever heard of a prospector carrying a sponge?" he would say. "If you must have such a thing, you might at least keep it out of sight!"

Well, Mooween put an end to the sponge business, for he ate my sponge, every fragment of it, then went down to the creek and drank about a gallon of water, and according to Joe one could see him swell as the sponge became saturated inside! Needless to say, all this occurred when I was away from camp, and I am inclined to think that there was a certain amount of co-operation in the disposal of that sponge.

Every man has his weaknesses, and one weakness of Joe's was that he *would* remember what was the day of the week. Every evening he would tell me solemnly that it was Tuesday or Saturday, or that tomorrow would be Sunday. It annoyed me immensely. Not being of a mathematical turn of mind I did not care what day it was, and did not want to know. What matter the day, there in God's vast infinite forests, where one's duties were set, anyway—the great distances, the clear sunsets, and just to awake with the dawn? Moreover, Joe possessed one outstanding vice—he *would* shave on Sundays! He would get busy with his hunting-knife and hack off the topmost straggling growth of beard; then, with endless soap and lather, would come the final painful task of clearing away the undergrowth! Other prospectors are content to let their whiskers grow till they get back to civilization, and then pay a barber to do the job properly in having an all-round trim-up. Not Joe. Sunday was Sunday, and meant having a shave!

But Mooween put an end to all that nonsense.

One morning when I went back to camp after hauling in the fish-net, I found Mooween moaning and lathering, but nevertheless making steady headway with Joe's shaving-soap. He had already eaten half of it, but though the spirit was still willing the flesh was beginning to weaken, so I put some sugar on the remaining bit of shaving-soap and Mooween lathered and slobbered right through it.

When Joe came back after his dip in the creek, I told him that the cub had eaten his shaving-soap, and thereupon there occurred one of the worst rows we ever had in a long partnership. We did not have many rows. Our friendship was of the kind which man makes but once, or at the best twice, in a lifetime. Truly we had rows of a kind. Sometimes we hated each other with a very deadly hatred; then Joe would be late back from the creek, or I would be late back, and then the other would think about the danger of rapids, and the many manifold perils which beset a man travelling alone in such places. And when the one who was absent for so short a time from the camp fire finally turned up, the other would wave cheerily and shout the greeting: "Come on, old son. Supper's ready. Thought you'd drowned your ugly old self!"

"Joe," said I, "the bear cub's eaten your shaving-soap," and Joe stared at me. For some seconds, he was speechless, then he stammered out: "Darned little varmint!"

I never saw a man so het up. "Eaten it *all*," I went on re-
morselessly, "silver foil and everything. That's the end of your
shaving business, anyway."

Joe glared. "You gave it him!" he accused me.

"I never did," I asserted. "You evidently left it on the ground.
You know he thinks anything on the ground is his for the
taking." Joe sat on a log and thought. "Bet you encouraged
him!" he finally said. "Bet you put sugar on it or something!"
We faced each other squarely. "What about my sponge?" I
asked, "Bet you soaked it in maple syrup and let it drop off its
hook."

"Your *sponge!*" sneered Joe.

"Your shaving-soap!" I hissed; while meantime Mooween,
seated at the tent entrance, made quite the strangest bubbling
and hissing noises.

"It's a dirty trick, anyway!" rumbled Joe.

I laughed. "How can eating a bit of soap be called a dirty
trick?" I demanded. It struck me as hugely funny. I lay down
to laugh, and Mooween at that moment, while Joe sat and
glowered at him, was physically ill—if you understand my
meaning!

It was customary for one of us, last thing in the evening, to
climb to the highest available point in order to survey the surrounding country for forest fires, and some of the views thus
obtained live in my memory to this day. Often from some high
outcrop we overlooked thousands of miles of forest, the nearer
valleys touched with the most exquisite colouring—chains of
blue and green lakes, sweeping uplands of cedar, tinted with
the lighter green of birch and poplar, and fading into the distance, ridge after ridge of palest indigo, till one could not discern
where forest ended and the haze of sky began.

On one such perfect evening, Joe and I and Mooween climbed
to the rocky ridge together. For the most part our lives were
shut in by the eternal forests. We lived in the forest's shadows,
but at that high point there was for once open sky overhead

— sky of the clearest, deepest blue, across which white clouds were scudding.

For the first time Mooween noticed the sky. He sat on end and whined at it. He reached up at it with his forepaws, licking and sucking at the clouds, till he overbalanced backwards, and regaining himself forgot where the sky had been. He looked round for it in all directions, and Joe and I tried to point it out to him. We held him in our arms tummy upwards, but could not make him look any further than our chins and our sunhats. We sat him on end and pointed his nose to the sky, but he could not see it. We did everything possible to make him look up, but Mooween had got the focus once by accident, and he never got it again. I don't suppose that from that day on he ever again noticed the sky.

One thing Mooween knew — that our canoe was a safe rendezvous. When we were travelling he would sleep for hours in the waist of it among the packs, and never stir. On land he usually ambled about within close touch of us, but he possessed an uncanny instinct for knowing if it were to be a serious landing or whether we were just going ashore for a look-round. In the latter circumstances, he would remain sleeping in the canoe till we returned, for he possessed a wonderful capacity for sleep. Given one good meal, he would sleep for long periods, and never trouble about food for several days unless it came his way. When it came his way he was invariably ready for it.

The turn-back must be made, and though one was longing for the sight of one's fellow men, for the comforts of civilization, for the glimmer of the street-lamps and the crowded pavements, it was always with a sense of sadness that the turn was made. Yet as the days pass, and the grub pack becomes slighter still, one paddles with growing haste to be back to the city again — but how soon its charm dies, how soon the great silence calls once more! And it is a strong call, which takes many years — nay, more than half a lifetime — to die!

So back we had to go, and one day, when we were nearing civilization, Joe broached the question which was in both our minds. Little Mooween was much like a dog to us. "He'd be far better off in his own woods," said Joe. "How can we get rid of him?"

We were thinking of the tame bears we had known in the mining-camps — bears which as cubs were every man's darling, but they outgrew that stage. One sees them in later life, mangy, chained among mud and garbage heaps, fed on offal by the "cookie", or anyone who happens to think about them — robbed of their natural powers, and dependent upon man, who has no further use for them.

But both of us knew that the city would not claim us for long, and when we returned to the woods Mooween could return with us. Meantime we had taught him to feed himself. We had rolled over logs for him to reveal the insects underneath, till he had learnt to roll logs for himself. He was dependent upon us for very little, for goodness knows we had little to give. If we were in the canoe all day, we trolled a spinning bait for fish, and Mooween always got his share of the catch. For some time past he had received nothing from us save such fish and game as might be to spare, so when given his freedom he could very well feed himself.

Yet Mooween accompanied us back to civilization. We struck an outlying mine, where the three of us were feasted. Mooween was given a large blueberry tart, but he did not like the mine very much. There was too much noise and stir, too many strangers; and having eaten the tart he went into a corner and growled, looking up at the roof and round at the walls.

The manager's wife gave him a bottle of cider-pop, which proved to be some kind of sweet cider. Mooween knew just how to deal with bottles, and he drank it all. But it made him helplessly tipsy, and in the end he fell into a ditch and lay there on his back with his legs in the air. We carried him back to the canoe.

Next morning he went down to the creek and drank gallons and gallons of water, and while he was at it the purr of a motor-launch sounded in the distance. Mooween listened, and when the launch appeared he sat spellbound, staring at it — a canoe without paddles! He watched it pass within fifty yards of him, and when it was past and gone, he ran to Joe in such a state of alarm that he knocked Joe's legs from under him. It occurred to us that had there been a "sportsman", of the kind not unknown in the north country, aboard the launch, Mooween, sitting there, might have got a rifle bullet, so we tied a crimson handkerchief about his neck to show that he belonged to someone.

That day we got back to Porcupine, and with us a very unhappy and uneasy little bear cub. He was not heavy to carry, but we managed him in turn, and when anyone came to speak to us he would poke his head out of sight under our arms. He saw a white motor-boat lying keel upwards on the shore, and that disturbed him immensely. Human laughter filled him with fear and dread, though goodness knows Joe and I had been laughing at him nearly all his days. He was terrified of losing sight of us, and if for a moment we put him down, he would paw and drag at our legs till we took him up again. He did not want food, he did not want to be amused, he only wanted to hide his face under Joe's or my jacket, and all the time he seemed to be saying: "Come on. Let's go back to the woods, just you and me and Joe!"

They would not accept a bear cub at the hotel, so we went to another prospector's cabin, and finding him away from home we broke in and took possession of his quarters. We got a box for Mooween and made him comfortable in a corner, and for a whole week he slept off the effects of the bottle of cider.

Then one day I took him in the canoe to see a friend who was in charge of an outlying mine, and on the way out Mooween bucked up, for he knew well enough that our faces were towards the Great Unsurveyed. Only he was worried at Joe's absence; he could not understand a canoe with only one man in it, and kept walking about and looking under my pack for Joe. Finally we reached our destination, and as we walked up from the landing-stage towards the mine I heard the familiar call of "Fire!" rather nearer to us than I cared for. A few seconds later there was a terrific explosion of dynamite only a few yards away, and great boulders of rock went crashing through the trees over our heads. At that moment I looked around for

Mooween. He was sitting in the centre of the trail just behind me, looking at me with his little pig-like eyes, and in that look there was a world of meaning. It said: "Strangers, motor-boats, houses with roofs—all these things have I endured, but dynamite I cannot stand. Good-bye, old chum! I'm off!"

He turned and dashed into the bush, his nose towards the North Pole, his red handkerchief about his neck, and I knew from his manner of going that he would not turn back. He was seen at Mattagami next day, still running towards the north. He fell into the river without noticing it, and swam across. Maybe he is still running—I do not know, but at all events he took the wise choice of returning to his own people and to his own land.

Much water has passed under the bridge since then, but often I wonder—is Mooween still living among those forests we knew and loved so well?

Even as I think of him the vividness and fragrance of it all come back to me—the memory of a period which one might term the War of the Sponge and of the Shaving-soap—and, perhaps, most vividly of all, I recall a little barrel-shaped bear cub, reaching up and trying to suck the sky.

FOUR

BEARS IN THE
WILD

The Battle of the Bears

EGERTON R. YOUNG

The tendency among children's writers has been to see bears as people in fur coats. The writer here relates a story of two rivals in love who settle their differences finally, violently, as humans might.

"Chist! Oomah! Look there!" Thus whispered Curlyhead in two languages.

My gazing had been in another direction, and so before I could see what had excited my Indian canoemen, with their strong paddles they had arrested the onward movement of our canoe and had paddled back behind a great rock.

"What is the matter now?" I asked, for, from my lack of alertness or duller vision, I had failed to observe anything unusual. But these keen-eyed hunters, whose very existence often depended upon their alertness, had caught the one glimpse for which they had been eagerly looking. It was that of a great black bear far ahead of us, sunning himself on the shore.

We had had signs of bear during the last two or three days. Not only were there numerous tracks on the sandy shores of the different lakes and rivers, but at several points where the whitefish, pike, mullets, goldeyes and other fish are abundant in the waters we found the fishing grounds, or rather flat rocks, on which the clever bears seat themselves, from which, with a good deal of skill and cleverness, they succeed in throwing out of the water, with their long arm-like forepaws, numbers of the finny tribe.

Bears are very fond of fish, but they are more or less fastidious in eating them according to the quantity they capture. When a bear goes fishing, he does not generally, unless ravenously hungry, eat the first fish he captures. If he thinks he has secured a fishing spot, where his sharp, keen eyes, even if they are small ones, tell him that fish are here plentiful today, he patiently continues fishing, sometimes for hours, until he has skilfully thrown a goodly number of them out on the shore. His preference among all is the delicious whitefish. If at one fishing he is fortunate enough to catch a number of them, he is so dainty in his tastes that he will only bite out and eat the rich oily part of the fish just back of the head. If he has not caught a sufficient number to furnish him a hearty meal on those favorite parts he also eats the next best portions.

If his fishing luck has been poor that day and he has caught but few, he greedily devours them all, with the exception, perhaps, of a head or two, and it may be some tails and bones.

Thus it was that the Indian hunters, as they found these various places, where the bears had been fishing, and then dining, could always tell by the remains of the dinner what success they had had in their last fishing at that spot.

As I have mentioned, the watchful, experienced eyes of my Indians had detected several of these fishing rocks and dining-rooms of the bear, during our canoeing of the previous days, and so this early morning they were on the alert for a sight of these clever fish-catching bears. And now sure enough here was one of them, and a fine handsome fellow he was, as noiselessly gliding round the shoulder of the big rock, we surveyed him at our leisure. My telescope, which made my sight-seeing about equal to that of the Indians with their naked eyes, enabled me to see him perfectly, as there, at that early morning hour, he, after his night's rest, rolled himself about lazily in the sand like a great black Newfoundland dog. He was evidently in good humor and not hungry; and my men said, as they watched him, that he must surely be the bear whose fishing rock we had found the previous evening not many miles in our rear. As a matter of precaution bears do not generally sleep near where they have been fishing even if they have left there some fish that they could not devour. They prefer their fish fresh in the season, and, having satisfied themselves, and indifferent as to the future, they generally go away some distance ere they cuddle down to sleep in a cosy spot, exactly as does a dog. Contrary as it may seem to the impression of many, the black bear is naturally a peaceful animal and does not generally begin a quarrel unless he has some good reason for it. He is timid and alert and harder to approach than is a deer. Meet him unexpectedly on a trail in the forest, and he is as frightened as you are; and unless he is provoked by your wounding him, for he is very quick tempered, or by a great display of cowardice on your part, you will find him delighted with any reasonable excuse for retiring from your presence, with all alertness possible, consistent with his ideas of safety. For some time we watched the bear's antics as he rolled himself about in the warm sand and then by way of variation sat up on his haunches, and with his forepaws struck at the deer-flies and other similar pests that worried him.

Lest we should be discovered, or our presence even suspected by him, we again drew back behind the rock. There my men discussed the best means for his capture. I mildly protested again the delay. I said that a half day at least would be lost, and then game more agreeable to our taste than bear's meat had been so abundant that our canoe was well filled with the choicest of meat. I also added, that even if they did succeed in killing him, his skin would not be nearly so valuable now as it would be some months hence in the colder weather.

When my words and requests were emphatic, they were always listened to by my Indians and promptly carried out. But today, somehow or other, they seemed to lack the snap which always brought the prompt compliance with them, and these men, quick to read me, said, with the merest twinkle of the eye:

"Ookemou (master), wish to go on or see a bear hunt?" When there is a disposition to surrender we are easily conquered. So I capitulated and said: "Well, show me a first class one, and be quick about it."

The first thing they did was to withdraw the charges of duck-shot from their guns and reload them with bullets. Their flint guns will throw a ball about a hundred yards as well as an ordinary rifle. My Martini-Henry rifle was charged with a fresh cartridge, while my men gave a quick glance at their sheath knives to see that they were in perfect condition, for in a bear fight no one knows what may happen.

The next thing now was to get near that bear. This was no easy matter. Such was the nature of the muskegs or swamp behind him that there was no possibility of getting at him in the rear. There was, however, a small rocky island not more than sixty or seventy yards from the sandy beach on which he was now resting. The Indians, knowing the restless nature of bears, said that it was hardly likely that he would remain here very long, but they would try any way a scheme that might possibly work. So we began at once to carry it out. We paddled back a little further up the river and then quietly landed on the shore on the opposite side of the river from the bear. From this place where we landed we made a portage by carrying our canoe and its contents along in the forest parallel to the river but well out of sight and scent of the bear. When directly opposite that little island, which was now between us and the bear, we noiselessly launched and loaded our canoe and quietly paddled across the river and landed on that island on the op-posite side from the bear and therefore out of his sight.

Hardly had we landed and secured our canoe and then taken possession of our guns, before we heard the angry: "Woof! Woof!" of the bear. Thinking that in some way or other he had got some knowledge of us, we crouched flat on the ground. My Indians were surprised and perplexed. The wind was dead in our faces, so he had not got any scent of us and they were sure they had made no noise that could have been heard. So we lay low and waited. But we had not long to wait. The "Woofs! Woofs!" were repeated again and again, and so Cur-lyhead, our most experienced bear hunter, quietly crawled for-ward to see what was the matter.

As these ominous sounds were still heard we waited with some impatience for his return. The gleam of the hunter was in his eye when he, noiselessly like a snake, crawled between us and reported what he had seen. His story was that the bear, which he had already seen, was still about where he had first observed him on the sand, and that coming slowly toward him was a family of black bears consisting of the father and mother bear and a couple of cubs, about four or five months old. It was evident by the way that the two male bears were snarling at each other that they were enemies and, perhaps, had been rivals, and anyway a big fight would doubtless soon take place between them. He also added, from his experience of bears' battles, that as they were now so wild at each other they would not be so alert in watching against other enemies.

"We can carefully get higher up among the rocks and see the battle and then fire when we think best. But," he added, "be very careful for that old mother bear may act as sentinel and discover us if we give her a chance."

Strange, is it not, how some things excite us? Do what I could, I could not keep my heart from loud thumping or my breath from coming fast and hard. Christian or heathen, what is it in us that at the prospect of such a fight throws us into such agitation? It was not any idea of danger; for here on this island, heavily armed, we were absolutely safe. If those bears got one sight or scent of us they would rush away as speedily as the most timid deer. Yet here I was strung up with this almost uncontrollable excitement, as holding on to my rifle, I carefully crawled along under cover of the rocks ahead. We reached our points of observation before the battle began.

It was evident, Curlyhead whispered to me, that they were old fighters, who had met before, as like experienced gladiators they seemed to wait for an unguarded moment on the part of each other.

In the meantime the mother bear had settled down on her haunches on the sand in utter indifference as regards the fight. When either of her cubs, as they frolicked and wrestled with each other, happened to come near her, she seemed to delight in giving it a cuff that tumbled it over in the sand. Warily moving around on their hind legs, the two great bears kept up their growlings, evidently getting more angry and exasperated with each other, but each loth to begin the conflict. A quiet laugh from Curlyhead as we called him, but his right name was Mache-que-quo-nape, who was crouched close beside me, almost startled me. Quietly I listened while he whispered:

"Those old bears are just jawing each other. They both wanted the same wife. They had a big fight once before about her, and as one bear in the fight got a bad bite that made him lame, the other fellow ran off with her. We Indians," added Curlyhead, "say that the bear, because his paw is so like the hand, has a little human in him, and so there those two bears are scrapping just like two men about a woman." And again he chuckled quietly to himself, for he had had his own troubles.

How much more of this quaint Indian lore I would have heard I know not if it had not been abruptly brought to a close, for now the two bears suddenly sprang at each other and were locked in the terrible embraces of each other's great muscular arms. It was an awful struggle, and even my seasoned Indians could not keep from being intensely excited. Standing on their hind feet and wary, the bears struggled in the greatest wrestling match imaginable. The grip they had on each other was what the boys call a back-hold and of equal advantage, as each bear had one forearm under and the other over his opponent. As they put forth their enormous strength it did not seem to us that their efforts were so much directed to down each other as to try to squeeze out the very life. The power of the hug of a bear has enlivened and electrified many a yarn, and has to many a poor hunter been his death or nearly so. And now here to see two great, muscular, full-grown bears, full of jealous hate, practising these hugs on each other — well, it was a sight but seldom seen.

Strange to say, they did not use their teeth much on each other. They both seemed to hope that the hug trick would do its work. But as carefully balancing themselves on their hind feet, which they kept wide apart, as they continued the desperate struggle, they seemed both to realize that some other method of fighting was necessary, and especially as they were so horribly enraged. So in a short time they began most vigorously to tear at each other's head and neck as well as they could, altho not for a moment letting to their grip on each other.

Tough as bearskin is, it could not stand this very long, and so the end came very suddenly. All at once we noticed that the great forearms of the bear that had come with the family fell limp by his sides and then he quickly sank on the sands. The other bear, loosening his grip, watchfully stood over him as tho suspecting a trick, but as there was no movement beyond some convulsive jerkings he drew back a yard or two and watched him to his death. Then he moved away to the female bear and her cubs. A little conversation and some mutual explanation doubtless took place and they began moving away.

My Indians wanted to fire at them, but I positively forbade them. "Fire your guns to hurry them off but do not hit them," I said, and raising my own rifle I started the music by sending my bullet close enough to make the sand fly near them. The Indians also fired and away sped a newly organized or reorganized bear family.

We hurried back to our canoe and when we reached the dead bear we found that his opponent, with his sharp teeth, had cut thru his jugular vein, and so he had bled until exhausted, and then fell, as we saw him, on the sand.

Kootznahoo, Home of the Bears

FRANK DUFRESNE

While some hunters are becoming conservationists, the scientists just can't leave bears alone. The bears may still, on occasion, make their opposition to investigation known, however.

I'd spent enough time among the bears with the famous Alaska guide Hosea Sarber to realize this would be a day of danger. It was during the second week of our bear census in the dark wilderness of Admiralty Island, known to the Indians as *Kootznahoo*, Home of the Bears. We left our anchored patrol vessel at daybreak, rowed our skiff to the river mouth and began wading upstream toward an experience I have never forgotten.

Sarber, with his .30–06 rifle cradled across his arm in case of sudden attack, led the way. I followed with a bucket of plaster of Paris for casting sample bear tracks. Salmon so filled the shallows there wasn't room to set our boots without touching off a flurry of splashes. On the gravel shores, eagles and ravens and gulls haggled over the salmon scraps left by the bears.

It would be like this, Sarber said, all the way upriver for three miles to a point where we could see a cataract leaping off a flat mountain-top, bouncing from ledge to ledge and finally disappearing among the tree tops. At the bottom of this waterfall we'd find an almost solid mass of humpback and dog salmon churning and hurling themselves at the thudding column of snow water. In this mist-filled evergreen jungle, where scarcely a human had ever made a footprint, there'd be a concentration of salmon — and of sour-tempered grizzly and brown bears unequaled for variety and numbers anywhere else in the world.

That was why Sarber planned to reach the falls at sun high, when most of the bears would have had their morning fill of fish and be bedded down in the timber. We'd already worked out a formula for counting the bears without seeing them. We'd discovered that their pad prints were as individual as human fingerprints. Some were hamshaped, some oval, and some almost as narrow as the track of a human. Each track showed scratches, pore patterns, twisted and broken claws unlike those of any other bear. We recognized the cubs because their pad marks measured only four inches wide, whereas the old, half-ton boars left deep impressions we couldn't cover with our hats.

We wouldn't kill a bear unless we had to. In fact, it would be all right with us if we didn't even see one all day. But ten minutes later a rust-colored hulk erupted from the river with a salmon in its jaws, ambled ashore, and faced us across a gravel bar no more than forty paces away. Never taking its eyes off us for a moment, the bear spread itself flat across the stones like a wet rug and devoured its fish, leaving head, tail and backbone for the two gulls that were hopping and screaming within inches of its chomping jaws. Only after it had finished its meal did the bear turn its back on us and stroll casually into the forest shadows.

Hosea, who disagreed with the naturalists who credited five species of grizzly and brown bear to Admiralty Island, nevertheless made a stab at nomenclature. "Near as I can tell," he said, "that was the bear that Dr. C. Hart Merriam classed as *Ursus mirabilis*, the strange grizzly. It's trigger-tempered and unpredictable like all the grizzlies, but it isn't as big and dangerous as another one we'll be running into up at the falls."

He waited while I fixed a batch of plaster and poured it into a hind track. "Old native name for the big brute is Black Hoots,

239

the Killer," he offered. "The Indians weren't just flapping their lips, either, because I've helped carry some of its victims out of the woods on stretchers."

I lifted the plaster cast, an operation Hosea regarded with tolerant amusement, and marked it for identification. We moved on upstream past well-trodden bear trails leading down off the timbered spurs to the river. On either side of us the banks were cluttered with grizzly tracks, and their tunnelings led through salmonberry patches from one river bend to the next.

Beyond the last muskeg, Sarber watched carefully as he slipped along in the permanent gloom of the great spruce trees, the moss-draped hemlocks and old growth cedars. Their branches laced together across the river, leaving only occasional open patches through which the sun shafts came probing like search-lights to illuminate the hordes of spawning salmon. Schools of red-spotted Dolly Varden trout snapped at the pea-sized eggs floating among the thrashing humpies and dogs. The shadows were alive with flapping wings and shrieking birds come to join the summer feast. There were mysterious rustlings of un-seen things in the understory of brier and devil's-club thickets. It was an eerie place where a bear attack could come in a split second.

Though we had been but one bear, we'd passed the sign of at least twenty others that had winded us and chosen to steal quietly into the cover of the forest. Twice we saw sprinkled trails leading from the river across the dry pebbles, and once as we cut over a sandbar Sarber laid a forefinger against his lips and pointed to salmon in our path. A bite had been taken out of its back and it was still kicking.

As we neared the base of the cataract the stream canyon became almost opaque with mist. Giant trees wore swaying shrouds of gray moss. It was a place for bears, I thought, not people, and then a sudden squalling of gulls and ravens ahead brought Hosea's thumb to the safety of his rifle. But by the time we came sloshing around the river's turn there was nothing in sight except a hassle of birds around another flopping fish. My eyes were scanning about for a clean-cut pad print in the silt when Hosea spoke out of the corner of his mouth. "You want to see the biggest dang brute on the island, turn around real slow and look behind you."

I swung my head, not slow but fast, because I'd already caught a flash of its movement. It had pushed soundlessly out of the devil-clubs, and now it reared up alongside a big water-logged snag to study us, then dropped back on all fours. When my eyes met it full I couldn't help gasping. The animal was huge; it was black as a load of coal, and for all its bulk appeared to be nimble as a cat. It was a fearsome sight, yet Sarber did not shoot. He had noticed that the rounded ears of the beast were fanned erect, not buttoned back like those of a bear in a killing rage. Its teeth clacked loudly and drops of foam fell from its jaws, but the sideways hops it made toward us were more bluster than the headlong charge of a bear in full attack, and it appeared to be kicking up an unnecessary fuss in the water as it bounced nearer.

When it reached a shallow spot fifty feet away it jumped up and down stiff-legged until it had swatted the pool into bubbles, then abruptly froze in its tracks and glared at us like a giant ogre. Sarber, with rifle sights lined up on a spot between the two burning eyes, spoke comforting words. "The black devil is bluffing." But his cheek remained pressed against his rifle stock. "Maybe," he added. The great bear could change moods in an instant and we both knew it. If the ears of the bear went down, if it started licking its tongue across its lips, if it lowered its enormous head, if it came any closer, Sarber would have to shoot.

An accident broke the spell. The tin bucket suddenly slipped from my sweaty fingers and rolled clattering across the sloping rocks toward the river. The bear gave a startled *huff*! Neither of us moved a muscle as the monster swung its head ponderously, took another long look at us, then shuffled slowly away. Its shaggy rump looked as big and unreal as a hairy mammoth's as it disappeared into the underbrush. Sarber was only partly satisfied. "We'll see that big boy again," he promised.

Below the falls another sight as undisturbed by civilization as if it were still in the Ice Age greeted us. The pounding water of the lofty cataract had ground a deep basin out of solid granite, and it was now choked with salmon that had unknowingly reached the end of the line for them. Already past the last spawning gravel in the river, they continued to jump blindly, battering their shining bodies against the wet rocks, only to be hurled back into the boiling caldron where tons of them went washing around and around in a slithering mass.

Two yearling grizzlies, soaked as drowned rats, were dodging in and out of the showering falls, catching and releasing salmon and galloping over the slippery rocks in a furious game of tag. They went scooting into the dark timber when they caught our scent, and later we found enough morning sign to indicate that at least thirty bears had been feasting on the doomed fish.

Later, in going over our notes, Hosea and I figured our bear count for the three-mile stretch of river to be not less than sixty. If the rest of Admiralty Island's salmon streams averaged as well, we'd wind up our census with close to a thousand bears for this one island. To make the figures even more astonishing, all the bears were in a National Forest visible to tourists on steamers plying between Petersburg and Juneau on Alaska's Inside Passage.

"And five kinds of them," I reminded Hosea, though I knew that neither he nor any other Alaska guide would agree with the "experts" who named new subspecies sometimes from examination of a single skull. I started to name the Admiralty bears as listed by Dr. C. Hart Merriam: Island grizzly, Admiralty grizzly, crested bear, strange grizzly . . . Hosea cut me off. For him there was but one bear on Admiralty. It was the massive, almost pure black Shiras bear, one of the most striking-looking predators in existence.

As long as he lived, Hosea Sarber never changed his mind about this dark, brooding giant found only on Admiralty Island. And Ralph Young of Petersburg, the man who succeeded Hosea as the most active bear man in Southeastern Alaska, shares his old friend's views. Like Hosea, Ralph Young scoffs at the "swivel-chair biologists" who ascribe five species of brown and grizzly bears to an island only eight-five miles long and barely twenty-miles wide. Young recognizes, at most, a medium-sized, brownish grizzly weighing from 500 to 700 pounds and the black form weighing half a ton or more at full growth.

"If there are five kinds of bears on Admiralty Island," says Ralph Young wryly, "someone has forgotten to tell the bears about it. I've seen big black ones traveling with little brown ones. I've seen a yellow sow-bear with three cubs of different shadings. I've even seen a blue-colored bear on the island." Adds Young with logic, "I think we ought to give up trying to catalogue the Admiralty bears, because when mating time comes they won't obey the rules. We ought just to go along with the fact that here at the mercy of the United States Forest Service is the greatest collection of grizzly bears the world will ever know. We ought to be more concerned on how this Federal organization protects these bears from its logging crews."

At the base of the thundering falls I could find no pad marks to match those of the giant Shiras black; so while Hosea amused himself by counting salmon-gorged eagles sleeping in the snags I dropped down around the bend with my bucket of plaster. A few feet from a stump I found and measured a hind track 10 inches wide by 14 inches long, not counting the claw marks. I sprayed it with gum arabic, poured in the wet plaster reinforced with strips of cloth, and was waiting for the stuff to set when I became aware of a penetrating stench. For a moment the full meaning of it escaped me. Then, suddenly I knew fear. The owner of the huge track had stalked me in dead silence. Somewhere, very close, it was watching me.

Fighting a natural urge to get away from there fast, or to yell out to Hosea, either of which could get me killed quickly, I picked up my bucket as casually as I could and began backing slowly toward the river. As I straightened up I found myself staring directly at a broad, black head that looked as big as a wheelbarrow. The bear had been close enough to breathe down my neck as I worked absorbed over its track, and now I was almost within reach of its great hooked claws. But it was the beast's eyes that held me. They were glaring into mine with a malevolence that I had never seen in those of another wild thing.

I must have gasped aloud at the horror of it. The bear's response was to drop heavily from its squatting position to all fours. I had no possible defense in mind other than flinging the bucket of plaster in its face and diving for the river when I heard Sarber's level voice. "Just keep backing away. Easy."

Hosea had come around the bend, pebbles crunching steadily under his boot soles. The black brute watched his every step until we converged at the water's edge. At that instant it covered half the distance between us in two prodigious bounds. It skidded to a stop in a crashing of stones and let go with belly-deep coughs that echoed through the forest. As it faced us stiff-legged, jaws clacking, I was confident that Hosea could have split its skull with a single bullet, because he was a cool, deadly shot. But he had the ice-water judgment to hold his fire.

It wasn't until we had managed a further retreat to the middle of the river the Hosea spoke again. He said he guessed we were in the clear if we kept moving along and didn't stop for any more foolishness with the plaster bucket. It was midafternoon, I remember. All the bears on the river were heading down from their beds in the timber to fish through the twilight hours.

We sloshed downcurrent, keeping well out from the brush-screened banks. After a while Hosea said somewhat illogically, "You know, these bears really are a peaceable lot; they don't want any trouble." He swung around for a look at the giant Shiras bear huffing and snorting its anger on the gravel bar. "Of course, you got to keep out of their way."

I agreed with this latter remark, and then I said something about our having accomplished our mission on the river, anyway; that we'd got everything we went up there for.

"Not quite," said Hosea with sly humor. "You forgot to pick up your plaster bear track."

Grizzly Tracks

SID MARTY

Bears live mostly in parks, now, where they are protected. But a grizzly is still a grizzly, and a grizzly's charge can still make a man quake.

Few animals are as well adapted as the grizzly bear for survival in an inhospitable environment that is only free from snow for three or four months of the year. The grizzly is a prodigious and eclectic eater of almost anything, equipped with the killing tools of a predator, the opportunistic instincts of a scavenger, and the omniverous tastes and digestive tract which allows it to exist on a largely vegetarian diet. It will graze on grass high on an avalanche slope, acting more like an old cow moose than a fierce predator, licking up any insects it encounters along the way, and digging up plants with its powerful claws to eat the succulent roots. It loves carrion most of all, relying on the wind to bring news of food to its highly developed nose, since, with its dim eyesight, it may not see the message of the wheeling ravens. Grizzlies don't often kill big game animals because, unlike wolves, they lack the instinct to hunt together and drive the quarry into a pocket where it can be cut down. But when conditions are right, if the game is in some natural corner, or is weak or sick, the bear has the speed to run it down, and will kill it with crushing bites of its powerful jaws. A grizzly has the speed to outrun a horse for a short distance and the stamina to run straight up an avalanche slope for a thousand feet without stopping. But it is a careful opportunist; it won't expend energy on the chase unless its instincts tell it the chase will be rewarded.

Both the grizzly and the black bear have a built-in respect for man. Only one thing draws bears to man and that is the smell of human food, including garbage, which to the bear is a delicacy.

Fortunately, there were no campers left in the Tonquin Valley. The rain that had preceded the snow had sent them packing down to the highway. But there was always the chance that more people would be hiking in via Portal Creek and Maccarib Pass, coming in to the Tonquin where Maccarib Creek flows in at the north end of the lake. The bear was headed that way so I decided to follow her and learn what I could about her routes and her temperament. If I met any hikers on the way, there'd be good opportunity to prevent run-ins with the bears by making sure they kept a clean camp, with their grub tied up in a tree.

The horses were out of sight. "Ho, boys!" I called and heard the "pong" of Toby's old brass bell float to me across the meadows, but the sound echoed from the mountains on both sides of the valley, and you could never fix his direction from the first note. "Oats, Toby!" I yelled, like every morning, and heard the bell go "pong, pong," as he lifted his head and nodded a yes to his belly at the prospect of grain. The horses had drifted up the lake shore toward Tom's camp. I thought tonight I'd feed them in the corral, in case they tried to pull out on me, and head down Meadow Creek for Dominion Prairie. That was down on the Yellowhead Highway, safe from early snow. Even with hobbles, they'd pull out if they sensed a blizzard coming, jumping like kangaroos with the front feet moving together, a trick any mountain horse knows well.

I went out with a halter to where they had turned to watch for me, the snow still clinging in patches on their rumps, steam rising from their wet backs. I slipped the hobbles and haltered my saddle horse and the others followed, walking stiffly at first, taking small, shuffling steps as if the hobbles were still on their front feet. We went up to the cabin.

Myrna had seen the tracks. "I'm going to follow her for a while," I told her. "I want to see where she goes, figure out her range a bit better."

"I guess you'll have to bushwhack," she said.

"Probably. I doubt she'll stay on the trails. I may have to lead the horse and climb if she goes up high."

"It's all right. I wouldn't mind taking it easy today. Really," she added, seeing my contentious look.

I'd been expecting more of an argument; she fooled me, as usual.

After breakfast, I buckled on my leather chaps, then went out and tightened Toby's cinch. Myrna brought our coffee out on the porch and we drank it in the sunlight, savouring the flavour of the brew and the smell of spruce and wet meadow grass. I watched the horse pawing impatiently at the snow, anxious to be moving in the chill air. I finished my coffee and set my cup down.

"Hold the fort, sugar," I told her and went over to the horse and untied his lines, "it may be dark before I get back."

"Write if you find work," she said, watching me swing on. "Shouldn't you take the rifle?"

"Naw. The trouble with that rifle is that once you have it, you have a tendency to think you're safe. Bears don't like the smell of gun grease. Best not to get close enough for them to smell it in the first place."

"Good advice," she said. "Just see that you follow it."

I grinned and rode out on the track of the bears. The snow made it easy work, but it would be melted by mid-afternoon, so I took a short-cut across the meadow at the trot, aiming to pick up her sign on the far side again. Just before the tracks led into the woods, Toby shied at a dark object half hidden in the willow shrubs. It was a dark green pile of bear crap, splashed with the brilliant red of soapberry. I got off to have a look at it because a bear's droppings will often give insights into a bear's state of health that would be dangerous to try to obtain by

means of a more intimate inspection of the animal. The crap
on hand was still conveniently firmed up by the night's cold,
despite the enematic effect of the soapberries on the bear's digestive tract. What they see in those acridly bitter lumps of poison
is beyond me, but they will spend days gorging themselves at
berry time, using their claws as rakes to gather in the berries,
or simply eat them branches and all. The size of the scats identified them as the sow's and not the cub's, and the green colour
meant she'd been feeding almost completely on vegetable matter, not flesh, which gives a characteristically dark blackish
colour to the stool. With a stick I broke it up, looking for bone
fragments and animal hair and checking for parasites, but found
nothing but vegetable fibre. The sow was healthy, which was
good, since it made her less likely to try and steal human food
out of desperation.

A big rock fell and clattered down the wall of Paragon Peak
on the far side of the lake. It rolled down the talus slope and
into the lake with a splash. The sun was fully up, and the good
tracking would not last long. Tom Vinson's chainsaw rattled
a half mile to the left, as he cut deadfall on the wood permit
I'd issued to him. He would buck it into eight-foot logs to be
skidded to his camp when the snow was deep enough for them
to slide easily.

The bear tracks led into the dark woods, and I reined in for
a moment to let my eyes adjust to the dim light, after the dazzle
of snow in the bright meadow. The tracks meandered indeci-
sively on the trail of a marten, backing up in disgust from the
marten's pissing post where the pungent weasel scent had as-
saulted the sow's nose. We came out into a narrow meadow at
the foot of an avalanche slope. Here the trail, which had been
steadily gaining altitude, as if to bypass the campground, de-
toured abruptly down a creek to the first tent site, where much
scuffling and arguing had gone on over some fish guts that
somebody had heaved into the creek, and where one cub had
been roundly cuffed out of the way and sent rolling down the
slope like a ball to learn some manners. There were a few bright
scales clinging to the rocks; other than that, the camp's water

supply, fouled by man, had been purified again by the bears, our resident sanitary inspectors.

The sow knew all about campgrounds. She had taken the cubs on a tour all around the tent sites, and their tracks were in the snow on top of the camp tables. I had cleaned up that campground just a few days ago, burning the paper and bagging cans and bottles to be packed out on the horses. The place was spotless, free of human pollution, or at least that's how it appeared to me. The critical nose of the bear mocked my efforts. All through the campground there were little pockets of snow and earth dug up and in each one was a garbage souvenir that campers had buried under a pile of leaves, covered with a rock or stuffed down a ground-squirrel burrow. The sow had scented each one out and dug it up for me; an orange peel, a chocolate bar wrapper, chewed into a wad and spat out again, tin cans, plastic bags, beer bottle caps, and Kleenex — soggy, pink, and ubiquitous — all scattered obscenely on the immaculate white of the snow. I slumped in the saddle and sighed when I came to the old garbage pit that one erstwhile group had dug with their trusty war surplus trenching tools. They had filled the pit in behind them with a couple of feet of dirt, probably figuring that the garbage had been neatly disposed of for all time. Two feet of loose dirt is not even a fair test to a bear's nose. Contemptuously she had raked it all out, spreading broken glass, tinfoil and plastic bags from hell to breakfast for me to clean up.

I tied the horse up and worked for an hour gathering up the smaller bits and pieces that would fit in Toby's saddlebags. The rest I stuffed into a burlap sack carried for that purpose, which I cached in the fork of a tree to be packed out later. Patches of grass were showing through the snow by the time the job was done, and the tracks were erased from the meadow beyond the camp. Back in the saddle, I circled the camp until we cut her sign, picking it up on a higher contour where the snow was shadowed from the melting warmth of the sun under a canopy of spruce. She'd gone up the mountain in a straight line, headed for timberline and the higher meadows that lay beyond. The trail was an overgrown tunnel through the forest, the moss deeply indented by the feet of her ancestors, made impassable to us by the overhanging limbs and deadfall. A big spruce at the entrance was blazed and gouged by the claws of bears that had come this way over the years. A tuft of black hair was stuck to the trunk, glued in a stream of pitch that had flowed out of the wounded tree; memento of some old humpback that had paused to rub its back against the rough bark, relieving a colossal itch.

Toby stopped, his nostrils twitching, smelling bear. "Gitup," I told him, and we went switchbacking up the mountainside, working our way through the trees as we climbed back and forth across her trail, snapping off dead limbs and being generally about as quiet as a bull moose in rut as the horse lunged through the shintangle. The end of a snag slipped under the stirrup leather and Toby stopped, breathing hard. I got off and pulled it out, then began climbing up on foot, leading him. The sweat was running down my face by the time we made it out to timberline, walking through a stand of larch trees, their black branches wrapped with the spun gold of their changed needles. We contoured across to the north until I picked up her trail coming out of the timber near the edge of an old rockslide. She was hunting ground-squirrels and the hunting had been good. We came to a fresh dig where she had shifted a boulder weighing a quarter of a ton to get at the burrows beneath it. There were blood stains and a wisp of gold fur on the dirty snow, all that was left of the ground-squirrel colony.

The horse snorted and backed up nervously. Even I could smell the musky taint of grizzly bear in the ravished earth. An afternoon sun was warming the slopes, and the wind had changed in favour of the sow; blowing up my neck and carrying our scent towards her. A pika, a diminutive relative of the rabbit, squeaked and chittered with alarm from its vantage point halfway up a rockslide. Sensing the bear was near, I quickly got back on the horse and spurred him forward below the slide to where I could see a good line of escape leading down toward the valley of Maccarib Creek. Toby was skittish, worried now that he could no longer get wind of the bear, and not knowing in what direction to look.

She was watching us, but from where? I was sure that she wasn't below us in the timber; she would feel safer if she kept above us. There was nothing in sight on the steepening arc of the horizon; the green line of the meadow was marked only by scattered patches of dwarf spruce and the sharp ridges of Mount Clitheroe rising beyond it. I reined the horse in and waited; no sense moving until we figured out where she was. A flight of pink snow birds spiralled up from the forest below and flitted in a rose-coloured cloud across the patchy snow to land, noisily quarrelling on a clump of dwarf spruce two hundred feet above us. The sow stood up then with a roar and the small birds scattered and tumbled like pink fluff from her shoulders with high pitched, frightened cries.

Toby's ears went up like rockets and he took one step back and froze with his front legs braced. My feet tightened involuntarily in the stirrups, as I began to ease his head to the left again, wanting him pointed the right way, in case he ran into the timber, bucking. Standing seven feet high with her yellowed claws held out in front of her, the sow dominated the horizon, her black form etched against the snow and the blue of the sky, her silver-tipped ruff fanned out in the light. She weaved her head gently back and forth and sniffed sharply, reading our scent, and the sound shivered the air like a bone whistle or the note the wind will make on the lip of a chimney. I shook the reins lightly and Toby took a step sideways, wanting to keep his head toward her, watching. The cubs walked out of the bush then and stood up beside her. One of them dropped to all fours and walked a little ways down the hill towards us, curious to find out what we were.

Her hair was up. "Easy Toby," I said and kicked him around, urging him forward. She noticed the cub, dropped to all fours and came down the hill without warning, letting out a bellow when she ran over the cub in her haste, continuing on in a line that would take her to the right of us. The speed of her charge precluded any motion from us until she had already pulled up and turned to go back to the squalling cub. She cuffed him once, driving him uphill, and he shut up fast, scurrying after his siblings. Then they were gone over the crest and I knew the charge had been a bluff, made out of fear for the cub.

There had been no time to feel fear but now that she was gone I saw my hands trembling on the reins and felt the slightly nauseated churning in the gut that follows a surge of adrenalin and an accelerated heartbeat. "Close enough, Toby," I told the horse and he stepped quickly down the slope following the tree line by way of an answer, snorting and shaking his head as if to say, "I told you so." In a few minutes we reached the mouth of a steep-walled ravine. Looking up, I saw the bears a quarter of a mile above us, moving quickly across the top of the meadow at the base of the cliffs. But she would have to go lower for a while to feed before taking them up to dig a winter den high on an avalanche slope. How long she stayed out after that would depend on her fat and the weather.

Bears

BEN GADD AND JOHN CHALMERS

In the spring of 1984, a radio talk show host invited his listeners to send him their favorite true bear stories. These two represent a very small part of their response.

Here's a bear story from Jasper National Park. The incident occurred along the Icefields Parkway, the road between Jasper and Banff. A young couple were driving along on a warm day in the summer of 1980. They stopped not far from Athabasca Falls and headed into the woods with some wine, some cheese and amorous intent.

Everything was perfect. The sun shone steadily and the wine went down well. Presently the couple had taken their clothes off and were lying in the grass.

Time went by. Then something made the young man look up — right into the face of a bear. The couple jumped up and ran. They didn't stop to get dressed or even to grab their clothes off the ground.

Rushing across the highway, they tried to jump into their car. Ah, but the car was locked, and the keys? The keys were up in the woods in a pants pocket. And here came the bear, which had followed them.

What to do? They climbed up on the car. And there they were, stark naked on the roof, with the bear going round and round the car on its hind legs as carload after carload of incredulous tourists drove by.

Someone reported the situation to the warden at the Athabasca Falls station, just a few minutes' drive down the road. The warden brought his dog, who chased the bear up a tree. The young lady put on the warden's jacket, while the man, still naked, accompanied the warden to the spot where the clothes had been abandoned.

Meanwhile, the bear had climbed down from the tree, ignoring the dog, to defend the clothes. It was all the warden could do to recover the man's clothes; the woman's the bear would not surrender until he had ripped them up. Then he retired, carrying off one of her shoes as a trophy.

And that is how there came to be an occurrence report on file at the Jasper warden's office entitled "The Bare Facts."

Ben Gadd
Jasper, Alberta

Two, imbued with sudden passion,
  By a mountain highway parked,
Locked their car in careful fashion,
  Sought a glade that they had marked.

Hidden by a screen of bushes,
  Underneath the summer sun,
By a lakelet edged with rushes,
  Shed their garments one by one.

But a disapproving critter,
  Clothed in fur like other bear,
Muttered imprecations bitter,
  Though it wasn't his affair.

"Dress as I do" was his motto.
  (Bruin was a hide-bound prude.)
Swift he chased them to their auto,
  Ending their behaviour lewd.

Naked though they were, they scampered,
  Leaving all behind them far,
Lacking keys, they then were hampered,
  Gained no entrance to their car.

To escape the angry ursine,
  Climbed they to their car-top high.
Long that bear they stayed there cursing,
  But delighting passers-by.

John Chalmers
Edmonton

Two Weeks in a Polar Bear Prison

FRED BRUEMMER

When the polar bears gather in autumn, the naturalists gather to watch them.

Day 1—October 21st: The pilot waves, the helicopter rises with a metallic roar and vanishes into the ash-gray void of gently falling snow. John Kroeger and I are alone on the cape. A broad, pebble-covered esker meanders across the cape from east to west, flanked on the north by shallow lagoons, already frozen, and on the south by marshy tundra ponds, hemmed by willow thickets. Two miles to the east, the cape ends in a crescentic, boulder-strewn spur that hooks out into the dark waters of Hudson Bay. Moist snow falls softly, evenly; our world is gray and silent.

A forty-five-foot tower stands on the esker, topped by a tiny hut, our home for the next two weeks. While we haul our provisions up, a polar bear shambles along the esker toward us. He walks slowly, ponderously. He stops, raises his elegant, triangular head; sniffs, weaving slightly from side to side; then shuffles on. He is a young male, high-rumped and low-shouldered, his long fur deep yellow in the gloomy evening light. He seems neither afraid nor aggressive, just intensely curious.

Polar bears assemble near this cape in early winter to wait for ice to form on Hudson Bay. The British explorer David Hanbury camped at this spot in 1898 because "polar bears were said to be numerous here. . . . " It was early September and the bears had not yet come; he waited for ten days and did not see a single one.

Most polar bears of this region spend winter and spring on the ice of Hudson Bay hunting seals. Recent aerial surveys carried out by Thomas G. Smith of Canada's Arctic Biological Station show that Hudson Bay is home to about half a million ringed seals, the polar bears' principal prey.

In July, the prevailing northerly winds drive the disintegrating ice, and the bears, toward the southwest coast of Hudson Bay. Marooned on shore, the polar bears — the largest carnivorous land mammals, with the possible exception of the Kodiak bear — eat anything available: grasses, sedges, seaweed, carrion, berries. They raid eider colonies and eat the eggs. A few wander south as far as Moosonee at the head of James Bay, nearly on the latitude of London, England. Many just sleep, often in shallow pits scooped out on sandy ridges near the sea, living off the fat reserves accumulated during the bountiful hunts of winter and spring.

In fall the bears amble northward, bunching at capes like this, where they impatiently await the freeze-up that will enable them to move onto the seal-rich ice of Hudson Bay again. Surveys by Ian Stirling of the Canadian Wildlife Service, Canada's foremost authority on polar bears, indicate that about 600 bears mass along the 100-mile coastal stretch between the Nelson River south of us and the Churchill River to the north. It is the largest concentration of polar bears in the world.

Our hut sways gently. Beneath us in the dark a polar bear is leaning against the tower.

Day 2 — October 22nd: Three bears sleep near our tower. All are young males, weighing between 250 and 400 pounds. As we clamber down the tower skeleton, they glance up with lazy indifference. One bear rises, yawns, stretches luxuriously, and comes slowly to investigate. He rears up directly beneath us, leans with his huge, sharp-clawed, fur-fringed paws against the tower for support, and looks at us with small, deep-brown, slightly slanted eyes. In an odd way, it's a zoo in reverse. We are the captives, and the bears come from time to time to watch our antics.

Farther north Eskimos who used to hunt polar bears with highly trained huskies now use deadly efficient snowmobiles, and most bears are wary. The quota for the entire Canadian Arctic is nearly 650 bears per year. Along this coast of Manitoba, the bears are protected and, as a rule, show little fear of man. But they are very cautious with each other.

Male polar bears, said the explorer-writer Peter Freuchen, are among "the loneliest creatures on Earth. . . . " They always "keep some distance apart and never approach each other." Our bears not only meet, they spar and play and wrestle. But they do this only after proper introductions have been made. Initial encounters tend to be formal, ritualized, and tinged with mutual apprehension.

A new bear approaches across the dark, wind-polished ice of the lagoon. He stops. His long, sinuous neck sways back and forth, his coal-black nose twitches. His sense of smell is extremely acute. He lives in a world of smells; each breeze carries with it myriad messages. In spring, polar bears are able to detect "nunarjaks," the oval birth lairs of ringed seal pups, beneath three to six feet of hard, compacted Arctic snow.

Our bear trio dozes, but when the newcomer appears on the esker, they rise abruptly, worriedly. One walks toward the new male, and they begin a peculiar slow-motion, ursine pas de deux. They circle and sniff very slowly, heads held low, mouths closed, looking slightly past each other, signaling peaceful intent and mutual respect by subtle body movements, presumably evaluating by smell and sight each other's size, power, temper, and hierarchical standing. They halt and face each other, the hairs on neck and back slightly abristle, an outward sign of latent hostility and fear. They approach each other, the smaller bear, slow and submissive, taking the initiative. They sniff, dark noses touching, jaws agape. They paw and push, rise up on their hind feet and spar, lose their balance and, for one hilarious moment, stand locked in what looks like a passionate embrace. One topples and lies on his back, big paws pedaling in the air. The other, mouth wide open, throws himself on top. But they are very careful, very gentle, like two gigantic, shaggy puppies having a marvelous romp.

By nightfall, our coterie of bears has grown to twelve. All are young males, ranging in age from about three to eight years. All have been mutually "introduced," identified, and classified, and now they largely ignore each other. Most of the time they sleep.

Day 3—October 23rd: The weather continues to be vile. Yesterday it drizzled. Today an icy wind drives hard, granular snow across the land. It hisses past our hut and patters on the panes. A dark-gray gyrfalcon flies low along the esker, soars up, and lands on our hut. It is his lookout in this treeless land. Because gyrfalcons prey heavily on ptarmigan, governors of the Hudson's Bay Company at Churchill, reported the eighteenth-century explorer Samuel Hearne, used to "give a reward of a quart of brandy for each of their heads. Their flesh is always eaten by the Indians and sometimes by the English. . . ." The ptarmigan lie low today. We hear them cackle in the willows, but none appear, and after a while the gyrfalcon flies off.

Toward noon a huge, emaciated bear comes to the tower. We call him Cassius; he has that lean and hungry look. He appears both evil and pathetic. Both ears are torn, and the left one is nearly missing; his eyes are bleary and bloodshot; his head and face are heavily scarred; his nose, broken in some past encounter, has healed askew, giving him a permanent leer; his fur is ragged and smeared with dirt. He walks all hunched up, as if he had a stomach ache. Perhaps he has, for he suffers from diarrhea and squirts out jets of liquid feces from time to time.

He walks directly toward us, hardly pausing to sniff. Our resident bears rise in alarm, circle the gaunt giant, but stay at

FRED BRUEMMER

a respectful distance. He ignores them. He shuffles straight to
the tower, rears, reaches up as high as he can, and tries to hook
John off his perch. He almost succeeds, for he is much taller
than we thought, but John, despite his sixty-seven years, is as
nimble as a squirrel and swings one rung higher. For a moment
the great bear seems baffled. Then he begins to rock the tower
rhythmically, whether in frustration or in the hope of dislodg-
ing us, we shall never know. He looks ancient and decrepit,
yet his strength is awesome. The entire structure shakes and
clatters; the steel guys alternately go slack and tauten with a
crack.

After three minutes he stops and chews for a while on one
of the girders—but not hard enough to damage his teeth—
while frothy saliva oozes from his mouth. Then he sits, staring
at us with a certain yearning. He is at least eleven feet long and,
when fat, might weight 1,200 pounds. In his present state he
probably weighs barely 800 pounds. He hunkers down near the
tower and falls asleep. The other bears keep well away from
him.

Day 4—October 24th: Far out on the lagoon a bear tries to
break the ice. He rears, pounds down with stiff front legs, and
repeats this movement rapidly at least a dozen times. He scrapes
the shattered ice away and picks something from the water,
perhaps sculpins, small bony fish common in these shallow
lagoons, or maybe just a few fronds of seaweed. It seems a lot
of effort for such a small reward.

Given the opportunity polar bears are voracious eaters. A
large male can devour a hundred pounds of blubber at one meal.
The high-calorie blubber is their favorite food. When hunting
is good they eat only blubber and skin, and they do this, as
Stirling has observed, "in a very exacting manner." He watched
a bear in the high Arctic who, after killing a seal, was "carefully
using its incisors like delicate clippers to remove only the fat
from the carcass, leaving the meat." Successful bears leave a
trail of bounty for Arctic foxes, who often follow them in
winter and spring in hopes of leftovers, and for younger, less-

experienced bears. But summer and fall are lean times for the land-bound bears. They sleep a lot, expending a minimum of energy.

Cassius the gaunt came again this morning to give the tower a good shake, but with less conviction and perseverance than yesterday. He has dug a shallow pit in a snowbank and sleeps in it. A young male ambles over in a friendly, inquisitive, diffident sort of way. Cassius wakes and gives him the evil eye. Slightly perturbed, the young bear pauses, sniffs, then very cautiously walks on. The great bear lunges from his pit and glissades across the hard snow like a gigantic penguin, on chin and chest and belly, forepaws pressed to his sides, rump high, hind paws pushing in unison. The young bear wheels and flees. During the day a few more young males walk over to inspect the sleeping Cassius. They get a rude reception, and from then on all our bears leave the old grouch alone.

In the evening a huge bear arrives from the south and walks leisurely down the esker, immense power in slow motion, thick wads of muscle rippling beneath his immaculate, silver-glistening coat. He is not as long as Cassius but is round and sleek and must weigh close to a thousand pounds, a great male at or near his prime. Our entourage of younger males circles him with conspicuous caution and deference. Since he appears regal we call him Caesar.

He snuffles around the tower, licks the pebbles where we have poured down bacon fat with his long purplish tongue, then shuffles toward the snowbank where Cassius sleeps. The old bear gets up instantly. The hairs rise on his neck and back. He puffs out his upper lip and huffs and hisses menacingly, like a cornered cat. The newcomer halts, sniffs, then inches forward. The old bear champs loudly, rapidly; froth trickles from his muzzle. He seems to become more compact. It is the steely tension that precedes a lightning charge. But the great white male does not want to fight. He stands still, head slightly averted, and yawns ostentatiously, which seems to be a signal of appeasement. He slowly backs up and walks off with feigned indifference. Henceforth the two avoid each other.

Day 5 — October 25th: The sun rises, a pale-orange disk over a land infinitely still and serene. A faint roseate blush suffuses the air and delicately tints the sea and ice and bears. In this pearly Monet light, a large flock of ptarmigan settles on the willows near the frozen pond and busily snips the buds. They look like bolls of cotton on the bare bushes.

A polar bear who slept nearby gets up and wanders over, not really hopeful but idly intrigued. The birds seem to ignore him. His walk becomes a stalk, cautious now and tense. At twenty feet he charges, an explosion of fantastic force, a blur of yellow across the ground. The ptarmigan cackle in alarm, clatter upward in a parabolic arc, and settle on bushes farther away. The bear lies down and falls asleep; then, beguiled by the smell of sizzling breakfast bacon, he gets up and ambles toward the tower. Dark clouds shift across the sun. Our world, so briefly luminous, is triste again and gray.

Our morning count is twenty-nine bears. This is not unusual. As many as forty-six bears have been seen at the cape at this time of year. Our presence and our meager gifts of food, particularly sardines — of which, for some reason, polar bears are inordinately fond — no doubt help to attract the bears. Feeding bears is strictly and rightly taboo in the North. In our case, Manitoba conservation officers do not really mind, for any bears we detain at the cape will not wander on to the town of Churchill, where their presence arouses some pride and some anxiety but very little prejudice.

The attitude toward bears was vastly different when I first came to Churchill to study them in the 1960s with Charles Jonkel, then with the Canadian Wildlife Service and now with the University of Montana. Churchill was a boom town then, home to army, navy, and a plethora of government offices. Its population was nearly 6,000, and the annual fall invasion of bears was regarded as a threat that ought to be eliminated or, at best, as a nuisance.

But Churchill has changed. The military has gone, most offices are closed. The population has dwindled to about 800, but these are generally permanent residents, people who like to live in the North. Tourism has become important. Situated at the sea and on the treeline, with birds of coast and taiga and tundra, Churchill is a birdwatcher's paradise. Hotels are full in June and July. More than 1,000 white whales spend the summer near town, in the mouth of the Churchill River.

And fall brings the bears. Churchill now calls itself "The Polar Bear Capital of the World," and visitors come from all over North America and even from Europe and Japan to admire the bears. John guides a tour each fall to see "The Great White Bears." Tourists watch them from the safety of rented cars, from buses, or ideally from all-terrain vehicles that creep along the coast and seem to attract the curious bears rather than frighten them. Town sentiment now is nearly solidly pro-bear. The hotspurs who used to chase the bears with snowmobiles, the killers who shot them from cars at the dump at night, the dumb kids who peppered them with .22s for kicks, have either left or changed their ways.

Our bears rest. Two young males who earlier wrestled and romped now share a snow pit and sleep entwined like lovers. The others lie scattered on snow patches some distance apart, rumps high, hind legs tucked under on either side, heads flat on the ground or, more often, pillowed on folded paws. They are light sleepers. A tiny sound, a whiff of food will rouse them.

At dusk an Arctic fox moseys down the esker, quick and nervy. Like a grayish shadow he slides silently past the sleeping bears, but most awake, glance up, then fall asleep again. The fox searches eagerly around the tower, but our bears have not left a smidgen; they lick the stones where food has fallen and eat the snow touched by a sardine. Disappointed, the fox hurries on and vanishes into the gloom.

Day 6 — October 26th: Our bears are still with us. Some come, some go, but most of those we now know so well remain in the vicinity. Great Caesar sleeps nearby, and Cassius the grouch rarely stirs from his pit. Several bears, including Caesar, have tags in their ears, and I wonder whether Caesar is one of the youngsters I helped to tag back in the 1960s.

The polar bear's realm is immense — five million square miles of circumpolar land and frozen sea. In the vivid imagery of their poems, Eskimos call the polar bear "pihoqahiaq," the ever-wandering one. Once, it was thought that polar bears roamed the top of the world from continent to continent, eternal nomads of the North. They do turn up in the remotest places.

In May 1926 the explorers Lincoln Ellsworth and Roald Amundsen crossed the frozen Arctic Ocean in the airship *Norge* from Spitsbergen to Alaska. Near the "Ice Pole" (86°N, 157°W), "the most inaccessible spot in the Arctic regions," they saw "one lone polar bear track." In 1961, when I traversed the icecap of Spitsbergen with a British expedition, we came across polar bear tracks at the base of Newtontoppen, the highest mountain of the Spitsbergen Archipelago.

But the recapture of tagged bears and recent genetic and morphological studies indicate that most polar bears belong to geographically discrete populations. Bears tagged near Churchill are caught or observed in the same area in subsequent years, and some of the bears we now watch will, no doubt, be here again next fall.

The younger bears often play together, but they avoid the three great males (the third arrived this morning). Casesar has tried repeatedly to make friends with some of the subadults, bears of between 250 and 500 pounds. He walks toward them, slow, friendly, inquisitive, but the smaller bears are tense and apprehensive. They back off and sometimes run.

As soon as food is involved, though, this respect for rank and hierarchy declines. We scatter lunch. Three young bears come immediately and so, a bit behind, does Caesar. The small bears growl but do not budge. They pick and lick the bits of stew and noodles from the rocks. The big bear does not charge or even threaten. He eases sideways and keeps pushing in until his muzzle is only inches from the nearest bear who, still growling and very reluctant, slowly begins to yield. Prior presence at a source of food seems to confer some rights. When the young bears are first, the big males muscle in but are cautious and circumspect, and the meal is usually shared, albeit in a rather tense atmosphere. When a big bear is first and a small bear comes near, the big one growls a warning and, if this is ignored, may turn on the intruder with a roar and chase him away.

Day 7 — October 27th: Until today, all bears at the cape have been males. We have seen females with cubs only in the distance. They shun the cape, for males may kill cubs and have been known to kill the mother as well. Since males usually cluster at the capes, females with cubs tend to wait for freeze-up farther inland.

In the winter of 1969–70, Charles Jonkel discovered a major polar bear denning area in the forest and lake region between the Broad and Nelson rivers to the south of us. Stirling estimates that about 80 females den in Manitoba each winter and roughly 150 cubs are born, usually in December or January.

The cub that now follows a female along the esker is ten or eleven months old, a chubby miniature edition of its massive mother. She is extremely cautious. She walks a bit, with the cub directly behind her or close to her side, stops often, and sniffs. She came from upwind but now has circled to leeward to test the breeze, to take warning from the multitude of messages it carries.

Our resident bears sleep within a few hundred yards of the tower, yellowish humps upon patches of snow. If we scatter food, they may trot up; if threatened by a big male, they may jump aside and trot off. At all other times they move slowly and deliberately. (Because of the polar bear's rolling, ponderous gait, nineteenth-century whalers called it the "farmer.") It should be easy for us to keep track of all bears in the vicinity. Yet they have a disconcerting ability to appear and disappear unexpectedly. Ten minutes ago, I counted fourteen bears near us. Then I watched the female and cub. Now I count again and two are gone, and no amount of searching reveals their whereabouts. For all their bulk and seeming slowness, the bears can move with amazing speed and stealth. They pad along in utter silence, vanish behind a knoll, lie still, and blend with land and snow.

The female and her cub come closer, the mother worried, the cub intensely curious. A young male slowly ambles toward them. The female "talks" to her cub in low grunts. The cub hides behind her but peeks around her broad rump from time to time.

As the young male draws near, the female becomes increasingly hostile: ears flat against her head, hairs slightly raised, head lowered, staring directly at the advancing bear. The male is inquisitive but cautious and signals "peace" as explicitly as he can with every nuance of body posture and movement. He reaches her. They sniff, the female tense and defensive, the male cautiously curious and friendly. The female growls, and the young bear backs off and walks away. The female and cub lie down, but she is nervous. In the evening they leave. Near a little bush, the cub smells something interesting and pauses to poke and sniff. The female walks on, then turns and calls the cub, which obediently joins her.

Day 8-9 — October 28th–29th: It storms. Our tower sways and clanks and groans; the wind wails eerily in the guys and girders. We seem suspended in a swirling world all white; at times we cannot even see the ground. Five bears sleep near the tower, oblivious, it seems, to the icy gusts that reach 70 mph and to the stinging, wind-whipped snow. Triangular drifts build up against the bears; they sleep blissfully. Their thick layer of insulating blubber and dense, oily wool covered by a long, shaggy coat of guard hairs make adult polar bears virtually impervious to the worst Arctic weather.

Only the cubs seem singularly ill-prepared for their midwinter birth: they weigh barely one and a half pounds and are blind, deaf, and naked. In November the pregnant female digs a den in a deep snowdrift, usually in an area that has been used by denning polar bears for untold generations and, most likely, not far from the place where she herself was born. The den may be a simple oval, five to ten feet long and about three feet high, or it may have several chambers. As in Eskimo igloos the entrance tunnel slopes upward so warm air will not escape, and drifting snow usually seals it. Since snow is an excellent insulator, the temperature inside the den may be 40 degrees warmer than the temperature outside. The cubs snuggle into their mother's deep-pile fur and suckle her fat-rich milk. She reclines on her back and cradles the cubs upon her chest with her massive furry paws. When the cubs are cold they cry, and the mother curls up protectively and hugs them closer. The cubs grow quickly. At two months they weigh about eleven pounds, are densely furred, and begin to explore their gloomy world.

The Canadian scientist Richard Harington opened a den on Southampton Island in northern Hudson Bay. "A glistening black eye and twitching muzzle were instantly applied to the aperture by the mother bear. While she paced the den floor beneath us, uttering peevish grunts, we were just able to discern her two young cubs huddled against the far wall of their snow house." When they emerge from the darkness of their den into the dazzling glitter of the Arctic in late March, the cubs weigh a chubby twenty pounds.

During brief lulls in the storm we try to spot the other bears. It is nearly impossible; they have become as one with the land. Old Cassius, buried in his pit, is now just a slight hump on the snowbank, visible to us only because we know the exact spot where he sleeps.

Toward evening of the second day, the storm abates. Here and there, like mounds of snow come to life, polar bears rise and shake themselves. They seem itchy after their long rest. They roll and rub in the snow, twisting and turning with sensuous pleasure, great paws wagging limply in the air. One backs into a willow bush to rub his rump, another slides back and forth across the stunted willows to scratch his belly. Four young males have left the cape; two newcomers, also young males, have joined us. They make the rounds and "introduce" themselves, sniffing the bigger males from a respectful distance, pawing and romping with their peers.

At night the northern lights are spectacular. Constantly changing streamers and whorls and curtains of greenish-white shift and sway across the sky, silent and superb. They flare and flow in eerie splendor against the velvet-black of night, changing to deep violet and back to pale green, the silent dance of spectral fire. They are, say Eskimo legends, the souls of the dead at play.

Day 10—October 30th: It is a glorious day, our first and last. The air is as cool and clear as chilled champagne, the sky a gentle blue, the snow and ice aglitter. Near the coast a red fox pesters a bear. It is a silly game and seems a trifle risky, but the fox keeps it up for more than half an hour.

The bear, a young male, sleeps. The fox traipses past. The bear charges, not really in earnest but in a sort of rolling trot. The fox skips nimbly away. The bear lies down, the fox comes mincing back. The bear looks but does not charge. The fox sashays past just feet away. Up goes the bear, a lumbering lummox, and off goes the fox with a lithe pirouette. The bear lies down, but the fox will not give up. Closer and closer he comes, enticing the bear to charge. And the bear does charge, again and again, but finally he has had enough and walks away. The fox tries his wiles on another bear, a big male who charges once, then goes to sleep and will not budge. The fox makes a few more passes, is completely ignored, and trots off.

Day 11–14—October 31st–November 3rd: We've had the single magnificent day of our entire stay. It is gloomy now and gray. It snows a bit and blows. The bears begin to leave.

Some wander to the very tip of the cape. Others just amble away. Even Cassius, who has slept nearby for eleven days, shuffles off, looking very old and ailing. The plane arrives and bounces along the esker, chasing the remaining bears away. Our captivity is over; for the first time in fourteen days we come to earth again.

The Grizzly's Rage to Live

DOUGLAS H. CHADWICK

Outlaw grizzlies may be "teachers offering us a last, rare occasion to learn humility."

Old Two Toes had 18 toes. The two that gave him a name came off in 1898 in Ricks' trap. While the toes still held, leg, trap, chain and anchor tree were dragged by the grizzly for a quarter of a mile through down timber. Then he ate his leg loose. Like all animals, he was absolutely honest with himself.

It might have become harder for him to get at natural foods with an injured foot. It might have been something as simple as revenge. Anyway, Old Two Toes began to work Montana's Swan Valley, the Mission Mountains and the Flathead Range. He would come swinging down into the bottomlands, keeping to the edge of the spruce, moving his nose, moving his ears, now wading pigeon-toed into the tall meadowgrass feed while the fat animals began to call to one another; now rising to stand like a man, so quick and imminent you can't imagine it. He gouged into herd after herd of cattle and sheep, and ran down horses in the brush.

In the spring of 1903 Old Two Toes emerged in the melt and killed 15 calves and three cows before the valley had even greened. One of the cows died alongside her calf after a struggle in which her neck was broken; a brave animal. The rest died alone, feeling terror in their dim way. Those that survived Old Two Toes had sledgehammers crush their skulls just above the thin bones of the nose after a long drive to slaughterhouses in the Midwest. The reward on Old Two Toes went up, bringing in a new man, Kline, to the high country. Kline found the grizzly one day in some timber by the river and shot him. The wounded bear circled and pulled Kline down, tore his leg all to hell before he passed out, then broke the leg and bent the trapper's gun barrel back on itself. Like all animals, he was absolutely forthright in his dealings. Kline lived but did not see Old Two Toes again.

The Fergusons probably came closest to him next. They happened on his tracks while hunting up missing horses near timberline in the Missions. They too had lost stock to Old Two Toes and were eager to shorten up his trail. They were closing, about to follow fresh-laid claw prints through a pass when they spotted other bad company: smugglers bringing Chinese south from Canada along the mountains. Because Chinese were bringing around $1,000 a head in Butte and Anaconda, the Fergusons figured the smugglers would be quick to protect their investment. So they hid in some mountain alder and agreed to turn for home. Lawmen and a rancher posse that included the Fergusons finally caught the smugglers because they were running rustled stock back north after bringing Chinese south, but Old Two Toes took 55 more range animals that year before he slept.

Other men, ranchers mostly, saw the grizzly over the many years he raided. Some got off a shot or two at him, and some, like Hawkey and Moore, claimed a hit after seeing the bear bawl and swipe at himself. But Old Two Toes kept on moving, going toward wherever it was he wanted to go. Belieu was another trapper the ranchers financed for a time. He set out after Old Two Toes with his two prize dogs, and the bear disemboweled the dogs before Belieu ever saw him. The trapper swore certain revenge, but he never got it. The bear went to sleep that fall high up where the little creeks start, and the snows covered him for half a year while Belieu cursed and killed wolves and then disappeared.

Old Two Toes never was old. When he was killed in 1906 in a panic of pitching horses and rolling rocks, he was middle-aged—between 15 and 20, it was figured. Many of his teeth were broken from chewing Ricks' trap and he carried at least four bullet wounds along with his other scars. His life among other bears was unknown: with whom he mated, whether or not he might share berries in a good August, how he felt about things when he died.

The Blackfeet and their brothers the North Piegans and the Bloods believed that a special spirit existed within Real Bear and they left it mostly alone. But the white men came and sheared the West with their slow-moving animals. The bear race was systematically killed and forced toward those lands no one had any other use for—not even Indians—and it was then that a few native Montanans like Old Two Toes, Peg Leg, Slaughterhouse and Old Roughhouse fought their lonely fights. White men were hoarding all the meat that remained on the range, so competition over flesh was inevitable. But several stock-killing bears seemed rarely to eat the results of their work, making interpretation of their motives more difficult. Peg Leg, like Old Two Toes, stepped early into a trap and lost a paw before he began raiding. Slaughterhouse and Old Roughhouse were named for the distinctive styles with which each swatted bleating woolies around, their true personalities unguessed, their real purpose untranslated.

I've lived in some of the places Old Two Toes scourged 70 years back. Certain traditions remain. For about three years I stayed in a cabin near Meadow Creek Gorge at the northern end of the Bob Marshall Wilderness. Then I lived in a log shack by the Swan River between the Flatheads and the Missions. Grizzlies tore up the Meadow Creek cabin three times, the Swan River shack twice. The refrigerator door in the Swan cabin was crumpled nearly double like Kline's gun barrel. The grizzlies broke windows and broke preserve jars, tore apart soup cans and chewed holes in kerosene tins. After I put a lodgepole barricade with sharpened spikes over all the doors and windows at the Meadow Creek cabin, a bleeding bear slammed straight through its side. It may not even have been angry. I don't know. I was always gone when the bears came, and when I returned there were squirrels, jays, wood rats and, once, deer inside the cabin eating.

A she-bear lived with her two-year-old cubs along Bruce Ridge, which leads into Lost Creek. When she came at me her mouth was red and dripped spittle and she was flanked by her big offspring. They all whuffed each time their legs grabbed the ground. I clenched far into myself and screamed "Nooooo, nooooo," realizing as I did that I had seen her running at me before in a dream, with the sun coloring her back just so and her cubs on either side, the wind-bent white pines on the ridgeline, the gentians underfoot, and I had screamed 'Nooooo, nooooo," awakening the woman next to me.

The bears — what had they known of this? — turned aside. After two more mock charges by the young alone, again so close I could smell nothing except them, they lumbered away, and I, full of heat and unguessed hormones, was walking after them, yelling threats — invulnerable. Stepping on bright metal, I discovered that I had hurled an antenna, with which I had been trying to locate radio-collared mountain goats, at the she-bear. This had not been in the dream, or premonition, or whatever it had been the first time the bears exploded in my mind. Now I looked up from the metal and the bears had vanished. I understood then that I was, like all animals, absolutely alive, possibly in ways I did not fully understand.

So there is still competition for food and space in what is known as grizzly country: cabin break-ins, garbage strewn about, encounters on the trail. But there has not been much grizzly country and there have been few grizzlies of any note since the turn of the century. Montana bears these days are mere flashes in the pan, one-shot deals. Worse, with only a few hundred Real Bear left in the lower 48 states we've hardly enough to keep heads and humpless rugs snarling from our barroom walls, much less good stories to tell while standing beneath them, much less again the chance to stride through grand spaces. It makes you wonder if there hasn't been a change in the nature of the beast. Are bears still made of the same stuff? While whittling down a race from many thousands to a few hundred it is a fairly routine matter to weed out those traits that make for brawlers, activists or free-thinkers — enemies of the state. There is a more dreary explanation: it is the same critter but there are too many roads, too many pickups with gun racks, too few hole-in-the-wall hideouts for an outlaw to put together a long string of successes.

Take the Little Griz that started scrounging salmon guts left by fishermen along the confluence of the Flathead's North and Middle forks not long ago. It was young, without much weight for a fall bear; away from home, probably a subadult which, hungry, had gone to look on the other side of the mountain. Soon the locals were patrolling the riverbanks with their guns, and Little Griz fled south toward the new homes, trailers and small quick-sale lots which were edging north. The locals took to their pickups. Moving quickly along the straight lines of the road hatchwork and making serious talk on their CB radios, they closed on the bear and got eight shots away. Wounded, still hungry, Little Griz fled south again and was banging garbage out of cans when a man stepped from his house and shot her or him, I forget which. Garbage and fish guts, taking its wounds to pilfer our wastes.

Old Two Toes, bless his brown and powerful heart muscles, would have snatched a few choice steers, torn the wheels off the first pickup to challenge him, and kept the world at bay with his fearsome roaring. Here was a resource for the imagination! Little Griz came as a bread thief; no outlaw but an apologetic burglar, trying to get by. It didn't work. No one listens to a loser, and no one speaks. Not one word to the bear from the most vocal of animals. So the bear died and nobody knows anything more than he did before, nothing having been learned or taught here.

By now it is evident that there is a great deal riding on the Giefer Grizzly. He is to give us hope for the monumentally free spirit of Real Bear. Without a doubt, as you will hear, his breast remains savage; without a moment's vacillation, his will remains indomitable. Without a trace of remorse, he is a go-to-hell, shaggy, bad-ass bruin in the best tradition. He can tell us what we need so badly to know, and he is strong and smart and unrelenting enough to make us listen to him.

His origins are obscure. We know only that two or more years ago he was a nameless digger of sleeping ground squirrels, an eater of grubs. Then he began taking some of his food from cabins around Giefer Creek near where it flows into the Middle Fork of the Flathead. He did not come to the cabins merely because they were there. Something attracted him. Where he was first reported to have entered a cabin, game officials found food and garbage scattered around. He was soon caught at cabin-raiding. Game officials removed one of his teeth to discover his age, tattooed his lip and put a metal disc through one ear for identification, then transported him 50 miles across a mountain range into the South Fork of the Flathead. By the standards of Old Two Toes' time, he got off easy. He came back after a year; homing by the stars or sounds or smells or other things he knew, and polished off a few more cabins at Giefer Creek. They caught him again. Capital punishment of grizzly bears had been outlawed in 1975 with federal designation of the animal as an endangered species (it is technically a threatened species, a few households away from being endangered by extinction). So the Giefer Grizzly was taken away again, unconscious but unharmed. His other ear was tagged and he was placed up the one fork of the Flathead they had not tried him in: the North Fork, where I also live.

The Giefer Grizzly did not find his way home again, but while looking he ran into more cabins. People, myself included, are crowding into the North Fork too, putting their homes throughout the rich bottomlands where bears traditionally spend the spring and fall. Soon one resident after another returned home to find his cabin ransacked by the Giefer Grizzly, the bear that twice lost his own home to people. He hit cabins just to the north and south of me. I waited to meet him, for he rarely left one in between like that.

Wardens were called in to kill the bear after he had entered cabins 15 times, capital punishment having been temporarily reinstated for this particular beast. The locals hunted him on their own time, of which there is more here than in other places. After his 25th invasion, the wardens called in full-time professional government hunters; and after the 35th they began an even more intensive search, using a light plane, pickup trucks and electronic communications networks. The locals kept after him on their own time, which they increased. They hunted in vain. Before long the Giefer Grizzly had broken into cabins some 55 times and he still, by God, stormed between them at will. The mythmaker in all of this — the thing that moves this bear toward the company of Old Two Toes and Slaughterhouse — is that ever since his arrest in Giefer Creek the bear had borne around his neck a radio transmitter collar that revealed his position to those chasing him. Butch Cassidy, Peg Leg, Billy the Kid, Old Roughhouse, Jesse James, Sundance — Old Two Toes even — these were hombres who could see everything they had to fight. Pre-radio, pre-plane, pre-pickup truck heroes. Which of them, and who among us, could so long and successfully wage lawlessness in the face of spaceage technology — with a beacon sealed around his neck?

The Giefer Grizzly, pronounced Guyfer by some and Mr. Geefer Goddam Griz by others, covered a hundred square miles of the North Fork, sometimes traveling up into the high country; sometimes, when the heat was really on, he moved into nearby Glacier Park, which has almost no roads and where there is little inclination to kill bears. Then he would come back to the cabins. In his approaches, in his forced entries, in his narrow escapes, he avoided jawed leg traps, cubby sets with snares, poisoned meats, culvert traps, bullets and the Lord knows what else laid across his path. Other more law-abiding bears were unable to avoid them, although it is hard to sort through the stories to learn how many died.

English Tom is farther upstream toward the Canadian border. He showed me his shed. It was made of poles and weathered one-by-eights, a loose wire held the sagging door, and inside were black smells and shadows. "Loose, so Mr. Giefer can get in easy this time," he said with a sort of smile. "I got a little present fixed up for him in there." I could see nothing in the dark space. English Tom never would let on what the shed held for the bear. The grizzly had come through the screen door and into the porch by the time English Tom awakened, waving his flashlight and hollering. The bear had left at once but returned when English Tom went to visit a neighbor and raked the windows out of the cabin on his way in. Like everyone else here now, English Tom has spiked boards on the doorsills and beneath the windows, though they say the bear has learned to bend them. I had to stretch across nails to place my hand over the grizzly's paw marks. They were not especially long or wide. He is, by all accounts, a medium-size bear living by his wits beyond his strength.

As a scientist hopeful of discovering truths through inquiries into the natural world, I find the Giefer Grizzly embodies that factor most essential to discovery: the allusion to something beyond the experiment. The first thing that becomes clear in this is the inadequacy of trying to understand such a being within the dwarfish framework we have allotted the animal world. When we report on bears sliding down a snowbank on a warm afternoon, we describe this — for God's sake — in terms of non-directed thermoregulatory behavior. Itch-scratch; stimulus-response. Like looking for electrons with a magnifying glass, we have been trying to explain why bears do what they do by examining their turds and counting the number of times they feed in meadows with green rushes as compared to spruce forests, or dividing the number of cubs born each year by the total number of adult females in the dwindling population. The central problem, it seems to me, lies in the great assumption, never proven, that all ideas originate in the minds of men. Yet clearly much of what Real Bears respond to must originate within their own brains. By disrupting our daily lives and shattering our sense of security, if only to get our attention; by then steadfastly disputing our absurd claim to ownership of every concept and hillock and manner of being on this globe, the outlaws force us to judge their race anew; and they ask us, demand us, to credit them with free will and imagination and to accord the wild places an existence of their own. The outlaws are spokesmen, but the message is carried by all bears in their own way. I saw a straw-colored bear in huckleberry time immerse its big muzzle in a stream to blow bubbles and then prick them with the tip of its claw.

If the grizzly does possess an imagination, what is it then that it imagines? Having listed some of the trials and pitfalls along the path of the Giefer Grizzly, we have not really examined where this path leads. What is his progress toward, and does he despair of reaching his goals? Perhaps he is after social reform. No one else could have demonstrated with our own transistors how enormously humans subjugate and destroy other ways of life, other visions of existence. Or maybe the outlaws are merely teachers offering us a last, rare occasion to learn humility. Love, the Real Bear is saying, needs a loss of pride. Love between the races: his goal may be nothing less. No easy back-to-the-earth jive, but a revolutionary theme, which with any luck may spread to the whales and their system of beliefs, the tigers and the cranes with their huge wings. Someone has to lead and, as in all revolutions, a lot of cabins must get smashed before a new Bill of Rights is written.

A short time ago the official hunters said they had killed the Giefer Grizzly. We had a wake for him at the Northern Lights Saloon, those of us who live along the North Fork, Tory and revolutionary together.

It turned out to be the wrong bear. Another grizzly, a little smaller maybe, a slightly different color, had been accidentally overdosed with drugs by the government hunters. When they got a closer look at it, it wasn't the Giefer. We nursed our own overdoses after the wake, and the Giefer Grizzly ambled on where he chose to, swinging his head, making his plans.

Why, we wondered, couldn't they tell that it wasn't the Giefer Grizzly before they overdosed it? After all, the Giefer should have had on the collar that cried out his whereabouts day and night. What we didn't know at the time of the wake was this: several days before the other bear was killed, the radio signal had become fixed in one area. Had the outlaw tired of running? Was he going to make his stand against the professional hunters, pilots, radio operators and game biologists in pickup trucks? Would he take his rest from a bullet or a drug overdose? The trackers searched, talking back and forth in code through the transistors, until in one cabin, past a shattered door, beyond strewn furniture and broken glass, there was the collar, lying on the floor in a heap of food the bear had pulled from a cupboard.

The Giefer Grizzly was somewhere else. We heard this news after the wake. And even the grizzly-haters marveled. You got to admit he beat 'em, by God. Beat 'em flat out, beat 'em every whichaway, beat 'em at their own game. He plumb snookered those smart government boys, no way around it. That's some goddam bear! And then the talk inevitably drifted to how many thousands of dollars had been wasted by these empty-handed officials. I moved off. I hadn't said much, wishing to keep good relations with my neighbors by keeping my opinions on bears as teachers to myself. But when I passed behind a building there at the Mercantile I slapped my knees and struck my forehead, exclaiming, "Lord Almighty, it can still be done! It can still be done! That's some goddam bear!" Now, I thought, he will move back to the Middle Fork and secure a home on the north slope where he can keep an eye on developments around Giefer Creek. Free.

The way the collar was found amidst the bear's handiwork, it seemed certain the bear had hooked the collar on something or used his claws to wrench it from his neck. Then a new rumor filtered to us that a local had killed the bear and left the collar in the broken cabin. Shoot, shovel and shut up. I refused to believe it, preferring to think that game officials had invented the story to save face and at least make us believe the bear was dead. No one stepped forward to claim the kill, not even in the bar, but the stories persisted.

There were many stories. Before long, everyone came to believe that the bear was dead after all. I too assumed that someone else knew more than I and began to agree that the Giefer Grizzly had gone under. Sure, that's the way it's bound to end for these guys. We had another wake at the saloon, and those of us who had become involved with the bear's aspirations toasted him at home for a while after that, often and well into whatever worlds follow this one.

It had got hairy toward the end. Everyone was carrying guns. Few of us moved unaffected after dark and we put off leaving for town until we really needed something. We were stuck here in wild country, existing on its own terms. It was like the old days. We could no more own the night than we could scatter unused food in back of the cabin, and we could no more move through the willow brush in our arrogant, careless way than we could control the movements of that one bear. So many cabins had been broken into that details became jumbled. Two or three cabins were said to have had things stolen from them, suggesting that human predators were taking advantage of the confusion. Not surprisingly, there were one or two break-ins after the collar was found. Were there others like myself who, upon hearing this, suddenly looked downward and moved away to think? And then weeks later as I was working at Glacier Park the local reporter who comes each Monday to collect events mentioned that there had been still two more break-ins up the North Fork. A grizzly was responsible, he said, and plaster casts of its tracks matched those of the Giefer Grizzly. I had dared hope it! Our bear lives still, a being capable of transforming the very dimensions of the night and the mountains around him — teacher, prophet, outlaw, wanted bear. Mr. Geefer Goddam Griz. This was in November, just before denning-up time. The legend grows. We shall see next spring, after a long sleep, what direction it will take.

EPILOGUE: This story was written in December, around Christmastime. In northern Montana, the short, snowbound winter days are a good time for visiting and telling stories. We often talked about the Giefer. Two men, one a logger and one a rancher, all but admitted outright that they had had a hand in killing the bear. They had seen him dead. Tracks found by the Fish and Game people were from a similar bear, they said. It turned out to be a light winter, easy traveling for the elk and deer. Few died, and because there was so little carrion on the early spring ranges, everyone was predicting that the bears would be down in the cabins. But there were no bear problems here in the North Fork during early green-up. A big grizzly was killed in the Swans. A man shot at it through the closed door it was trying to open. The shot hit its throat and the bear went a little way from the cabin and died in the brush. The bear had a lip tattoo. It had been captured before and was probably the same one that had broken into my cabin and the neighbors' when I lived there.

I was in town for supplies in early May when I saw the town paper in the store window with the headline THE GIEFER CREEK GRIZZLY IS DEAD. "I guess they really got him this time," said the clerk as I began reading the story. She was right. He had spent the winter undisturbed in his den. He had emerged sometime in April, and, like other fugitives before him, had gone north into Canada. There is a spring grizzly hunting season in Canada. Near sundown, on April 24, a Sunday, a hunter killed him with three shots from a .340 magnum rifle while he was feeding in an opening. The hunter was an American, a grocery store owner from McConnellsburg, Pa. He was guided into the area.

The bear is being mounted by a taxidermist now. He was larger than when he was first captured, and the hunter is hopeful that the skull will qualify for the trophy record book. "Maybe they got the wrong one," said another person in the store. No. They have the tags from his ears and the skull is missing the tooth they pulled. His story is over.

ACKNOWLEDGMENTS

Care has been taken to trace ownership of copyright material contained in this book. The publishers will gladly receive any information that will enable them to rectify errors or omissions affecting references or credit lines in subsequent editions.

"The Bargain Trap" by Andy Russell (page 144). From *Grizzly Country*, by Andy Russell. Copyright © 1967 by Andy Russell. Reprinted by permission of Alfred A. Knopf, Inc.

"The Battle of the Bears" by Egerton R. Young (page 231). Reprinted from *The Independent* (July 25, 1907).

"Bear-Chasing in the Rocky Mountains" by Frederic Remington (page 44). Reprinted from *Harper's New Monthly Magazine* (July, 1895).

"Bear Customs of the Cree" by Alonson Skinner (page 26). Reprinted from *Papers and Records* of the Ontario Historical Society (Toronto, 1914).

"A Bear Hunt in Montana" by Arthur Alvord Stiles (page 113). Reprinted from *The National Geographic Magazine*, Vol. XIX, No. 2 (February, 1908).

"Bears" by Ben Gadd and John Chalmers (page 253). Reprinted from *The Morningside Papers*, edited by Peter Gzowski (Toronto: McClelland & Stewart, 1985). Reprinted by permission of the authors.

"Bears in New Brunswick in the Olden Time" by Venerable Archdeacon Raymond (page 21). Reprinted from *Collections* of the New Brunswick Historical Society (Saint John, N.B.: Barnes & Co., 1928).

"The Bear That Came for Supper" by Robert Franklin Leslie (page 212). Copyright © 1964 by The Reader's Digest Association, Inc. Reprinted by permission.

"Black Bear Honking in the Valley of Kashmir" by J.C. Grew (page 79). Reprinted from *The Outing Magazine* (August, 1907).

"Black Bear in Chamba" by Shikari (page 33). Reprinted from *The Cornhill Magazine*, Vol. XLIX (July – December, 1920).

"The Cabin Where Terror Came Calling" by Keith McCafferty (page 119). Reprinted by permission from *Field & Stream* (September, 1984). Copyright © 1984 by Keith McCafferty.

"A Colorado Bear Hunt" by Theodore Roosevelt (page 85). Reprinted from *Scribner's Magazine* (October, 1905).

"The Dentist and the Bear" by Michael V. Dickinson (page 132). Copyright © 1986 by Michael V. Dickinson. Reprinted from *The Calgary Herald* (14 December, 1986) and *The Edmonton Journal* (December, 1986).

"A Dirge for the Polar Bear," Anonymous (page 207). Reprinted from *The Spectator* (24 November, 1894).

"The Grizzly and the Golden Rule" by James Oliver Curwood (page 139). Reprinted from *God's Country* (New York: Cosmopolitan Book Co., 1920).

"A Grizzly Chase" by Winnifred Weir (page 127). Reprinted courtesy of *Outdoor Canada* magazine.

"The Grizzly's Rage to Live" by Douglas H. Chadwick (page 269). Copyright © 1977 by Douglas H. Chadwick. Reprinted from *Sports Illustrated* (18 July, 1977).

"Grizzly Tracks" by Sid Marty (page 245). From *Men for the Mountains* by Sid Marty. Used by permission of The Canadian Publishers, McClelland & Stewart Limited, Toronto.

"Guaranteed Unpredictable" by Ralph W. Young (page 161). Reprinted from *Grizzlies Don't Come Easy*. Copyright © 1981 by Ralph W. Young. By permission of New Century Publishers, Inc., Piscataway, N.J.

"How to Cope in Bear Country" by Stephen Freligh (page 135). Copyright © 1984 by the National Wildlife Federation. Reprinted from the August – September, 1984, issue of *National Wildlife* magazine.

"Hunting the Great Alaskan Bear" by Andrew J. Stone (page 107). Reprinted from *Scribner's Magazine* (February, 1907).

"Kootznahoo, Home of the Bears" by Frank Dufresne (page 238). Reprinted by permission of Harold Ober Associates Incorporated. From *No Room For Bears*, copyright © 1965 by Frank Dufresne.

"Memories of Mooween" by H. Mortimer Batten (page 218). Reprinted from *The Children's Hour Annual* (London: Hutchinson, 1936).

"Now You Take Bear" by Russell Annabel (page 151). Reprinted from *Field & Stream* (February, 1943 and March, 1981). Copyright © 1943 by Russell Annabel.

"Polar Bear Shooting on the East Coast of Greenland" by Fridtjof Nansen (page 55). Reprinted from *Littell's Living Age* (4 August, 1894).

"The Rubber Bear" by Ray W. Lane (page 200). Copyright © 1986 by Ray W. Lane. Reprinted from *The Calgary Herald* (14 December, 1986) and *The Edmonton Journal* (December, 1986).

"Two Weeks in a Polar Bear Prison" by Fred Bruemmer (page 256). Copyright © 1981 by Fred Bruemmer. Reprinted from *Audubon*, the magazine of the National Audubon Society, New York, N.Y.

"The War in the Woods" by Edward Hoagland (page 178). Copyright © 1970 by Edward Hoagland. Reprinted from *The Courage of Turtles*, by Edward Hoagland, by permission of Random House, Inc.

"The White Bears" by William H. Wright (page 11). Reprinted from *The Grizzly Bear* by William H. Wright (London: T. Werner Laurie, 1909).

"Yukon and the Bear" by R.D. Lawrence (page 169). From *The North Runner* by R.D. Lawrence. Copyright © 1979 by R.D. Lawrence. Reprinted by permission of Henry Holt and Company.